BEAUTY AND MISOGYNY

Should western beauty practices, ranging from lipstick to labiaplasty, be included within the United Nations' understanding of harmful traditional/cultural practices? By examining the role of common beauty practices in damaging the health of women, creating sexual difference, and enforcing female deference, this book argues that they should.

In the 1970s feminists criticized pervasive beauty regimes such as dieting and depilation, but in the last two decades the brutality of western beauty practices has become much more severe. Today's practices can require the breaking of skin, spilling of blood and rearrangement or amputation of body parts. Some "new" feminists argue that beauty practices are no longer oppressive now that women can "choose" them. This book seeks to make sense of why beauty practices are not only just as persistent 30 years after the feminist critique developed, but in many ways more extreme. By examining the pervasive use of makeup, the misogyny of fashion and high-heeled shoes, and by looking at the role of pornography in the creation of increasingly popular beauty practices such as breast implants, genital waxing and surgical alteration of the labia, *Beauty and Misogyny* seeks to explain why harmful beauty practices persist in the west and have become so extreme. It looks at the cosmetic surgery and body piercing/cutting industries as being forms of self-mutilation by proxy, in which the surgeons and piercers serve as proxies to harm women's bodies. It concludes by considering how a culture of resistance to these practices can be created.

This essential work will appeal to students and teachers of feminist psychology, gender studies, cultural studies, and feminist sociology at both undergraduate and postgraduate levels, and to anyone with an interest in feminism, women and beauty, and women's health.

Sheila Jeffreys is Associate Professor in the Department of Political Science at the University of Melbourne where she teaches sexual politics, international feminist politics and lesbian and gay politics. She is the author of five books on the history and politics of sexuality, and has been active in feminist and lesbian feminist politics since 1973.

WOMEN AND PSYCHOLOGY

Series Editor: Jane Ussher

School of Psychology

University of Western Sydney

This series brings together current theory and research on women and psychology. Drawing on scholarship from a number of different areas of psychology, it bridges the gap between abstract research and the reality of women's lives by integrating theory and practice, research and policy.

Each book addresses a "cutting edge" issue of research, covering such topics as post-natal depression, eating disorders, theories and methodologies.

The series provides accessible and concise accounts of key issues in the study of women and psychology, and clearly demonstrates the centrality of psychology to debates within women's studies or feminism.

The Series Editor would be pleased to discuss proposals for new books in the series.

Other titles in this series:

THIN WOMEN
Helen Malson

THE MENSTRUAL CYCLE
Anne E. Walker

POST-NATAL DEPRESSION
Paula Nicolson

RE-THINKING ABORTION
Mary Boyle

WOMEN AND AGING
Linda R. Gannon

BEING MARRIED DOING GENDER
Caroline Dryden

UNDERSTANDING DEPRESSION
Janet M. Stoppard

FEMININITY AND THE PHYSICALLY ACTIVE WOMAN
Precilla Y. L. Choi

GENDER, LANGUAGE AND DISCOURSE
Ann Weatherall

THE PSYCHOLOGICAL DEVELOPMENT OF GIRLS AND WOMEN
Sheila Greene

THE SCIENCE/FICTION OF SEX
Annie Potts

JUST SEX?
Nicola Gavey

WOMAN'S RELATIONSHIP WITH HERSELF
Helen O'Grady

BODY WORK
Sylvia K. Blood

BEAUTY AND MISOGYNY

Harmful cultural practices in the west

Sheila Jeffreys

LONDON AND NEW YORK

First published 2005
by Routledge
27 Church Road, Hove, East Sussex BN3 2FA

Simultaneously published in the USA and Canada
by Routledge
270 Madison Avenue, New York NY 10016

Routledge is an imprint of the Taylor & Francis Group

Typeset in Sabon by Garfield Morgan, Rhayader, Powys
Printed and bound in Great Britain by TJ International Ltd, Padstow, Cornwall
Paperback cover design by Anú Design
Paperback cover photo: Tom Schierlitz/Getty Images

This publication has been produced with paper manufactured to strict environmental standards and with pulp derived from sustainable forests.

British Library Cataloguing in Publication Data
A catalogue record for this book is available from the British Library

Library of Congress Cataloging-in-Publication Data
Jeffreys, Sheila.
Beauty and misogyny : harmful cultural practices in the West / Sheila Jeffreys.
p. cm. – (Women and psychology)
Includes bibliographical references and index.
ISBN 0-415-35182-0 – ISBN 0-415-35183-9
1. Feminine beauty (Aesthetics). 2. Body, Human–Social aspects. 3. Women–Social life and customs. 4. Women–Health and hygiene. 5. Women in popular culture. 6. Misogyny. I. Title. II. Series.

HQ1219.J44 2005
306.4'613–dc22
2005004366

ISBN 0-415-35183-9 (hbk)
ISBN 0-415-35182-0 (pbk)

Beauty and Misogyny is dedicated to my partner, Ann Rowett, with my love, and with respect for her lifelong, determined resistance to beauty practices.

CONTENTS

Acknowledgements viii

Introduction 1

1 The "grip of culture on the body": beauty practices as women's agency or women's subordination 5

2 Harmful cultural practices and western culture 28

3 Transfemininity: "dressed" men reveal the naked reality of male power 46

4 Pornochic: prostitution constructs beauty 67

5 Fashion and misogyny 87

6 Making up is hard to do 107

7 Men's foot and shoe fetishism and the disabling of women 128

8 Cutting up women: beauty practices as self-mutilation by proxy 149

Conclusion: a culture of resistance 171

References 180

Index 195

ACKNOWLEDGEMENTS

I am grateful to the Australian Research Council for the large grant that enabled me to do the research for this book. I was able to employ two wonderful research assistants, Carole Moschetti and Jennifer Oriel, who not only collected and annotated materials but discussed them with me and made suggestions. I appreciated their enthusiasm for this project and their support in looking at the sometimes difficult materials that had to be analysed.

I would like to thank those friends who read and commented helpfully on the manuscript, Ann Rowett, Heather Benbow, Iva Deutchman. My students in Sexual Politics over the last few years have contributed very useful insights about the impact of beauty practices such as high-heeled shoes on their lives and I have enjoyed my discussions with them very much.

I would like to acknowledge my debt for the ideas in this book to the work of the radical feminist theorist Andrea Dworkin. Her untimely death in April 2005 was a terrible loss to feminist activism and scholarship. I am very sad that she will not be able to read this book and know how her ideas on beauty practices continue to inspire those who survive her.

INTRODUCTION

In the 1970s a feminist critique of makeup and other beauty practices emerged from consciousness-raising groups. The American radical feminist theorist Catharine A. MacKinnon called consciousness-raising the "methodology" of feminism (MacKinnon, 1989). In these groups women discussed how they felt about themselves and their bodies. They identified the pressures within male dominance that caused them to feel they should diet, depilate and makeup. Feminist writers rejected a masculine aesthetics that caused women to feel their bodies were inadequate and to engage in expensive, time-consuming practices that left them feeling that they were inauthentic and unacceptable when barefaced (Dworkin, 1974). "Beauty" was identified as oppressive to women.

In the last two decades the brutality of the beauty practices that women carry out on their bodies has become much more severe. Today's practices require the breaking of skin, spilling of blood and rearrangement or amputation of body parts. Foreign bodies, in the form of breast implants, are placed under the flesh and next to the heart, women's labia are cut to shape, fat is liposuctioned out of the thighs and buttocks and sometimes injected into other sites such as cheeks and chins. The new cutting and piercing industry will now split women's tongues in two as well as creating holes in nipples, clitoris hood or bellybuttons, for the placement of "body art" jewellery (Jeffreys, 2000). These developments are much more dangerous prescriptions for women's health than the practices common in the 1960s and 1970s when the feminist critique was formed. It might be expected, then, that there would have been a sharpening of this critique and a renewed awareness of its relevance in response to this more concerted attack on the integrity of women's bodies. But this is not what happened. Instead, the feminist perspective, which caused many thousands of women to eschew beauty culture and products, came under challenge in the 1980s and 1990s.

The challenge came from two directions. Liberal feminists, such as Natasha Walter (UK) and Karen Lehrman (USA), argued that there was nothing wrong with lipstick or women making themselves look good, with all the products and practices of beauty culture (Walter, 1999; Lehrman, 1997). Feminism itself had created choice for women, they said, and enabled women now to "choose" lipstick where once it might have been thrust upon them. Meanwhile the influence of postmodern ideas in the academy led to some rather similar rhetoric about "choice", usually in the form of "agency", emanating from some feminist theorists and researchers (Davis, 1995). Bolder propositions were made as well, such as the idea that beauty practices could be socially transformative. Postmodern feminist theorists such as Judith Butler (1990), with their ideas on gender performativity, inspired the notion among queer theorists that the beauty practices of femininity adopted by unconventional actors, or outrageously, could be transgressive (Roof, 1998). Other postmodern feminists such as Elizabeth Grosz argued that the body is simply a "text" which can be written on, and that tattooing, cutting, let alone lipstick, are just interesting ways of writing on it (Grosz, 1994). It is in response to this recent defence of beauty practices against the feminist critique that this book has been written.

In *Beauty and Misogyny* I suggest that beauty practices are not about women's individual choice or a "discursive space" for women's creative expression but, as other radical feminist theorists have argued before me, a most important aspect of women's oppression. The feminist philosopher Marilyn Frye has written incisively of what makes a theory feminist, and why it is not enough to rely on women's individual assurances that a practice is OK with them and in their interests:

> One of the great powers of feminism is that it goes so far in making the experiences and lives of women intelligible. Trying to make sense of one's own feelings, motivations, desires, ambitions, actions and reactions without taking into account the forces which maintain the subordination of women to men is like trying to explain why a marble stops rolling without taking friction into account. What feminist theory is about, to a great extent, is just identifying those forces . . . and displaying the mechanics of their applications to women as a group (or caste) and to individual women. The measure of the success of the theory is just how much sense it makes of what did not make sense before.
>
> (Frye, 1983, p. xi)

In this book I attempt to identify some of the "forces which maintain the subordination of women to men" in relation to beauty practices.

I seek to make sense of why beauty practices are not only just as pervasive 30 years after the feminist critique developed, but in many ways are more extreme. To do this I use some new approaches that are suited to explaining this escalation of cruelty in what is expected of women in the twenty-first century. One impetus towards my writing this book lies in my growing impatience with the western bias of the useful United Nations concept of "harmful traditional/cultural practices". In United Nations (UN) documents such as the Fact Sheet on "Harmful Traditional Practices" (UN, 1995), harmful cultural/traditional practices are understood to be damaging to the health of women and girls, to be performed for men's benefit, to create stereotyped roles for the sexes and to be justified by tradition. This concept provides a good lens through which to examine practices that are harmful to women in the west – such as beauty practices. But western practices have not been included in the definition or understood in international feminist politics as harmful in these ways. Indeed there is a pronounced western bias in the selection of practices to fit the category such that only one western practice, violence against women, is included (Wynter *et al.*, 2002). The implication is that western cultures do not have harmful practices such as female genital mutilation that should cause concern. I argue in *Beauty and Misogyny* that western beauty practices from makeup to labiaplasty do fit the criteria and should be included within UN understandings. The great usefulness of this approach is that it does not depend on notions of individual choice; it recognizes that the attitudes which underlie harmful cultural practices have coercive power and that they can and should be changed.

Another approach I use is to look at men's involvement in two ways in the beauty practices of femininity: in transvestism/transsexualism, and in the role of designers and photographers in the fashion industry. There are useful clues to the cultural meanings of feminine beauty practices, and the ways in which they are enforced, to be gleaned from looking at the behaviour of the men who practise them and the men who design them. I use insights gleaned from books and Internet resources aimed at men who gain sexual excitement from appropriating a form of femininity for themselves. In the decades since the 1970s the male practice of transvestism/transsexualism, that is, appropriating clothes or body parts usually allotted to members of the subordinate sex class under male supremacy, has gained much wider public exposure and influence. The Internet has enabled the websites of individual practitioners and support groups, as well as commercial makeover sites and pornography devoted to these masculine practices, to proliferate. This provides a good opportunity to show that "feminine" beauty practices are neither natural, nor confined to women. There is also much useful information about what such practices represent for men, the sexual excitement of ritualized subordination. I make use of such websites in several chapters, analysing the creation of femininity by men or "transfemininity". With the insight that such an analysis offers I argue that this practice of men is influential in the construction of harmful beauty practices for women through the influence of male fashion designers, fashion photographers and makeup artists who have vested interests in transfemininity.

Another approach I use to investigate beauty practices is an analysis of the influence of the pornography and prostitution industries in their creation. I suggest that in the late twentieth century, the growth of these industries had a considerable effect on the beauty practices that are required of women. As these industries have moved above ground and become respectable, through the development of new technologies such as the Internet, and laissez-faire government policies, the cultural requirements for the construction of beauty have changed. The stigmata of sexual objectification for sale have become de rigeur in the beauty industry. Pressures from pornography have created new fashion norms for women in general, such as breast implants, genital waxing, surgical alteration of labia, the trappings of sadomasochism in the form of black leather and vinyl, and the display of increasing amounts of flesh including naked breasts and buttocks.

Beauty and Misogyny concludes with a chapter on the degree of serious physical harm to women and some categories of men that has now become normalized through the sex industry, through celebration in art and fashion circles and through Internet networks. This harm, I suggest, needs to be understood as self-mutilation by proxy. It includes cosmetic surgery in which the proxies are cosmetic surgeons, and the cutting and piercing industry in which the proxies are to be found in piercing studios. From the 1990s onwards it has included extremely severe practices such as limb amputation for which the proxies are surgeons and other practices of sadomasochism in which body parts are removed. Some of these practices are suffered by vulnerable categories of gay men as well as by women. There does not seem to be a limit to the varieties of cutting up that members of the medical profession are prepared to engage in for profit. The defence of the "consent" of the victim is being employed in such dubious circumstances that the whole notion of consent must be thrown into doubt. I argue that, consent notwithstanding, limits should be constructed to the swathe of attacks on the integrity of women's and some men's bodies in the name of beauty or dissatisfaction with appearance that are taking place in the early twenty-first century.

1

THE "GRIP OF CULTURE ON THE BODY"*

Beauty practices as women's agency or women's subordination

In the 1990s a fundamental disagreement emerged between feminist scholars regarding the extent to which western beauty practices represent women's subordinate status or can be seen as the expression of women's choice or agency. Ideas emerge in particular time periods because of a concatenation of social forces that make them possible. In the 1960s and 1970s the new social movements of feminism, black power, animal liberation, lesbian and gay politics came into being in response to a mood of hopefulness about the possibility of social change. These social movements were fuelled by a belief in social constructionism and the idea that radical social transformation was possible in the pursuit of social equality. These ideas underpinned the thoroughgoing radical feminist critiques of beauty that emerged from that period.

In the 1980s, however, the ideas of radical feminism, like those of other socially transformative ideologies, were treated to the contempt of right-wing ideologues who called them "political correctness". A new ideology of market fundamentalism was developed to provide the ideological support for the expansion of a newly deregulated rogue capitalism. This stated that the free market, controlled only by the choices of empowered citizens, would create an ideal social and economic structure without interference from the state. Citizenship, in this new worldview, was not about rights but about responsibilities, and the citizen was empowered by consumer choice (Evans, 1993).

By the 1990s these ideas about the power of choice influenced the thinking of many feminists too. The idea that women were coerced into beauty practices by the fashion/beauty complex (Bartky, 1990), for instance, was challenged by a new breed of liberal feminists who talked about women being empowered by the feminist movement to choose beauty practices that could no longer be seen as oppressive. The new language that penetrated feminist thinking from the pervasive rightwing rhetoric was that of "agency", "choice" and "empowerment". Women

* Bordo (1993, p. 117).

became transformed into knowledgeable consumers who could exercise their power of choice in the market. They could pick and choose from practices and products. Feminists who continued to argue that women's choices were severely constrained and made within a context of women's relative powerlessness and male dominance were criticized with some acerbity as "victim feminists"; that is, making women into victims by denying their agency (Wolf, 1993).

In this chapter I examine the ideas of the radical feminist critique of beauty and show how these came to be challenged both by the new liberal feminism and by its counterpart in the academy, a variety of postmodern feminism that emphasizes choice and agency in a similar way. I consider the tensions that have developed between the advocates of "choice" and those who emphasize the role of culture and force in exacting women's conformity to the beauty practices of femininity. I conclude with the ideas of some of those feminist theorists and researchers who have provided persuasive explanations of the constraints that restrict the possibilities of women's agency around beauty practices in male dominant cultures founded on sexual difference/deference.

THE FEMINIST CRITIQUE OF BEAUTY

Feminist critics of beauty have pointed out that beauty is a cultural practice and one that is damaging to women. For writers such as Andrea Dworkin the most important question was not the extent to which women could express agency and "choose" to wear makeup but what harm beauty practices did to women. Her book *Woman Hating* is a good example of the powerful critique that radical feminists were making of the notion of beauty in the 1970s (Dworkin, 1974). She analyses the idea of "beauty" as one aspect of the way women are hated in male supremacist culture. Dworkin indicts woman-hating culture for, "the deaths, violations, and violence" done to women and says that feminists, "look for alternatives, ways of destroying culture as we know it, rebuilding it as we can imagine it" (1974, p. 26).

Dworkin sees beauty practices as having extensive harmful effects on women's bodies and lives. Beauty practices are not only timewasting, expensive and painful to self-esteem, but rather:

> Standards of beauty describe in precise terms the relationship that an individual will have to her own body. They prescribe her mobility, spontaneity, posture, gait, the uses to which she can put her body. *They define precisely the dimensions of her physical freedom.*
>
> (Dworkin, 1974, p. 112, emphasis in the original)

And, she continues, beauty standards have psychological effects on women too because "the relationship between physical freedom and psychological development, intellectual possibility, and creative potential is an umbilical one". Dworkin, like other radical feminist critics of beauty, describes the broad range of practices that women must engage in to meet the dictates of beauty:

> In our culture, not one part of a woman's body is left untouched, unaltered. No feature or extremity is spared the art, or pain, of improvement. Hair is dyed, lacquered, straightened, permanented; eyebrows are plucked, penciled, dyed; eyes are lined, mascaraed, shadowed; lashes are curled, or false – from head to toe, every feature of a woman's face, every section of her body, is subject to modification, alteration.
>
> (Dworkin, 1974, p. 112)

Interestingly this list omits cosmetic surgery, and that would not make sense today. This shows the progress there has been in making cosmetic surgery simply another form of makeup in the 30 years since Dworkin embarked on her analysis (Haiken, 1997). The other oppressive elements of beauty that Dworkin remarks on are that it is "vital to the economy" and "the major substance of male–female role differentiation, the most immediate physical and psychological reality of being a woman" (Dworkin, 1974, p. 112). Beauty practices are necessary so that the sexes can be told apart, so that the dominant sex class can be differentiated from the subordinate one. Beauty practices create, as well as represent, the "difference" between the sexes.

Sandra Bartky, who also developed her ideas in those heady days of the 1970s when profound critiques of the condition of women included an analysis of beauty, addressed the issue of why women could appear to "choose". She explains why no exercise of obvious force was required to make women engage in beauty practices. "It is possible", she says, "to be oppressed in ways that need involve neither physical deprivation, legal inequality, nor economic exploitation; one can be oppressed psychologically" (Bartky, in a collection of previously published pieces, 1990, p. 23). In support of this she utilizes the work of the anti-colonial theorist Frantz Fanon who wrote of the "psychic alienation" of the colonized. The psychological oppression of women, Bartky says, consists of women being "stereotyped, culturally dominated, and sexually objectified" (1990, p. 23). She explains this cultural domination as a situation in which, "all the items in the general life of our people – our language, our institutions, our art and literature, our popular culture – are sexist; that all, to a greater or lesser degree, manifest male supremacy" (1990, p. 25). The absence of any alternative culture within which women can identify a different way to be a woman enforces oppressive practices, "The subordination of women, then, because it is so pervasive a feature of my culture, will (if uncontested) appear to be natural – and because it is natural, unalterable" (1990, p. 25).

The bedrock of this cultural domination is the treatment of women as sex objects and the identification of women themselves with this cultural condition. Bartky (1990) defines the practice of sexual objectification thus: "a person is sexually objectified when her sexual parts or sexual functions are separated out from the rest of her personality and reduced to the status of mere instruments or else regarded as if they were capable of representing her" (p. 26). Women incorporate the values of the male sexual objectifiers within themselves. Catharine MacKinnon calls this being "thingified" in the head (MacKinnon, 1989). They learn to treat their own bodies as objects separate from themselves. Bartky explains how this works: the wolf whistle sexually objectifies a woman from without with the result that, "The body which only a moment before I inhabited with such ease now floods my consciousness. I have been made into an object" (Bartky, 1990, p. 27). She explains that it is not sufficient for a man simply to look at the woman secretly, he must make her aware of his looking with the whistle. She must, "be *made* to know that I am a 'nice piece of ass': I must be made to see myself as they see me" (p. 27). The effect of such male policing behaviour is that, "Subject to the evaluating eye of the male connoisseur, women learn to evaluate themselves first and best" (Bartky, 1990, p. 28). Women thus become alienated from their own bodies.

The "fashion–beauty complex", representing the corporate interests involved in the fashion and beauty industries, has, Bartky argues, taken over from the family and church as "central producers and regulators of 'femininity'" (1990, p. 39). The fashion–beauty complex promotes itself to women as seeking to, "glorify the female body and to provide opportunities for narcissistic indulgence" but in fact its aim is to "depreciate woman's body and deal a blow to her narcissism" so that she will buy more products. The result is that a woman feels constantly deficient and that her body requires "either alteration or else heroic measures merely to conserve it" (p. 39).

Dworkin and Bartky produced their critiques of beauty in the 1970s and early 1980s. The most powerful feminist work on beauty to be published since then, Naomi Wolf's *The Beauty Myth* (1990) provides an interesting example of how the times had changed. Despite, or perhaps because of, the power of her critique, Wolf felt it necessary to publish within 3 years another book, *Fire with Fire* (1993), which substantially removed the sting from her analysis and set out to distinguish her from the ranks of radical feminists. Wolf argues that women are required to engage in beauty practices and that this requirement was tightened in the 1980s as a backlash against the threat of the women's liberation movement and the greater opportunities, particularly in the workforce, that women were now accessing. As she explains, "The more legal and material hindrances women have broken through, the more strictly and heavily and cruelly images of female beauty have come to weigh upon us" (1990, p. 10). Wolf's analysis suggests that women are coerced into beauty practices by expectations of women in the workplace. Women might have entered workplaces in great numbers in the 1970s but in order not to threaten men, and in order to meet the requirement that they should be objects for the sexual delight of their male colleagues, they were required to engage in painful, expensive and time-consuming procedures that were not expected of their male counterparts if they wanted to get jobs and keep them. There was a "professional beauty qualification" which accompanied women into the workplace. Interestingly, despite the strength of Wolf's critique of beauty practices she does not consider them to be harmful in their own right, but only if they are forced on women rather than freely "chosen". In her last chapter "Beyond the Beauty Myth" she asks "Does all this mean we can't wear lipstick without feeling guilty?" (1990, p. 270); then answers, "On the contrary". She explains:

> In a world in which women have real choices, the choices we make about our appearance will be taken at last for what they really are: no big deal.
>
> Women will be able thoughtlessly to adorn ourselves with pretty objects when there is no question that we are not objects. Women will be free of the beauty myth when we can choose to use our faces and clothes and bodies as simply one form of expression out of a full range of others.
>
> (Wolf, 1990, p. 274)

Wolf's analysis does not suggest that there is a problem with the fact that women, and not men, have to do beauty practices at all, only that they are not free to choose to do so. It is this failure to ask the fundamental questions of why beauty practices are connected with women and why any women would want to continue with them after the revolution, that makes *The Beauty Myth* a liberal feminist book rather than a radical feminist one. *Fire with Fire* made her liberal feminist credentials clear (Wolf, 1993). In this book she asserts that women can not only choose to wear makeup, but also choose to be powerful. The material forces involved in structuring women's subordination have fallen away to leave liberation a project of individual willpower, "If we do not manage to . . . reach parity in the twenty-first century, it will be because women on some level have *chosen* [her italics] not to exert the power that is our birthright" (1993, p. 51).

Wolf's description of her clear distress at the negative reactions from audiences to the radicalism of her book on beauty may offer a clue as to why she evolved so swiftly into a fully fledged liberal feminist. After publication she said, "My job involved engaging, on TV and radio programs, with people who represented the industries I was criticizing. Many were, understandably, angry and defensive. Hosts were sometimes confrontational . . . I was acutely uncomfortable" (1993, p. 238). Her experience was a shock because, "I had always thought of myself as warm, friendly, and feminine", and, "after a vigorous debate, I would come home and cry in my partner's arms". Wolf's experience shows how difficult it is to criticize something so fundamental to male dominant western culture as beauty practices. Her reaction to it helps to explain why she chose to write *Fire with Fire* so soon thereafter, a book which appears to contradict the strong message of *The Beauty Myth*. She set out to create an unthreatening form of feminism and castigate radical feminists. Radical feminists who campaign against male violence become "victim feminists" who "identify with powerlessness", are "judgmental" particularly of "other women's sexuality and appearance" and "antisexual" (1993, p. 137). She seeks to soothe the masculine breasts that might have been ruffled by *The Beauty Myth* by proclaiming, "Male sexual attention is the sun in which I bloom. The male body is ground and shelter to me, my lifelong destination" (p. 186). Wolf overcompensated for what she may have seen as the youthful folly of writing a book on beauty which threatened the interests of male dominance. She retreated into a firm public/private distinction which exempts the area of "private" life from political scrutiny and turns it into an arena for the exercise of women's choices.

THE PERSONAL IS POLITICAL

The feminist critique of beauty starts from the understanding that the personal is political. While liberal feminists tend to view the realm of "private" life as an area in which women can exercise the power of choice untrammelled by politics, radical feminists such as Dworkin and MacKinnon seek to break down the public/private distinction which, they argue, is fundamental to male supremacy. This distinction provides men with a private world of male dominance in which they can garner women's emotional, housework, sexual, reproductive energies while hiding the feudal power relations of this realm behind the shield of the protection of "privacy". The private world is defended from the point of view of male dominance as one of "love" and individual fulfilment that should not be muddied by political analysis. It is a world in which women simply "choose" to lay out their energies and bodies at men's disposal, where they remain, despite whatever violence or abuse is handed out to them. The "private" nature of this world has long protected men from punishment because it has been seen as being outside the law that only applies in the public world. Thus marital rape was not a crime in this worldview, and domestic violence was a personal dispute.

Radical feminist critics argued that, on the contrary, the "personal"; that is, the behaviours of this "private" world, were indeed "political". Recognizing the "personal as political" allowed women to identify, through consciousness raising groups and the exchange of experiences, that what they took to be their own personal failings, such as hating their plump stomachs or feigning a headache when they wanted to avoid sexual intercourse without their male partner getting angry, were not just individual experiences. They were the common experiences of women, constructed out of the unequal power relations of the so-called "private" world, and very political indeed. The "private" world was recognized as the basis of the power men wielded in the "public" world of work and government. Men's public power and achievement, their citizenship status (Lister, 1997), depended on the servicing they received from women in the home. Not only did women provide this vital backdrop to men's dominance but they lacked a class of persons who would do the same for them, thus they were doubly disadvantaged in the public world in comparison with men. The concept that the personal is political enabled feminists to understand the ways in which the workings of male dominance penetrated into their relationships with men. They could recognize how the power dynamics of male dominance made heterosexuality into a political institution (Rich, 1993), constructed male and female sexuality (Jeffreys, 1990; Holland *et al.*, 1998), and the ways in which women felt about their bodies and themselves (Bordo, 1993).

"NEW" FEMINISM

Radical feminism, which identified the workings of male dominance throughout women's lives, was always opposed by varieties of feminism that sought to privatize and depoliticize sexuality and beauty practices. In the 1980s, for instance, there was a move to insulate sexuality from the radical feminist critique by both "liberal" and socialist feminists (Vance, 1984). In the 1990s there was a surge in publication by mainstream publishers, who had not been so keen to publish radical feminist work, of books that were said to embody a "new", "power" or "sexy" feminism (Wolf, 1993; Roiphe, 1993). These books had in common the furious repudiation of radical feminism and of the notion that the personal was political. They sought the radical depoliticization of sex and "personal" life. "New" feminism argued that women had achieved huge advances by the late twentieth century towards equal opportunities with men in the public world of work. This "new" feminism was influenced by radical American liberal individualism such as that expressed by a 1986 book which argued that "gender justice" could be achieved entirely through the facilitation of women's choices by the removal of barriers so that "individuals have the opportunity to choose" (Kirp *et al.*, 1986, p. 133). In the "new" feminism women's private lives were now simply the result of "choice" and should be off limits for feminist analysis or action.

A British example of these "new" feminists is Natasha Walter. She explains that she was able to learn from "cultural icons" such as Madonna about women's independence and sexuality. Madonna's contribution to creating a new sexualized feminism clothed in the costumes and practices of pornography will be discussed later in this volume. Walter's "new feminism" is based on a firm reinstatement of a line between the personal and the political. The personal, which should be exempt from political critique, covered "dress and pornography". The problem with feminism, she says, is that it "has sought to direct our personal lives on every level" (Walter, 1999, p. 4) and this "new feminism must unpick the tight link that feminism in the seventies made between our personal and political lives" (p. 4). Women were now free in their personal lives because, "Most women feel free, freer than their mothers did. Most women can choose what to wear, whom they will spend their lives with, where to work, what to read, when to have children" (1999, p. 10). She agrees with Naomi Wolf (1993) that what women really need is the "power" that will come when they are earning more. When they have "power" then they will apparently still have the desire to, "spend time waxing their legs or painting their nails" (Walter, 1999, p. 86) but feminists will feel "easier" about it. Women will be able to indulge the, "real, often wickedly enjoyable relationship they have with their clothes and their bodies" without being made to feel guilty by puritanical feminism (p. 86). In relation to beauty, Walter takes a similar view to that of the American libertarians above, "Respect for individual choice, however mysterious its origins, is a necessary condition of social justice" (Kirp *et al.*, 1986, p. 15). In other words the context in which "choices" are made is less important than the opportunity to explore them. This eschewing of rational interrogation of the mystery of such "choices" and pleasures to which most men seem immune, and what they might mean for women's lives, renders beauty practices into an aspect of the natural world beyond political concern.

The American equivalent of this brand of liberal feminism is Karen Lehrman's *The Lipstick Proviso* (1997), which argues that makeup is entirely compatible with feminism. Lehrman considers that there has been a return to femininity in the USA so that, "In recent years many women have also returned to practices that were once thought to subsidize male oppression. They're wearing provocative clothes and heels again, painting their faces and nails, treating their skin and hair to the latest styles and fads" (1997, p. 8). Feminists, she says, need to, "learn to respect women's choices – from wearing sensuous Galliano gowns to staying at home to raise their children" (1997, p. 13). She blames women's oppression on their failure to exercise their personal power. Women must just stop being self-destructive and give up "acting helpless" (p. 41). Beauty, she says, is "a reality, a gift of God, nature, or genius that, to some extent, transcends culture and history" (p. 68). In line with traditional male sexologists and sociobiologists she argues that women and men desire beauty because it is necessary to reproduction. Women want to be chosen, and men are programmed to choose "beautiful" women. Lehrman argues that "beauty", in the form of sexiness, gives women power they can use to advance themselves. The power derives from "wearing sexual clothing". Women "strut" she says, "because sexuality is a form of power, a strength, an asset . . . The difference now is that it's not women's only power" (1997, p. 94). Women are not, she says, "victimized by diets, exercise, beautiful models, fashion designers, high heels, makeup, compliments" (p. 23). Rather, they have, "a great deal of control over their lives" (p. 23). The problem for women, it turns out, is that there is intrusion into the sanctity of their personal lives, not just by the government but by something called "society" which "includes feminist theorists" (p. 23).

Nancy Etcoff's book *The Survival of the Prettiest* (2000) expresses almost identical sentiments. Beauty is inevitable and universal, a "basic instinct" (Etcoff, 2000, p. 7). Etcoff has a harsh diagnosis for those, like feminist critics of beauty, who fail to respond to "physical beauty". This lack of response is "one sign of profound depression" (2000, p. 8). Men inevitably respond to "young, nubile girls" because of a "reproductive imperative". She agrees with Lehrman that women can achieve "power" through beauty practices because "isn't it possible that women cultivate beauty and use the beauty industry to optimize the power beauty brings?" (Etcoff, p. 4). These liberal feminists do not acknowledge the forces that restrict and can even eliminate women's ability to choose. They do not consider the limitations of the "pleasure" and "power" that beauty practices offer, or the ways in which they contribute to women's condition of subordination. Thus they can be seen to protect the status quo of the cultural sexual objectification of women.

THE CULTURAL TURN

The invigoration of liberal feminism is but one aspect of an upheaval in the way oppression could be spoken about that took place in the 1980s and 1990s. A change took place in the academy too. The move towards putting emphasis on women's capacity to choose and express agency than on the forms of coercion that caused women to engage in beauty practices is an aspect of that postmodern takeover of leftwing thinking that Fredric

Jameson has called "the cultural turn" (Jameson, 1998). Postmodern thinking rejects the notion that there is such a thing as a ruling class which can create dominant ideas. Marxist cultural theorists who reject postmodernism, such as Fredric Jameson and Terry Eagleton, explain that this set of ideas emerged to serve a particular stage of the history of capitalism. Eagleton, for instance, argues that postmodernism took root in response to the perceived failure of the left, and the death, among so many of its members, of any idea of revolution or serious social change (Eagleton, 1996). Eagleton invites his readers to imagine that a political movement has suffered a historic defeat:

> The governing assumption of such an epoch, one imagines, would be that the system itself was unbreachable . . . there would be an upsurge of interest in the margins and crevices of the system . . . The system could not be breached; but it could at least be momentarily transgressed . . . Fascinated by fault-lines, one might even come to imagine that there *is* no centre to society after all.
>
> (Eagleton, 1996, p. 2)

In particular the overtaking of critical thought by postmodernism meant a discarding of the notion of ideology because this notion implies that there are such things as agents or interests responsible for oppression. Australian radical feminist theorist Denise Thompson has argued powerfully the case for retaining the concept of ideology for feminist theory. She answers what she considers to be postmodern mystification thus: "to abandon the concepts of 'agents and interests' is to abandon politics. If there are no 'agents', there are no perpetrators and beneficiaries of relations of domination, and no one whose human agency is blocked by powerful vested interests" (Thompson, 2001, p. 23). Thompson criticizes the effect this abandonment of the concept of ideology has on feminist theorizing of popular culture. One important understanding of postmodern cultural theorists is that there is little to choose between low and high culture, so that soap operas and sometimes porn movies come to be seen as equal in value to other cultural products. This belief is bound up with the notion that the consumers of this popular culture are knowledgeable and discriminating, imbued with agency and choice, able to select and reject from the smorgasbord of offerings in their own interests. Thompson shows the problem of this tendency in the work of Michele Barrett, a British socialist feminist theorist in whom the socialism has been overtaken by postmodernism. Barrett criticizes feminist theorists for regarding "cultural phenomena such as soap opera, royalty or romantic fiction" as representing a subordinating ideology for women because, as Barrett says, this ignores the "passionate enthusiasm of many women for the products of which they are alleged to be victims" (quoted in Thompson, 2001, p. 24).

Beauty and Misogyny could well fit into precisely those feminist writings which are being criticized because I am arguing here that ideologies of beauty and fashion such as those circulated through popular culture do subordinate women, however passionately those women may adhere to them and cut up their bodies in response. Indeed, as Thompson says, "passionate enthusiasm is the way ideology *must* operate if it is to operate at all" (2001, p. 24). Thompson suggests that the "only criterion for judging whether something is ideological is whether or not it reinforces relations of ruling" (p. 25). This test of whether or not they reinforce relations of ruling is a useful one to apply to the beauty practices such as makeup, fashion and labiaplasty that are examined in this book.

The "cultural turn" entered the discipline of women's studies too. Postmodern ideas became dominant over the way in which women's oppression and sexuality could be thought of and written about in the academy. The takeover of postmodern understandings, in combination with a decline in the strength of feminism and other social movements for radical change, undermined the feminist critique of beauty. The emphasis in the work of some feminist research changed from examining how beauty practices work to oppress and harm women to the question of how women could enjoy these practices and be empowered by them (Davis, 1995; Frost, 1999).

Some feminist researchers have found the ideas of one "postmodern" theorist, Foucault, helpful in addressing the complexities of the construction of women's "subjectivities" or understandings of themselves. Both Susan Bordo (1993) and Sandra Bartky (1990) use Foucauldian approaches to explain the way in which women are subjected to the regime of beauty to the extent that they engage in self-policing. However, as Bordo herself notes, the problem with the adoption of postmodern ideas in general is that they have led some writers to disregard the materiality of power relations. Bordo identifies the extrapolations and adaptations of Foucault that she considers unhelpful "misrepresentation", because they make it hard for many feminist thinkers to place women's actions in a context of power relations. She says of "liberated postmodern subjectivity" that, "This abstract, unsituated, disembodied freedom . . . celebrates itself only through the effacement of the material praxis of people's lives, the normalizing power of cultural images, and the sadly continuing social realities of dominance and subordination" (Bordo, 1993, p. 129). She suggests that postmodern cultural studies theorists may have been captured by the *Zeitgeist* of the very television chat shows that can be the object of their analysis. The triviality and superficiality of such cultural forms have been absorbed by the cultural critics and have substantially deradicalized their analysis:

> All the elements of what I have here called "postmodern conversation" intoxication with individual choice and creative

> *jouissance*, delight with the piquancy of particularity and mistrust of pattern and seeming coherence, celebration of "difference" along with an absence of critical perspective differentiating and weighting "differences," . . . All have become recognizable and familiar elements of much of contemporary intellectual discourse.
>
> (Bordo, 1993, p. 117)

She criticizes a "celebratory, academic postmodernism" which has made it "highly unfashionable – and 'totalising' – to talk about the grip of culture on the body" (Bordo, 1993, p. 117). The "totalisers" are seen as representing "active and creative subjects as 'cultural dopes,' 'passive dupes' of ideology" and seeing dominant ideology as "seamless and univocal, overlooking both the gaps which are continually allowing for the eruption of 'difference' and the polysemous, unstable, open nature of all cultural texts" (Bordo, 1993, p. 117).

The effect of the cultural turn on feminist ideas about beauty is three-fold. Women are seen as having choice and agency in relation to beauty practices, or even being empowered by them. Women are represented as having the power to "play" with beauty practices because instead of being oppressive they can now be reinterpreted as fun. Fashion magazines and popular culture are reinterpreted as fascinating resources from which girls and women can be inspired and creative rather than playing a role in the enforcement of dominant ideology.

The work of Kathy Davis is a good example of how a feminist theorist influenced by the cultural turn applies the concern with demonstrating women's agency to beauty practices (Davis, 1995). She researched women's reasons for having breast augmentation surgery in the Netherlands, and explains that she is determined not to represent her interviewees as "cultural dopes" who have simply imbibed the negative messages of the beauty culture about the inferiority of women's bodies. She says that the surgery is "an intervention in identity" which can allow a woman to "open up the possibility to renegotiate her relation to her body and construct a different sense of self" (Davis, 1995, p. 27). Davis says that cosmetic breast surgery "disempowers" the "entrapment of objectification". It can "provide an avenue toward becoming an embodied subject rather than an objectified body" (1995, p. 113). By the end of her book Davis takes the notion of respecting women's agency to new extremes by arguing that cosmetic surgery is a means of achieving moral and just outcomes for women, "Cosmetic surgery is about morality. For a woman whose suffering has gone beyond a certain point, cosmetic surgery can become a matter of justice – the only fair thing to do" (1995, p. 163).

Liz Frost is an exponent of this approach in relation to makeup. She describes the activity of "doing looks" as something "which cannot be avoided" (Frost, 1999, p. 134); that is, natural and inevitable. She does not see the requirement to "do looks" as ideological or in the service of male dominance. She derides feminist theorists for being critical of the practice and thus making women feel guilty and ambivalent. Such negativity, she argues, is in league with patriarchal religion which says that women should not be vain. She sees "doing looks" as a source of pleasure for women as well as empowerment. She uses postmodern concepts to argue that "doing looks" is vitally necessary for women:

> For women to feel powerful and in control, to feel a sense of agency and competence (all, I would argue, essential for mental health), doing looks can no longer be viewed as an optional extra but rather as a central identificatory process which can offer meanings such as pleasure, creative expression and satisfaction provided that women can appropriate a discursive space in which to contradict the silencing discourses of vanity, abnormality, superficiality and unsisterliness.
>
> (Frost, 1999, p. 134)

For Frost the feminist critique of beauty practices stands in the way of women's pleasurable agency in lipstick wearing.

The idea that feminine beauty and fashion practices can be seen as playful fun rather than oppressive owes something to the ideas of Judith Butler on "performativity". Butler argues in *Gender Trouble* (1990) that gender is socially constructed through the everyday doing of the rituals that constitute it, "Gender is the repeated stylization of the body, a set of repeated acts within a highly rigid regulatory frame that congeal over time to produce the appearance of substance, of a natural sort of being" (1990, p. 33). The idea that gender is socially constructed is not a new one for feminism, indeed it is fundamental to feminist understanding. Much of the excitement associated with her work stems from the way that it has been interpreted by queer theorists and activists as saying that the performance of gender by other than the usual actors, as in drag for instance, is a revolutionary tactic because it demonstrates the fact that gender is socially constructed. Her work has been the inspiration of a whole queer cultural project of playing with and swapping gender by actors who see themselves as doing political work when they wear the appurtenances of one gender on a body usually associated with its opposite. Butler has argued that this interpretation of her work – that gender can be subject to individual choice – is incorrect. In response she wrote *Bodies that Matter* (1993), arguing that gender performance is in fact the result of constraint and is not open to easy manipulation,

> If gender is not an artifice to be taken on or taken off at will and, hence, not an effect of choice, how are we to understand the

> constitutive and compelling status of gender norms without falling into the trap of cultural determinism?
>
> (Butler, 1993, p. x)

Though Butler argues that she has been misinterpreted, it is precisely that apparent misinterpretation that has been taken up by queer theorists to argue that drag, gender swapping, transgenderism and even sadomasochism, can be revolutionary ways of playing with gender and thus has made it harder for feminists to theorize beauty practices in a serious way.

Ruth Holliday's work on fashion is an example of this lighthearted queer theory approach. In a piece entitled "Fashioning the Queer Self" she argues that:

> postmodern fashion puts quotation marks around the garments it revitalizes, allowing them to be re-read in a space of ironic distance between the wearer and the garment. This opens up a space for "playing" with fashion which is the antithesis of being its victim, and thus the feminist arguments about the regulation of women's bodies through fashion decline in importance.
>
> (Holliday, 2001, p. 218)

Not everyone might notice the quotation marks, however, when they see the same old gender differences in clothing despite the fact that the players have "revitalized" them through postmodern inspiration.

Angela McRobbie's work (1997) is an example of another product of the "cultural turn", the idea that popular culture should not be seen as ideological but as presenting useful resources for women's creativity and agency. McRobbie is of the postmodern cultural studies school which tries to be relentlessly positive about women's and girls' relationships with culture and argues that women are not "cultural dopes" but negotiate the content of fashion and beauty magazines, interpreting what could be seen as patriarchal cultural messages in empowering, creative and diverse ways. Moreover, she argues, young women's magazines are actually involved in such postmodern practices as "parody" and "pastiche" and "irony" and "the readers get the joke" (McRobbie, 1997). Young girls reading *More* and *19* are not just internalizing the patriarchal scripts in the magazines but using them creatively.

These young women's magazines contain ever burgeoning amounts of sexual content, instructions for young women on what to do sexually and how to deal with sexual problems. This sexual content distinguishes these contemporary magazines from those of previous decades. McRobbie calls this "new sexualities in girls' and women's magazines" (1997). She writes about how the girls enjoy this sexual content because they have "pleasure-seeking sexual identities" (1997, p. 200). She advises that feminists are wrong to dismiss these magazines because so many hundreds of thousands of young girls enjoy them, and argues that the magazines themselves have "taken feminism on board" (1997, p. 207) and therefore feminists cannot straightforwardly condemn them. She concludes an article on these "new sexualities" by taking the postmodern line that there is no such thing as truth, and feminists need to accept that "Perhaps it is only by being willing to let go, and relinquish its grasp over the truth, that feminism earns an important place for itself in the magazines" (McRobbie, 1997, p. 208). Feminism, it transpires, can mean anything, as long as we manage to read irony, parody and pastiche into what might otherwise look like ordinary patriarchal ideology.

Unfortunately research by feminist social scientists into what is really happening to young women and girls in heterosexual relations does not support the gung-ho enthusiasm of relentlessly positive, postmodern, cultural studies buffs. The fashionable, post-Marxist, cultural studies of the present may be uninflected by the attention to material reality that concerns social scientists, but research on the experience of girls suggests that they are far from "pleasure-seeking" and certainly are not empowered. They are controlled in their relations with boys by the "male in the head" (Holland *et al.*, 1998). Lynn Phillips' research on young women and heterosex found that they were having to learn to split mind and body to stay in control of their sexual encounters and doing sex as a performance for men's sexual pleasure rather than meeting any desires of their own (Phillips, 2000).

Philips found that sexually violent experiences were common among the college age women she interviewed in the late 1990s. Indeed, 27 of the 30 women "described at least one encounter that fit legal definitions of rape, battering, or harassment" (2000, p. 7). But, despite the fact that many were taking women's studies courses and despite the work of feminists for 20 years challenging rape and trying to make it more possible for women to recognize and challenge violence against them, "only two women ever used such terms to describe a personal experience" (Phillips, 2000, p. 7). One reason, she suggests, is that young women today have been raised to believe in their own power and agency, precisely that which dominant cultural studies theory attributes to them, and this makes recognition of rape difficult:

> Whereas feminist scholars may speak of male domination and women's victimization as rather obvious phenomena, younger women, raised to believe in their own independence, invulnerability, and sexual entitlement, may not so readily embrace such concepts, even as they are raped, harassed, and battered by men.
>
> (Phillips, 2000, pp. 10–11)

Liz Frost, the writer we saw earlier declaring that "doing looks" was a positive "central identificatory process" for women, has, in other work, provided good evidence for why women "do looks" that relates clearly to oppression. In a book on the relationship of young girls to their bodies, she argues that young women in the west might be said to be suffering from "body hatred" (Frost, 2001, p. 2). She points out that though it might be expected that women who were losing their ability to represent the ideal of feminine beauty through age would be most vulnerable to body hatred, it is in fact the young who suffer most. She says that women's bodies are "inferiorised – stigmatized . . . within an overarching patriarchal ideology. For example, biologically and physiologically, women's bodies are seen as both disgusting in their natural state and inferior to men's" (2001, p. 141). Body hatred is manifested in self-harm and that harm is becoming more and more serious both in young women and in young lesbians and gay men. One of Frost's interviewees, when asked "Are there any young women who are happy with their looks?" responded, "Well if there is I don't know them!" (2001, p. 154). Bullying, in the young women's accounts, played a large part in creating the agonized relationships they had with their bodies. The constant humiliation of girls about their appearance from their school peers seems to be one element in the creation of body hatred. One interviewee explains that this leads to girls scrupulously trying to improve their appearance with beauty practices such as makeup. The "doing looks" that Frost celebrates can be seen, though she does not make this connection, as a way to ameliorate the shame and despair that a male dominant culture creates in women. The culture that young women in the west grow up in is not as diverse and open to playfulness as some cultural studies and queer theorists suggest.

SEXUAL DIFFERENCE/DEFERENCE

Western culture is founded on the notion of sexual difference: the idea that there is an essential difference between men and women, expressed in the behaviours of masculinity and femininity and their attendant practices. It is so dominant and all pervasive, allowing little place for alternatives, that the idea that women can positively "choose" the practices which express this difference makes little sense. Western culture, like all other male dominant cultures, requires that the "difference" be publicly demonstrated. For this reason the difference is regarded as truth. This is a most tenaciously enduring myth and difficult to challenge. The practice of different, masculine and feminine behaviours by men and women is based on the idea that there is such a thing as "sexual difference". French feminist theorists such as Monique Wittig (1996) and Colette Guillaumin (1996) argue forcefully that this difference is political and the very basis of male domination. Sexual difference is generally explained by biology as if there were two clear biologically distinct sexes that display biologically created differences of behaviour and appearance. Feminist theorists from various disciplines have pointed out with overwhelming force over the last 30 years that "sex roles", now more usually called "gender", are culturally constructed and this social constructionist analysis has more recently been extended to the idea of biological sex itself (Delphy, 1993). The phenomenon of intersexuality, where secondary sexual characteristics, hormones and/or genetic structure can incorporate elements of both supposedly distinct biological sexes, has lent force to the idea that the notion of two sexes is a political one. The idea of two sexes results from the need of a male dominant culture to be able to identify members of the ruling class of men and the subordinate class of women by slotting babies into one of these two status categories at birth. The genders of male dominance and female subordination are then foisted upon those occupying the appropriate status category.

The "difference" between men and women is created in and by culture but is regarded as natural and biological. The huge difficulty that so many women and men have in seeing femininity and masculinity as socially constructed rather than natural, attests to the strength and force of culture. The French feminist theorist Colette Guillaumin explains the difficulty with this cultural idea that women are "different" (Guillaumin, 1996). If women are "different" then there must be something they are different from. That something turns out to be "men" who are not themselves "different" from anything, they just *are*. It is only women who are understood to be different, "Men do not differ from anything . . . We are different – it is a fundamental characteristic . . . We succeed in the grammatical and logical feat of being different all by ourselves. Our nature is difference" (Guillaumin, 1996, p. 95). Women are, of course, understood to be "different" from men in many ways, "delicate, pretty, intuitive, unreasonable, maternal, non-muscular, lacking an organizing character", as Guillaumin puts it (1996, p. 95). But most importantly women are understood to be different from men in being both potentially "beautiful" and in being interested in beauty and enthusiastic to put in huge amounts of time, money, pain and emotional distress to be "beautiful". This is assumed in western culture to be "natural" to women and a most persuasive sign of women's difference from men.

The idea of biological sexual difference is the major obstacle to the recognition that men and women actually stand in relation to one another in positions of dominance and subordination. As another French feminist, Monique Wittig, puts it, "The ideology of sexual difference functions as censorship in our culture by masking, on the ground of nature, the social opposition between men and women" (Wittig, 1996, p. 24). The sex difference is created by a system of domination since in any system of domination, "The masters explain and justify the established divisions as a result of natural differences" (p. 24). Wittig argues that the concepts "man" and "woman" are political categories and would be abolished in a class struggle between women and men if women were successful. But women do not engage in this class struggle. They do not recognize they are dominated because the "oppositions (differences) appear as given, already there, before all thought" (1996, p. 25). Wittig quotes Marx and Engels on the way in which the ruling class of "every epoch" is "at the same time its ruling *intellectual* force" and the ideas of any time are the ideas of this class's dominance (1996, p. 26). It is the dominance of the political class of "men", according to Wittig, that teaches women that "there are before all thinking, all society, 'sexes' (two categories of individuals born) with a constitutive difference", which is both metaphysical and "natural" and adopted into Marxist thought in the form of the division of labour according to sex. This idea "conceals the political fact of the subjugation of one sex by the other" (Wittig, 1996, p. 26).

The category of sex into which humans are placed is the basis of compulsory heterosexuality (Rich, 1993) and it "founds society as heterosexual" (Wittig, 1996, p. 27):

> The category of sex is the one that rules as "natural" the relation that is at the base of (heterosexual) society and through which half of the population, women, are "heterosexualised" (the making of women is like the making of eunuchs, the breeding of slaves, of animals) and submitted to a heterosexual economy.
>
> (1996, p. 27)

The purpose of this compulsory heterosexuality is to enable men to "appropriate for themselves the reproduction and production of women, and also their physical persons by means of a contract called the marriage contract" (p. 27).

Wittig's analysis of the requirements of the "category of sex" for women is helpful for understanding beauty practices. She explains that women are made into sex itself:

> The category of sex is the product of heterosexual society that turns half of the population into sexual beings. Wherever they are, whatever they do (including working in the public sector), they are seen (and made) sexually available to men, and they, breasts, buttocks, costume, must be visible. They must wear their yellow star, their constant smile, day and night.
>
> (Wittig, 1996, p. 28)

Wittig suggests that we see this forced availability of all women, married or not, as "a period of forced sexual service, a sexual service that we may compare to the military one, and which can vary between a day, a year, or twenty-five years or more". It is beauty practices that mark out women as fulfilling the requirements of their sexual "corvée"; that is, the work that the peasants must perform for their feudal landlords without payment. The beauty practices give pleasure to men, enable their sexual excitement, in the office, the street, at the movies, in the bedroom. Men do not inhabit the category of sex as women do. Men are much more than sex, "the category of sex . . . sticks to women, for only they cannot be perceived outside of it. Only *they* are sex, *the* sex, and [it is as] sex [that] they [are] made in their minds, bodies, acts, gestures" (Wittig, 1996, p. 28).

This idea that women are sex is well described in the work of the male scientists of sex, the sexologists of the twentieth century who have played such an important part in giving the "category of sex" for women an authoritative base in science and medicine. The important sexologist Iwan Bloch, quotes in his 1909 *The Sexual Life of Our Time*, an author who, he says, has "well characterized woman's extended sexual sphere":

> Women are in fact pure sex from knees to neck. We men have concentrated our apparatus in a single place, we have extracted it, separated it from the rest of the body, because pret a partir [ready to go]. They [women] are a sexual surface or target; we have only a sexual arrow.
>
> (quoted in Jeffreys, 1985, p. 138)

The creation of sexual difference through beauty practices is essential to affording to men the sexual satisfaction that they gain as they go about the tasks of their day from recognizing "woman" and feeling their penises engorge. This may sound like an exaggeration of the way men think and behave but some are prepared to express it this clearly. J.C. Flugel in his *Psychology of Clothes* (1930/1950) puts quite baldly the reason why women are required to dress differently from men:

> the great majority of us doubtless will . . . admit frankly that . . . we cannot bear to face the prospect of abolishing the present system of constant titillation – a system which ensures that we shall be warned even from a distance as to the sex of an approaching fellow-being, so that we need lose no opportunity of experiencing at any rate the incipient stages of the sexual response.
>
> There seems to be no escape from the view that the fundamental purpose of adopting a distinctive dress for the two sexes is to stimulate the sexual instinct.
>
> (p. 201)

Emmanuel Reynaud, author of *Holy Virility*, offers an explanation of the difference in dress that supports the idea that it serves men's sexual satisfaction, "She must show her legs and make her vagina accessible, whereas a man does not have to reveal his calves or offer easy access to his penis" (Reynaud, 1983, p. 402).

Beauty practices show that women are obedient, willing to do their service, and to put effort into that service. They show, I suggest, that women are not simply "different" but, most importantly, "deferential". The difference that women must embody is deference. The way in which the sexual difference/deference is required to be expressed can vary considerably between male dominant societies, but there is no evidence that any societies exist in which the sexual difference/deference is irrelevant or in which the social order of male dominance is founded in anything but this difference. Indeed how could male dominance have any existence without a clear difference marking who is in the dominant class and who is not? In western societies it is expressed in the requirement that women create "beauty" through clothing which should show large areas of their bodies for male excitement, through skirts (although this is not such a pervasive rule as it was 20 years ago), through figure-hugging clothing, through makeup, hairstyles, depilation, prominent display of secondary sexual characteristics or creation of them by surgery and through "feminine" body language. Women are required to practise femininity in order to create sexual difference/deference. But the difference is one of power, and femininity is the behaviour required of the subordinate class of women in order to show their deference to the ruling class of men.

FEMININITY AS THE BEHAVIOUR OF SUBORDINATION

The beauty practices that women engage in, and which men find so exciting, are those of political subordinates. The sadomasochistic romance of male dominance, where sex is constructed from male dominance and female subordination (Jeffreys, 1990), requires that someone should play the girl. The feminist theorist of sexuality and sexual violence, Catharine MacKinnon, argues that the "genders" of male dominance, masculinity and femininity need to be constantly recreated to service the sexuality of male dominance; that is, eroticized power difference (MacKinnon, 1989). This understanding is helpful in explaining the existence and persistence of femininity. The sexuality of male dominance requires "fems" and women are trained and pressured into femininity to facilitate men's sexual excitement.

Feminist theorists have shown that what is understood as "feminine" behaviour is not simply socially constructed, but *politically* constructed, as the behaviour of a subordinate social group. Nancy Henley's work on body politics is a classic example of this approach (Henley, 1977). She shows clearly that the ways in which human beings are trained and expected to use their bodies derive from their place in a power hierarchy. The powerful express their privilege in certain ways that are forbidden to subordinates. Henley shows that it is not only men who act out the behaviours of power but human beings involved in other forms of hierarchy besides gender, such as employers and employees. The powerful take up more space. Not only do employers have larger offices but men will have more space in their homes and the world which is theirs alone. They take up more space with their bodies. Thus men may stretch out on a bus seat or on the sofa. Women are expected to keep their legs and arms tucked into their bodies and fit into the space that is left over. Similarly interviewees may not sprawl when in the subordinate position of applying for a job, but the interviewers may do so. Men, Henley shows, approach women more closely than they would approach other men because women are permitted less personal space around their bodies.

Touch is another area in which the powerful are privileged. The powerful may make physical contact while the subordinates may not. Thus employers may touch office juniors but the reverse behaviour would be presumptuous. Men may, and do, touch women but if women touch men it can be interpreted as a sexual comeon and is a dangerous behaviour. Eye contact is also a way of expressing power. Men may stare at women and women are not supposed to stare in return but to decorously cast down their eyes. But men may not stare at other men without inviting an aggressive, "who are you staring at" response. These behaviours are learnt both through direct instruction, such as mothers telling their daughters to keep their knees together, and through social interaction. But it is likely that by adulthood they are seen by those who practise them as "natural". The learning process is forgotten. The behaviours of space, touch and eye contact that are required of subordinates are then understood as the "natural" behaviours of femininity. It is on the base formed by these behaviours that beauty practices are grafted, and that high heels can seem natural on women but ridiculous on men.

The feminist psychologist Dee Graham has contributed significantly to our understanding of femininity as the behaviour of subordinates with her concept of "societal Stockholm syndrome" (Graham, 1994). In *Loving to Survive* she makes an analogy between femininity and the behaviour of hostages in situations of captivity and threat that has been named Stockholm syndrome. She explains that the idea of Stockholm syndrome comes from a hostage situation in Stockholm in which it became clear that hostages, instead of reacting with rebellion to their oppressors, were likely to bond with them. This bonding, in which hostages can come to identify the interests of their kidnappers as their own, comes from the very real threat to their survival that the kidnappers pose. Graham extends this concept to cover the behaviour of women, femininity, that is a reaction to living in a society of male violence in which they are in danger. Femininity represents societal Stockholm syndrome, "If one (inescapable) group threatens another group with violence but also – as a group – shows the victimized group some kindness, an attachment *between the groups* will develop. This is what we refer to as *Societal (or Cultural) Stockholm Syndrome*" (Graham, 1994, p. 57).

Graham states unequivocally that, "masculinity and femininity are code words for male domination and female subordination" (1994, p. 192). She says that women, like hostages, are afraid, and "use any available information to alter our behavior in ways that make interactions with men go smoothly" (p. 160). One of the things they do is change their bodies in order to win men over. She lists the harmful beauty practices that are considered in this book, such as makeup, cosmetic surgery, shaving and waxing body hair, high-heeled shoes and restrictive clothes, as examples. She says that these practices reflect:

> (1) the extent to which women seek to make ourselves acceptable to men, (2) the extent to which women seek to connect to men, and thus (3) the extent to which women feel the need for men's affection and approval and (4) the extent to which women feel unworthy of men's affection and approval *just as we are* (unchanged).
>
> (Graham, 1994, p. 162)

Graham also argues that, "femininity is a blueprint for how to get along with one's enemy by trying to win over the enemy" (1994, p. 187). The term "femininity", "refers to personality traits associated with subordinates and to personality traits of individuals who have taken on behaviors pleasing to dominants" (p. 187) and "those behaviors which male culture classifies as 'feminine' are behaviors that one would expect to characterize any oppressed group" (p. 189). These behaviours of the less powerful are necessarily indirect attempts to influence the powerful, "such as use of intelligence, canniness, intuition, interpersonal skill, charm, sexuality, deception, and avoidance" (p. 187); that is, those behaviours, except perhaps for intelligence, likely to be identified as essentially feminine.

Graham offers an explanation for why many women believe that their "femininity" is biological and inherent and why, "we believe that we would choose to wear makeup, curl our hair, and wear high heels even if men didn't find women who dressed this way more attractive" (1994, p. 197). Women believe this, she says, because "to believe differently" would require the acknowledgement that our behaviour is controlled by "external variables"; that is, men's use of force and its threat. Recognizing this would mean that women would have to "acknowledge our terror" (p. 197). She says that "It is scary for women to contemplate no longer being feminine" (p. 199) and concludes that examining what it is that is scary about giving up femininity may lead to the decision to give it up altogether.

Feminist social constructionists such as Henley and Graham understand the task of feminism to be the destruction and elimination of what have been called "sex roles" or "sexual difference" and are now more usually called "gender". When masculinity and femininity are understood to be the behaviours of dominance and subordination it does not make much sense to expect any aspects of these behaviours to survive the destruction of male dominance. Christine Delphy explains that the concept of androgyny as a way forward for dealing with gender difference – that is, both men and women could combine the behaviours now rigidly ascribed to either one or the other – is not realizable (Delphy, 1993). The behaviours of domination and subordination would not survive in an egalitarian future in order to be combined in any form. There may be aspects of ascribed behaviours that are not associated with power difference that may be more equally shared, such as nurturing behaviour, but all the behaviours of deference and privilege would become unimaginable.

I have sought to show the power of the cultural expectation that women should demonstrate femininity by engaging in beauty practices. The forces which exact this behaviour include a lack of any possibility of glimpsing alternatives, the belief that femininity and its practices are natural and inevitable, childhood training, bullying in school, the requirements of the workplace, the need to ameliorate the body hatred inculcated by male dominant culture, and the fear of male retaliation. As Karen Callaghan explains in her introduction to the collection, *Ideals of Feminine Beauty* (1994), social control in the contemporary west is not usually imposed on individuals by brute force but achieved through, "symbolic manipulation" which can include such things as advertising and women's magazines and "creates the guise of free will and choice" (Callaghan, 1994, p. x). The fact that some women say that they take pleasure in the practices is not inconsistent with their role in the subordination of women. This should perhaps be seen as the ability of some women to make a virtue out of necessity. In the next chapter I argue that western beauty practices need to be included in United Nations definitions of harmful cultural practices. This concept is a useful antidote to the debate on agency versus subordination that I have covered here because it is founded on an understanding of the power of cultural enforcement of practices that harm women and children. For practices that are identified as harmful, "choice" is no defence.

2

HARMFUL CULTURAL PRACTICES AND WESTERN CULTURE

I argue here that beauty practices in western culture should be understood as harmful cultural practices. Western beauty practices such as makeup and breast implant surgery involve different degrees of harm to women. Cosmetic surgery that removes body parts is more obviously similar to female genital mutilation than makeup wearing is, for instance. This chapter argues, however, that a continuum of western beauty practices from lipstick at one end to invasive cosmetic surgery at the other, fit the criteria set out for harmful cultural practices in United Nations understandings, although they may differ in the extremity of their effects. The concept of harmful cultural/traditional practices originates from UN concerns to identify and eliminate forms of harm to women and children that do not easily fit into a human rights framework (UN, 1995). It is gaining increasing recognition in the international human rights community but only inasmuch as it refers to practices such as female genital mutilation in non-western cultures. There is, however, no recognition of quite similar practices, such as the cutting of genitals to fit people into gender stereotyped categories in the west, as harmful. Indeed it is likely that the idea that the west has a "culture" that produces "practices" at all may seem foreign. Harmful practices in the west will most usually be justified as emanating from consumer "choice", from "science" and "medicine" or "fashion"; that is, the law of the market. Culture may be seen as something reactionary that exists in the non-west. The west has science and the market instead. In this chapter I argue that the culture of western male dominance does produce practices, including beauty practices, that are harmful to women.

In the last decade a particularly brutal western beauty practice, labiaplasty, has grown in popularity with cosmetic surgeons. An Internet search under the term "labiaplasty" turned up 2,200 websites, most of which were for US cosmetic surgeons offering the procedure. A labiaplasty surgeon describes the surgery as "a surgical procedure that will reduce and/or reshape the labia minora" (LabiaplastySurgeon.com, 2002). The websites list the practice routinely among the other surgeries offered which cut up the female body to conform to male desires. In western countries too, the practice of "gender reassignment" surgery, in which men and women are castrated, and breasts, penises, wombs are removed or constructed, is carried out by, often, the very same surgeons. But these practices are not understood to be clearly harmful and evidence of a reactionary culture. Transsexual surgical castration, for instance, is represented by the medical profession that profits from it as being treatment for a disabling medical condition of "gender dysphoria", rather than a cultural requirement that those who do not fit into one sex class category should be surgically transferred to another (Rottnek, 1999).

The concept of harmful cultural practices is helpful for analysing such practices in the west as well as in the non-west. Harmful cultural or traditional practices in UN terms are identified as: being harmful to the health of women and girls; arising from the material power differences between the sexes; being for the benefit of men; creating stereotyped masculinity and femininity which damage the opportunities of women and girls; being justified by tradition. This definition is well suited to beauty practices in the west such as cosmetic surgery. The concept enables the culture of male domination in which women live to be brought into focus and subjected to criticism instead of being regarded as natural, inevitable or even progressive.

HARMFUL CULTURAL PRACTICES

The UN concept of harmful cultural/traditional practices is aimed at identifying practices that are culturally condoned, as forms of violence and discrimination against women. The concept is enshrined in the very important and only "women's" convention – the Convention on the Elimination of All Forms of Discrimination Against Women (CEDAW; UN, 1979). Article 2(f) of CEDAW states that parties to the Convention will "take all appropriate measures, including legislation, to modify or abolish existing laws, regulations, customs and practices which constitute discrimination against women". CEDAW also enjoins States Parties to take measures to:

> modify the social and cultural patterns of conduct of men and women, with a view to achieving the elimination of prejudices and customary and all other practices which are based on the idea of the inferiority or the superiority of either of the sexes or on stereotyped roles for men and women.
>
> (UN, 1979, art. 5(a))

The definition of customary practices here is sufficiently wide to include beauty practices very well. Beauty practices are the main instrument by which the "difference" between the sexes is created and maintained. They create the stereotyped role for women of being sex and beauty objects, having to spend inordinate amounts of time and money on makeup, hairstyles, depilation, creams and potions, fashion, botox and cosmetic surgery. Men engage in most of the beauty practices described in this book only for the sexual satisfactions they gain from masochistic crossdressing. They are not required to wear makeup for work, or dress in high heels to please the dominant sex class. Indeed, as we shall see in Chapter 3, men's crossdressing causes considerable problems for women rather than stimulating sexual excitement. Unless we accept that women are biologically programmed to engage in beauty practices, then they need to be understood as cultural practices that are required of women. All practices required of one sex class rather than the other should be examined for their political role in maintaining male dominance.

The concept of harmful cultural/traditional practices was refined in several UN documents in the 1990s. An expanded definition of harmful traditional practices is offered in a 1995 UN Fact Sheet:

> female genital mutilation (FGM); forced feeding of women; early marriage; the various taboos or practices which prevent women from controlling their own fertility; nutritional taboos and traditional birth practices; son preference and its implications for the status of the girl child; female infanticide; early pregnancy; and dowry price.
>
> (UN, 1995, pp. 3–4)

Some of the practices described in the Fact Sheet have analogies in the west. Forced feeding, for instance, which prepares girls for marriage in cultures in which plumpness is considered by men to be attractive, bears some resemblance to western beauty practices. It is instructive to compare it with what is apparently its opposite, starvation, which is more likely to be engaged in by western girls and women in order to approach the cultural standard of attractiveness. In western culture women are likely to restrict eating for weeks or months in order to fit into their wedding dress rather than to increase their consumption. The Fact Sheet usefully explains how such practices originate and this can illuminate the origins of beauty practices too.

Harmful traditional practices are, in the UN definition, damaging to the health of women and girls. The damaging health consequences of practices such as female genital mutilation are well documented (Dorkenoo, 1994). The damage that results from harmful practices in the west may not be so immediately clear or severe. However, there is considerable evidence of the damaging health consequences of cosmetic surgery practices such as breast implant surgery (Haiken, 1997) that are common in the west. The psychologically harmful consequences of beauty practices are largely undocumented because such practices have not been considered problematic, but they are likely to be considerable, playing a part in the construction of a subordinate femininity for women.

The concentration on the health consequences of such practices arises from the tendency in the west to want harm to be subject to easy measurement. Harm to women's status as equal citizens is less easy to measure but is a likely result of all cultural practices based on women's subordination. Ruth Lister's work on women's citizenship, for instance, argues that the role of housewife with its accompanying requirements that women do various forms of unpaid labour severely damages women's status as citizens while supporting men's citizenship (Lister, 1997). The extra labour that women expend on beauty practices and the effects of these practices on the ways in which they are able to occupy public space, to feel about themselves, and to intervene in public life, could usefully be included in this analysis. Nirmal Puwar's work on the experience of women members of parliament in the UK shows that the practice of femininity in appearance is vital for them when trying to survive in that exceedingly masculine culture (Puwar, 2004). A woman MP she interviews explains that the women are being scrutinized and remarked on as sexual objects and "the women's sexuality is with them all the time" (Puwar, 2004, p. 76). The MPs are, Puwar argues, "under pressure to reproduce gender differences, through reified forms of bodily styles of dress, hence the emphasis on an acceptable form of feminine appearance" (p. 176). One impact is that they suffer constant remarks, but there are likely to be further effects, unexamined here, of having to be so clearly and conspicuously women, wearing the uncomfortable stigmata of their subordinate condition while seeking to be effective in government.

The Fact Sheet says that harmful cultural practices are, "consequences of the value placed on women and the girl child by society. They persist in an environment where women and the girl child have unequal access to education, wealth, health and employment" (UN, 1995, p. 5). In western cultures the value placed on women and girl children is clearly different from that placed on male humans. Unequal access to education may not be such a problem but unequal access to wealth and employment persists. The weekly average total individual income for women in the UK in 2000/1, for example, was £133, compared with £271 for men (Carvel, 2002). The lower value of women and girls is demonstrated in domestic violence and all the other practices of violence against women and girls, in the existence of pornography and other forms of the sex industry. Western beauty practices, I suggest, arise from this lower value. Makeup and high-heeled shoes, labiaplasty and breast implants are the result of the value placed on women and girls in the west, where women's bodies are changed and decorated to show that women are members of a subordinate class that exists for men's delight.

Other criteria the Fact Sheet gives for recognizing harmful cultural/traditional practices are that they "reflect values and beliefs held by members of a community for periods often spanning generations" and they are for the "benefit of men" (UN, 1995, p. 3). Beauty practices do reflect longstanding values and beliefs about women, although the precise practices to which women are subjected change over time. The requirement that women alter and adorn their bodies for the sake of "beauty" does not change, for example, though corsets as an instrument for shaping the female anatomy to emphasize the breasts may give way to breast implants (Summers, 2001). The idea of "beauty" as something that women should embody for men's sexual excitement, either naturally or by artifice, is deeply ingrained in western culture.

Beauty practices can reasonably be understood to be for the benefit of men. Though women in the west sometimes say that they choose to engage in beauty practices for their own sake, or for other women and not for men, men benefit in several ways. They gain the advantage of having their superior sex class status marked out, and the satisfaction of being reminded of their superior status every time they look at a woman. They also gain the advantage of being sexually stimulated by "beautiful" women. These advantages can be summed up in the understanding that women are expected to both "complement" and "compliment" men. Women complement men by being the "opposite" and subordinate sex. Women compliment men by being prepared to make an effort to adorn themselves for men's sexual excitement. Thus men can feel both defined in manhood and flattered by women's exertions and, if the women are wearing high heels for instance, pain endured for their delight. Those women who refuse beauty practices are offering neither complement nor compliment and their resistance can be deeply resented by members of the dominant sex class.

Harmful cultural practices "persist" the Fact Sheet tells us, "because they are not questioned and take on an aura of morality in the eyes of those practicing them" (UN, 1995, p. 3). Beauty practices in the west are certainly seldom questioned. They are understood to be natural and inevitable, justified cross-historically and cross-culturally as something inherent in women's biology (Marwick, 1988). The rejection of the practices creates anger and mockery, such as references to feminists as bra-burners, as ugly, hairy legged, can't get a man. Western beauty practices possess the morality of nature. Women who fail to practise them can be seen as "loose", disreputable, unnatural and threatening to the social fabric.

The UN Special Rapporteur on violence against women, Radhika Coomaraswamy, explains that attempts by states to modernize their economies often leave abuses of women's rights in the form of harmful traditional practices intact (Coomaraswamy, 1997). In the west there has been considerable development of what is, in western understandings, a "modern" economy, technology and democracy, and yet beauty practices that are arguably of considerable harm to women and girls thrive and form the basis of very significant industries. Instead of the modern economy leading to any decrease in harmful practices it exploits them, as in cosmetics and fashion, to make very considerable profits. In this way the modern economy greatly increases the difficulty of eliminating harmful practices. The global beauty industry was estimated by *The Economist* in May 2003 to be worth US$160 billion (*The Economist*, 2003).

In 2002 Coomaraswamy produced a new and lengthy report on harmful cultural practices. To a large extent the report continues the western bias of earlier documents, however western beauty practices do get a whole paragraph dedicated to them here. The report says that "In many societies, the desire for beauty has often affected women in diverse ways" (Coomaraswamy, 2002, p. 31). It specifically addresses beauty practices in the west in the form of the requirement of slenderness, "In the 'Western' world in the twenty-first century the beauty myth that a thin female physique is the only accepted shape is imposed on women by the media via magazines, advertising and television", and by sexist advertising. What the report calls this "culture of impractical ideals" results, it says, in "many practices that cause a great deal of abuse to the female body" and singles out for mention "cosmetic surgery of every part of the female body" which "has led to health problems and complications for many women". This passing mention, however cursory, may be an indication that the need to include some western practices among those which Coomaraswamy describes as violating "women's human rights to bodily integrity and to expression, as well as undermining essential values of equality and dignity" is being recognized (2002, p. 3).

She includes only non-western practices, however, in the category she identifies as most serious. This is the category of "cultural practices that involve 'severe pain and suffering' for the woman or the girl child, those that do not respect the physical integrity of the female body" and "must receive maximum international scrutiny and agitation" (Coomaraswamy, 2002, p. 8). It includes "female genital mutilation, honour killings, Sati or any other form of cultural practice that brutalizes the female body" (p. 8).

There are some non-western practices described in the report that might usefully be compared to very similar practices fast becoming ordinary components of beauty in the west. For instance we are told that "Tutsi women in Rwanda and Burundi undergo the practice of elongation of the labia, the aim being to allow the women to experience greater sexual pleasure" (Coomaraswamy, 2002, p. 12). This has something in common with the practice of labiaplasty in the west. In labiaplasty cosmetic surgeons cut off parts of the labia minora to "beautify" women's genitals. This is not a practice that can be explained or justified in terms of tradition, because it is of recent origin, but in degree of mutilation, pain and potential complications it does resemble female genital mutilation and forms a startling contrast to the Tutsi custom. In the west, in the advertising literature of labiaplasty surgeons, long labia are said to inhibit sexual pleasure and to be an embarrassment. Coomaraswamy uses the language of human dignity to describe the harm of traditional practices. These practices are said to violate women's dignity (Coomaraswamy, 1997). The concept of women's "dignity" is an important one and the idea of human "dignity" is fundamental to human rights theory and practice. It is a useful measure against which to size up western beauty practices such as labiaplasty. Though there are analogues in the west to many of the non-western practices described in the report (Wynter *et al.*, 2002), they are likely to be omitted in UN literature. This is, I suggest, because of a western bias that identifies the harmful cultural practices in the west as reflecting women's choice rather than being enforced by threat of punishment, or by religious edict.

WESTERN CULTURE PROVIDES "CHOICE"?

Harmful cultural practices are seen as existing in cultures in which women do not have choice. The idea that "chosen" harmful traditional practices can be distinguished from forced ones does not fit well with United Nations understanding of what constitutes such a practice. The notion of harmful cultural practices is based on the idea that culture can enforce and that women and girls are not free agents able to pick and choose. In the 1990s in the west, however, the ideology of western liberalism, and the economic systems of laissez-faire individualist capitalism defended by it, were potent forces in the deracination of political critiques that recognize inequality and oppression as constructing limits to choice and opportunity (see Jeffreys, 1997b). This ideology is so pervasive that it has even affected Radhika Coomaraswamy's discussion of harmful practices outside the west in her 2002 report. The report includes dress codes that enforce all enveloping clothing such as the burkha on women as harmful cultural practices. They are harmful because, "they restrict women's movement and their right to expression" and because they are harmful to health, "Such dresses may cause asthma, high blood pressure, hearing or sight problems, skin rashes, hair loss and a general decline in mental condition" (Coomaraswamy, 2002, p. 28). Recently another health concern has arisen. Doctors writing in the *Lancet* of the increasing incidence of rickets, in which bones are weakened by a lack of vitamin D, explain that, in the Middle East, there are "lots of mums there with the adult form of rickets and children with rickets as well" as a result of women being required to cover their bodies and getting no natural sunlight on their skin (Lichtarowicz, 2003).

Nonetheless, Coomaraswamy comments, such dress codes are a problem only if they are, "forced on women and if punishment is meted out for not wearing very cumbersome attire" because in that case "their rights of choice and expression are clearly denied" (2002, p. 29). The notion of choice she employs does not make allowance for the types of pressure towards wearing restrictive clothing that are discussed elsewhere in this chapter, such as harassment in public places that can only be alleviated in this way. Covering can reduce this kind of friction but is not therefore a sign of freedom so much as an accommodation to oppression. Coomaraswamy's introduction of the notion of "choice" is worrying because it waters down one of the most useful aspects of the notion of harmful cultural practices, the irrelevance of such western notions where cultural expectations and practices act as enforcers.

Even the well respected US feminist political philosopher, Martha Nussbaum, uses the "choice" argument to distinguish western beauty practices, dieting in particular, from those outside the west. Nussbaum argues that practices such as female genital mutilation (FGM) should not be seen as "morally on a par with practices of dieting and body shaping in American culture" (Nussbaum, 2000, p. 121). She argues that the differences between FGM and dieting are so considerable as to invalidate such an argument. The distinctions that she makes relate to the issue of choice, which she considers to prevail in the west in relation to dieting, and to the degree of damage to health involved in the practices. FGM is, she says, "carried out by force, whereas dieting in response to culturally constructed images of beauty is a matter of choice, however seductive the persuasion" (2000, p. 122). FGM, she argues, is irreversible whereas dieting is not. She says that FGM is performed in dangerous and unsanitary conditions, unlike dieting, and considers that the health problems linked to FGM, which can include death, are so much more severe that a comparison is inappropriate. Nussbaum also says that because FGM is usually carried out on children consent is not an issue. She details the distinctions in female literacy rates between the USA and some African countries as a basis for arguing that African women do not have access to choice and consent in the way that US women do. She says that FGM means, "the irreversible loss of the capability for a type of sexual functioning" which is, presumably, a greater loss than that connected with dieting. She argues, finally, that FGM is "unambiguously linked to customs of male domination" by which she implies that dieting is not. She has other broader arguments for seeing FGM as a more significant abuse of women's rights than beauty practices. She says that feminists in the USA have disproportionately criticized western beauty practices while giving less attention to FGM, and that it is the duty of feminists to be concerned for the fate of their sisters outside western culture rather than being concerned only with themselves.

It would be hard to disagree with Nussbaum that western feminists should be concerned with the human rights of their sisters in other countries. I would argue, however, that western feminist criticisms of harmful cultural practices in other cultures need to be founded on a profound critique of such practices within their own. Nussbaum's arguments as to why dieting should not be compared with FGM are not convincing. Western dieting inflicts lasting damage to health, particularly when it is taken to extremes in eating disorders that can cause death. A 2001 study reported in the *Lancet*, for instance, found that five (2 per cent) of the patients with eating disorders that were interviewed at the start of the research were dead at the time of a 5-year follow up (Ben-Tovim *et al.*, 2001, p. 1254). Similarly, cosmetic surgery practices can lead to serious health problems, as Elizabeth Haiken documents in the case of breast implants (1997). Labiaplasty, like FGM, can lead to difficulties in sexual functioning. Nussbaum's argument about the degree to which women in the west can "choose" could be seen as revealing a western bias, according to which women in the west are so advantaged that they can "choose" and thus whatever cultural practices they are required to engage in are not as severe as those in some African cultures. It is an underlying problem with liberal feminist thought that relations of power in western cultures are reframed as simply "pressures" which women have the education to withstand (Jeffreys, 1997b).

Some liberal individualist feminists can find evidence of women's "choice" even in the most unlikely situations. One of these is the practice of hymen repair surgery in the west. Hymen repair surgery is carried out to create an artificial virginity for women from cultures in which bleeding is required on the wedding night to avoid the shame that will descend on a bride and her family for lost "honour". The penalty for lost honour can be an "honour killing" in which the woman is killed by male family members. Immigrants to the west from such cultures can obtain hymen repair from the same surgeons who provide labiaplasty to women influenced by pornography to consider their labia ugly. In her article on the practice of hymen repair surgery in the Netherlands in the twenty-first century, Sawitri Saharso argues that girls who have hymen repair surgery are, "moral agents who can choose" (Saharso, 2003, p. 20). Feminists should, she says, respect "other women's choices, even if we do not agree with them. This in turn means that making hymen repair available is a deed of multiculturalism and good feminism" (p. 21). The girls are "morally competent actors who do have a choice and are able to state their preferences" (2003, p. 21). Hymen repair is currently available free from the public health service in the Netherlands and Saharso considers this to be a "policy measure that is culturally sensitive in that it acknowledges culturally informed suffering" (p. 21).

The concept of "choice" that Saharso puts forward is one that is so impoverished it is hard to work out why anyone would want to call it choice at all. For instance she quotes as a basis for her argument about girls "choosing" hymen repair surgery, a Dutch writer who argues that they can be said to be making a choice because they do have other options like leaving their community:

> She suggests that leaving the community does not necessarily mean becoming a prostitute, as there exist in the Netherlands shelters for runaway girls and women. So it is only if the girls want to remain within the family and community, and presuming the girl's family is indeed as mercilous as she presupposes, that the operation is the only solution available.
>
> (quoted in Saharso, 2003, p. 19)

Girls from immigrant communities are likely to need the support of families and communities more than those from the dominant culture. Thus the casual assumption that girls would be able to make a reasonable choice between outcast status in which they may have to hide for a lifetime from a family seeking vengeance for the shame brought upon it, and having surgery which would enable them to remain, is a rather surprising one. These "choices" are not equal in their implications and Saharso's suggestion that they should be considered so demonstrates the strange logic that can result from the fetishizing of choice in western liberal theory.

MAKEUP AND THE VEIL: SAME DIFFERENCE?

Rather than being two sides of the same coin of women's oppression, the veil and makeup are most usually seen as opposites. Makeup can even be seen as the liberated alternative to wearing the veil. Whereas there is apparently a difference, that is, respectable women in Islamic culture are expected to cover their heads and bodies so that men are not sexually tempted, while in the west women are expected to dress and makeup in such a way that men are sexually tempted and to create a feast for men's eyes, there can be seen to be a connection. These expectations reflect the traditional dualism with regard to women's function under male dominance. Women traditionally, even in the west, have been expected to fit into the categories of virgin/whore. Virgins were off limits until they married and were owned sexually by individual men, whereas whores existed to service men in general.

Unfortunately even feminist scholars are sometimes unable to think themselves out of this dualism to imagine an autonomous way of life for women that does not fall into one of these categories. Lama Abu-Odeh, for instance, in writing about the readoption of the veil in some Muslim countries, says that her assumptions as an Arab feminist are that "Arab women should be able to express themselves sexually, so that they can love, play, tease, flirt and excite . . . In them, I see acts of subversion and liberation" (Abu-Odeh, 1995, p. 527). But what she considered joyful the women who adopted the veil saw as "evil". In choosing the role for women of sexually exciting men over covering up, Abu-Odeh is stuck within the duality that is offered to women under male dominance, sex object or veiled one, prostitute or nun. There is a third possibility: women can invent themselves anew outside the stereotypes of western and non-western patriarchal culture. Women can have access to the privilege possessed by men of not having to be concerned for appearance and being able to go out in public barefaced and bareheaded.

Both the veil and makeup are often seen as voluntary behaviours by women, taken up by choice and to express agency. But in both cases there is considerable evidence of the pressures arising from male dominance that cause the behaviours. For instance, the historian of commerce Kathy Peiss suggests that the beauty products industry took off in the USA in the 1920s/1930s because this was a time when women were entering the public world of offices and other workplaces (Peiss, 1998). She sees women as having made themselves up as a sign of their new freedom. But there is another explanation. Feminist commentators on the readoption of the veil by women in Muslim countries in the late twentieth century have suggested that women feel safer and freer to engage in occupations and movement in the public world through covering up (Abu-Odeh, 1995). It could be that the wearing of makeup signifies that women have no automatic right to venture out in public in the west on equal grounds with men. Makeup, like the veil, ensures that they are masked and not having the effrontery to show themselves as the real and equal citizens that they should be in theory. Makeup and the veil may both reveal women's lack of entitlement.

In some cases the adoption of the veil is clearly the result of force and the threat of violence. In Iran covering up is compulsory and enforced by the state. As Haleh Afshar explains "The open defiance of hejab and appearance in public without it is punishable by 74 lashes" (Afshar, 1997, p. 319). There is no suggestion that women can "choose" to wear the veil since the enforcement process is so clear and so brutal, "Women who are considered inadequately covered are attacked by these men (members of the 'Party of God' the Hezbollahis) with knives, or guns and are lucky to survive the experience" (Afshar, 1997, p. 320). Makeup is not enforced with such brutality in western cultures.

However, as Homa Hoodfar points out, the veil may be worn for different reasons in different countries and even within the same country (Hoodfar, 1997). In some situations no obvious force is applied. Lama Abu-Odeh describes the readoption of the veil. She says that in the 1970s women "walked the streets of Arab cities wearing western attire: skirts and dresses below the knee, high heels, and sleeves that covered the upper arm in the summer. Their hair was usually exposed and they wore make-up" (1995, p. 524). In the 1980s and 1990s many, even some of the same women, adopted the veil, defined here as a headcovering or headscarf. Abu-Odeh tells us that, "their bodies seemed to be a battlefield" between the values of the west, the "'capitalist' construction in which female bodies are 'sexualized, objectified, thingified' and the traditional in which women's bodies were 'chattelized,' 'propertized,' and terrorized as trustees of family (sexual) honor" (p. 524). The women adopting the veil were those who needed to use public transport either for work or study. They were less likely to be sexually harassed by men. On occasions when they were harassed they would feel more comfortable objecting to this if veiled, because they could not be blamed for having incited this abusive male behaviour. It was easier for the veiled women and girls to feel outraged and for others to feel outraged on their behalf if they were seen as innocent victims who did not deserve such treatment. The adoption of the veil can thus be seen as a way to alleviate the harms suffered by women as a result of male dominance. Such a "choice", though, arises from oppression rather than indicating agency.

Hoodfar explains the readoption of the veil in Egypt where there is no threat of brutal punishment. Women who are, as Hoodfar puts it, "reveiling" tend to be lower-middle class, university educated and white-collar workers in public and government sector jobs. The reasons that Hoodfar gives for "reveiling" do not suggest that women had reasonable alternatives to making this decision. One woman Hoodfar interviewed expressed resistance to the idea of wearing the veil before she married but on the eve of her marriage encountered considerable pressure from her future husband's family against going out to work as a teacher, which she had trained to do and was looking forward to. Her in-laws argued that if she went out to work, "people would talk, and her reputation might be questioned" (Hoodfar, 1997, p. 323). Moreover she would suffer sexual harassment, "In overcrowded buses men who have lost their traditional respect for women might molest her and of course this would hurt her pride and dignity as well as that of her husband and brothers" (p. 323). To resolve these pressures she decided to become a *muhaggaba* (veiled one). This pleased the husband's family.

The reasons that Hoodfar gives clearly relate to women's attempts to accommodate themselves to male dominance. The veil, she says, demonstrates women's loyalty to the rules of male dominance, it "communicates loudly and clearly to society at large and to husbands in particular that the wearer is bound by the Islamic idea of her sex role" (Hoodfar, 1997, p. 323). Veiled women can work because they are demonstrating that they still respect "traditional values and behaviour". Women who wear the veil "lessen their husband's insecurity" and show their husbands that "as wives, they are not in competition, but rather in harmony and cooperation with them" (p. 324). In exchange for all these signs of obedience the veil "puts women in a position to expect and demand that their husbands honour them and recognize their Islamic rights". Thus husbands may let their wives keep the money they earn and keep their side of the bargain by "providing for the family to the best of their ability" (p. 324). None of the reasons given here suggest that the activity is chosen because it gives the woman any satisfaction that is separate from being able to alleviate the forces of male dominance. In order to have the right that men possess of working in the public world, women have to cover up and fulfil other stereotypes and expectations of women's subordinate role.

Another woman interviewed by Hoodfar adopted the veil directly to avoid sexual harassment when she worked late after studying and had to use the bus to get home, "So often people treated me badly that I would go home at night and cry". She decided on the veil so that "people would know that I am a good woman and that my circumstances have forced me to work late at night" (1997, p. 325). Seeking a strategy to avoid being attacked in the street by men is not an exercise of free choice but an accommodation to oppression. The ordinary men who would harass her in Egypt can be seen as the civilian equivalent of the Hezbollahis who lash women in Iran. Abu-Odeh explains the kinds of sexual harassment to which women have traditionally been exposed in Arab cities if not veiled:

> Unfailingly subject to attention on the streets and on buses by virtue of being women, they are stared at, whistled at, rubbed against, and pinched. Comments by men such as, "What nice breasts you have," or "How beautiful you are," are frequent . . . They are always conscious of being looked at.
>
> (Abu-Odeh, 1995, p. 526)

But Abu-Odeh reminds feminists who think that women should refuse the veil that this would be "socially suicidal" (1995, p. 529). Muslim women were in no position to speak out against the veil because they would be seen as defending the west. She adds the influence of Islamic preachers as another reason for reveiling: "A woman who decides to wear the veil is usually subjected to a certain ideological indoctrination (by a fundamentalist preacher), in which she is told that every Muslim woman needs to cover her body so as not to seduce men, and that in doing this she obeys the word of Allah" (p. 532). This can be seen quite clearly as religious indoctrination but it might be reasonable to ask whether it is necessarily more powerful in influencing girls to cover themselves in the veil than the magazines and fashion and beauty culture of the west are in getting girls to cover themselves in makeup.

WESTERN CULTURAL IMPERIALISM – EXPORTING HARMFUL PRACTICES TO THE NON-WEST

Women in an Afghanistan supposedly newly liberated from the rule of the Taliban, are trapped within the patriarchal duality of virgin/whore through being presented with only two choices for their appearance, covering up with the burkha or with makeup. Western beauty practices are seen as so obviously natural, inevitable and good for women that they have been held out as the holy grail to the women of Afghanistan. After years of terrible oppression in which they were only allowed outside in the all-enveloping burkha, could travel only in the company of men, were stripped of education and employment and could be beaten in the street by the male guardians of Islamic righteousness without redress, the ability to engage in western beauty practices, particularly for face and hair, does not seem an urgent need. Yet this is how it is being promoted.

The American beauty industry rushed in 2002 in the aftermath of war to infiltrate Afghanistan under the guise of urgently needed beauty "aid". This was represented in the western media as a positive help rather than as American cultural imperialism and capitalist enterprise. Women were offered the role of being covered in makeup and sexually objectified, rather than covered by the burkha to prevent them being seen as sex objects by men. The *New York Times* perspective on this is that despite two decades of war, "Afghan women have held on to their desire to look beautiful", but there is a "woeful shortage of beauticians. Also, they have no one to teach them and nowhere to lay their hands on a decent comb, let alone the panoply of gels, rinses, powders, liners and colors that spill from the shelves of the average American drugstore" (Halbfinger, 2002, p. 1). In response to this market opportunity, and the opportunity to show their companies dealing with an aid emergency, a "Who's Who" of the American beauty industry was soon "racing to the rescue" led by the editor of *Vogue*. The result of this generosity was that a school to teach practitioners of beauty was to open in the compound of the Afghan Ministry of Women's Affairs, as if beauty practices were indeed a crucial human rights issue for women, on a par with education, safety and work.

The manufacturers of American beauty products volunteered manuals and wares to help the venture. The *Vogue* editor, Anna Wintour, said that the beauty industry is "incredibly philanthropic" and the beauty school would "not only help women in Afghanistan to look and feel better but also to give them employment". Apparently the situation in the 20 beauty salons that did reopen after the removal of Taliban control constituted a health crisis because conditions were so unsanitary and dangerous. As one Afghan émigré who took a look at the situation reported:

> They're using rusty scissors, they'll have one cheap comb for the whole salon and they don't sanitize it, there's no running water or Barbisol, and there's a real lice problem. They'll use wooden sticks and rubber bands to do perms. And there's no cotton, so perm solution would just drip down a client's face.
>
> (Halbfinger, 2002, p. 1)

Perming hair could be considered a harmful cultural practice in its own right considering that the chemicals involved are toxic whether they run down the face or not (Erickson, 2002), but in the interests of capitalism it has been transformed into a human rights demand. Simply translating existing beauty education manuals was not sufficient in Afghanistan because so many women were illiterate, so a videotaped course of instruction in makeup was being prepared.

Though the cosmetics corporations vying with one another to make donations to the beauty school at a *Vogue* luncheon said they were not in competition for sales, one executive did say, "that the beauty school could not be judged a success if it did not create a demand for American cosmetics before too long" (Halbfinger, 2002, p. 1). It is not just in Afghanistan that US cosmetics corporations have seen a marketing opportunity. They swiftly entered the Soviet Union after the fall of the communist regime, to offer their service to formerly deprived women, and they are reaching out to China too. As the business historian Kathy Peiss puts it, even in "Amazon rain forests, women sell Avon, Mary Kay, and other beauty products" (Peiss, 2001, p. 20). But Peiss, like many of those involved in selling western beauty ideals in Afghanistan, conceals the oppressiveness of this colonizing activity by emphasizing that it provides employment for women who sorely need it. As she says, "as was the case a hundred years ago in the United States, these 'microbusinesses' have given some women a foothold in the developing market economy" (Peiss, 2001, p. 20).

COVERING WOMEN IN PATRIARCHAL RELIGION

Although the sexual objectification required of women in the west may seem very distinct from the covering up required by Islamic regimes, it is instructive to consider the identical cultural basis from which both western and Islamic cultures have developed. Covering the heads of women is a cultural practice of middle eastern tribes that found its way, via the monotheistic religions which originated in that region, to other parts of the world. The covering of heads and bodies was imposed on some Christian women in the west until quite recently. In my childhood in Malta in the 1950s, where my father was posted with the army, I remember the notices on buses that instructed women to "wear a Marylike dress". Women entering churches in many parts of Europe are still required to cover their heads. The Christian religion, like Islam, and the other patriarchal monotheistic religion, Judaism, has its roots in earlier patriarchal cultures that existed in the middle east. In these earlier cultures respectable women were required to be covered as in the Babylonian code of Hammurabi. Gerda Lerner explains in *The Creation of Patriarchy*, that the code, which predated the three religions, required women who were not prostitutes to cover themselves so that they could indicate that they were the property of individual men (Lerner, 1987). The prostituted women, usually slaves, were uncovered to indicate that they were the property of men in general.

In early Christianity a similar code was enforced. Thus in Paul's letter to the Corinthians in the New Testament he sets out the covering rule. He explains that the "head of every man is Christ; and the head of the woman is the man; and the head of Christ is God". This is to be demonstrated through head covering thus:

> Every man praying or prophesying, having his head covered, dishonoureth his head. But every woman that prayeth or prophesieth with her head uncovered dishonoureth her head: for that is even all one as if she were shaven. For if the woman be not covered, let her also be shorn: but if it be a shame for a woman to be shorn or shaven, let her be covered. For a man indeed ought not to cover his head, forasmuch as he is the image and glory of God: but the woman is the glory of the man. For the man is not of the woman; but the woman of the man. Neither was the man created for the woman; but the woman for the man.
>
> (Corinthians, 1957, 11: 3–15, p. 181)

Woman's headcovering would show that she was man's possession. Other harmful practices of early Christianity accompanied the dress code. Women were not to speak in church, though they were allowed to ask their husbands about anything they did not understand when they got home, and they were enjoined to "submit yourselves unto your own husbands, as unto the Lord" (Ephesians, 1957, 5: 22, p. 200).

One branch of the Christian religion today goes rather further than simply covering women. Women are actually excluded from the whole of Mount Athos in Greece, which is covered in Greek Orthodox monasteries, so that the monks may be protected from having to see them. In 2004 this ancient Christian practice received influential endorsement from a visit, reported in the media, of Prince Charles to a monastery on the mountain (Smith, 2004). The mountain has excluded women since the eleventh century and with the status of an independent theocratic republic is able to impose legal penalties on those who challenge the ban. Charles has visited several times since the death of his ex-wife, Diana, and is said to gain great solace from this refuge, a place where readings in the refectory "are frequently based on . . . the evil caused by womankind with the fall of Eve" (Smith, 2004, p. 3). The continued existence of this zone of exclusion despite attempts in the European Union to revoke the ban is a salutary reminder of the womanhating values that underlie patriarchal Christianity.

WHAT CONSTITUTES A HARMFUL CULTURAL PRACTICE?

I have suggested in this chapter that both western cultures influenced by Christianity and cultures influenced by Islam enforce harmful cultural practices on women. Only a determination to ignore the political origins, functions and consequences of western beauty practices would enable a belief that western culture is clearly superior in the freedoms it allows to women in relation to appearance. Whereas all three patriarchal religious cultures originating in the ancient middle east started off by enforcing the covering of women, this has changed in the west towards the apparently very different prescription that women perform their sexual corvée in public places. In some areas of the middle east and Asia where the covering requirement has been challenged or is dying out there has been a renewed enforcement of the rule. The end result is an apparently greater and greater divergence between the appearance rules for women east and west. Both sets of appearance rules, however, require that women should be "different/deferent", and both require women to service men's sexual needs, either by providing sexual excitement or by hiding women's bodies lest the men should be so excited. In both cases women are required to fulfil men's needs in public places and do not have the freedoms that men possess.

The concept of harmful cultural practices in relation to appearance should, therefore, not be restricted to non-western cultures. All the western beauty practices considered in this book, from makeup to labiaplasty, fit the criteria for identifying harmful cultural practices. I argue that they create stereotyped roles for the sexes, they originate in the subordination of women and are for the benefit of men and they are justified by tradition. It is certainly possible to argue, as I demonstrate in Chapter 6 on makeup, that even practices that appear to have the least effect on the health of women and girls, such as lipstick wearing, can be damaging. Although western beauty practices are seldom enforced by actual physical violence, they are all culturally enforced. The failure to wear makeup and depilate legs and underarms may not be "socially suicidal" in western cultures but it will, as I suggest in the makeup chapter, affect women's ability to get and keep employment and the degree of social influence that they may wield. The British women MPs I mentioned were required to wear feminine clothing and show their legs if they were to have any legitimacy in the legislature and they are unlikely to have survived if they allowed underarm hair to peek from their blouses or leg hair to show through their tights.

However I am aware that the degree of damage inflicted by such practices as cosmetic surgery and lipstick wearing is not the same. The implication of recognizing western beauty practices as harmful cultural practices is that governments will, as required by the UN Convention on the Elimination of All Forms of Discrimination Against Women, need to alter the social attitudes which underlie them. In the case of some cosmetic surgery practices the consequences are sufficiently severe and regulation so easily achieved by legal penalties on medical practitioners that they could be ended through legislative means. Lipstick wearing and depilation, however, should not be exempt from being considered as harmful and requiring remedies, although legal ones may not be appropriate. They mark women as subordinate and clearly demonstrate the stereotyped roles of the sexes even if not so severe in their impact on women's health. The role of governments committed to the ending of such practices, or even simply alleviating the impact of the cultural requirement that they should be performed, should therefore be to combat the creation of sexual difference, of ideas and attitudes, business practices, that inscribe this notion at the very foundation of western culture.

In later chapters I examine the practices of makeup, high heels and cosmetic surgery in some detail to show how they are enforced and what their consequences are for women's health and access to the ordinary prerogatives that men in western societies are likely to take for granted: to appear in public space barefaced, to run, to have leisure time free of the need for body maintenance. Readers will be able to make up their minds about the appropriateness of including these practices within the United Nations understandings. In the next chapter I enlarge on the meanings of feminine beauty practices in western culture through transvestism/transsexualism. The performance of beauty practices by men shows that this behaviour is not biologically connected with women. But it does more than that. As I seek to demonstrate here, male practitioners take sexual pleasure from these practices because they demonstrate subordinate status. This supports an understanding of beauty practices as behaviours of deference by a subordinate group.

3

TRANSFEMININITY

"Dressed" men reveal the naked reality of male power

Beauty practices and femininity go hand in hand but they are not essentially the properties of women. In this chapter I look at femininity as practised by men in order to illuminate the cultural meanings of this behaviour. The fact that men can be more ardent exponents of the practice of femininity than women has become clearer in recent decades as the medical profession, pornography and the Internet have spawned a massive cult of femininity among men in the form of transsexualism, transgenderism, transvestism. Femininity is sexually exciting to the men who seek it because it represents subordinate status and thus satisfies masochistic sexual interests. Men's femininity is very different from the femininity that is a requirement of women's subordinate status, because women do not choose femininity but have it thrust upon them. Femininity is not a form of sexual fantasy for women but the hard and often resented work required of those who occupy subordinate social status. However the forms that the outward appearance of femininity takes are quite similar in both cases, and the beauty practices are identical. Looking at what men make of it will show that femininity, rather than having any connection with biology, is socially constructed as the behaviour of subordination.

TRANSVESTISM/TRANSSEXUALISM – DEFINITIONS

The practice of "femininity" by men has been, and largely still is, defined and adjudicated by the medical profession. Nineteenth-century sexologists gave names and diagnoses to behaviours that did not fit their understandings of "correct" masculinity and femininity (Jeffreys, 1985). They were involved in the social control of deviant behaviour that was seen as threatening the heterosexual family that lies at the foundation of male dominance. In the twentieth century these "abnormal" behaviours became the domain of psychiatry. Until recent times the medical profession has tended to assert that there are clear and identifiable differences between transvestites, who simply like to dress in women's clothes occasionally, and transsexuals who want to live as women. The creation of this distinction was necessary in order that the doctors could identify those who were deserving of surgery and those who were not deemed to be "real" transsexuals. Transsexuals were identified as suffering from a medical condition of gender identity disorder in which they considered themselves to be female and this was explained as primarily a biological, or at least a distinct and essential, condition.

Feminist social constructionists have not accepted this biological explanation. In the first and still the most comprehensive feminist critique of the medical profession's construction of the phenomenon of transsexualism (first published in 1979), Janice G. Raymond explains that the "first cause" of the phenomenon is the political idea that there should be two distinct genders that founds patriarchal society (Raymond, 1994). She sees transsexualism as a construction of medical science designed to achieve three purposes: profit from the surgery, experimentation towards the achievement of mastery over the construction of body parts, and the political purpose of the allocation to acceptable gender categories of those gender rebels who are seen to be disrupting the two-gendered system of male dominance. The transsexual, she argues, simply exchanges one stereotype for the other and thus reinforces the sexist social fabric of society. Transsexualism, in this analysis, is deeply reactionary, a way of preventing the disruption and elimination of gender roles which lies at the basis of the feminist project, and "The medical solution becomes a 'social tranquilizer' reinforcing sexism and its foundation of sex-role conformity" (Raymond, 1994, p. xvii).

The feminist critique has, unfortunately, not caused the sexologists to pause in their ownership and enforcement of the categories of transfemininity. The distinction that the sexologists draw between transvestism and transsexualism has been suffering a great deal of strain in the time of the Internet as materials, groups and magazines on the web have spawned a proliferation of practices and broken down boundaries (McCloskey, 1999). Those who might once have been classified as transvestites – that is, heterosexual men who remain with their wives and occasionally crossdress for their pleasure – are now likely to have access to hormones too and more easily cross over into transsexualism. Some of these men now tell doctors that they want to be half transsexuals, so gaining breasts but keeping their penises (Blanchard, 1993). They then retain the ability to experience the excitements of masochism associated with having breasts, through their penises. Breast growth, or gynaecomastia, can be achieved through hormone treatment.

Though some crossdressers are keen to maintain that there is a clear distinction because they do not wish to be tainted by homosexuality, others are happy to say there is little difference. Charles Anders, author of *The*

Lazy Crossdresser (2002), tells us that there is very little difference between crossdressers and transsexuals, "There's a common joke in the transsexual community: 'What's the difference between a cross-dresser and a transsexual? Two years.' Sometimes the punchline is 'one year'. A lot, maybe the majority, of male-to-female transsexuals started out as cross-dressers, so they tend to see transvestites as their larval state" (Anders, 2002, p. 5). Peggy Rudd, author of an instruction manual for the wives of crossdressers, quotes a survey in which crossdressers were asked if they would have surgery if they could afford it (Rudd, 1999, p. 91). Apparently 24 per cent "left the question open" and what determined their answer was how much support they got from their wives and families for being cross-dressers; that is, nothing to do with whether they were "really" women at all. Rudd says, "So women must accept or men will have surgery" (1999, p. 91). Biology does not seem to have much to do with this. The men are making choices about how far they want to go.

In the 1990s a transgender movement arose in which men and some women, claimed that sex reassignment operations were not necessary to those who "transitioned" from one "gender" to another (Bornstein, 1994; Raymond, 1994) because they could transgender in their minds, and by assuming the outward appearance of the opposite gender, while keeping their body parts intact. The vast majority of those who now come under the umbrella of "transgender" politics, however, either have surgery or take hormones so that their bodies will be changed in some way. Some transgender activists claimed that their practice was revolutionary because they were showing that "gender" was socially constructed rather than "natural" by adopting feminine gender as physically entire biological males and vice versa. In fact, as I have argued elsewhere, the very idea of transing "gender" essentializes it by reinforcing the need for femininity and masculinity (Jeffreys, 1996). Bernice Hausman (2001) provides an effective critique of what she sees as the "queer" defence of transsexualism as a revolutionary activity that transgresses gender. She says that Kate Bornstein and other queer theorists of the practice:

> suggest a certain gender essentialism: that gender as a way of organizing identity is central to the human project, that each individual has a gender or belief in the self as a gender, or that gender in some fashion (as binary or plural) is necessary to or at least an inevitable part of the social fabric.
>
> (Hausman, 2001, p. 473)

Feminists who want to dismantle gender, because they see it as a product of male dominance, do not "trans" gender, they simply get over it. Trans-genders are so attached to the notion of gender, albeit to a different one from that in which they were brought up, that they spend huge amounts of time, energy and money in order to acquire their gender of choice. Transgender politics are fundamentally conservative, dedicated to retaining the behaviours of the dominant and subordinate classes of male supremacy – masculinity and femininity.

The transgender movement makes claims for legal, medical and social reforms, and to be exempt from political analysis, on the basis that transgenders are a mistreated biologically distinct minority. As such a minority, argues the US organization, National Transgender Advocacy Coalition (NTAC), they suffer:

> queer-baiting, the job loss, the difficulty in being rehired, the loss of insurance, the divorce and loss of visitation to children, the obscene phone calls and other hate violence, the parental–sibling ostracism, the cutoff from a person's place of worship, the hassles by police, and more.
>
> (National Transgender Advocacy Coalition, 2000)

NTAC campaigns for males-to-constructed-females (MTFs) and females-to-constructed-males (FTMs) to be able to have "gay" marriages and not to have to reveal genital status in order to be legally accepted as members of their "gender" of choice; that is, taking hormones without surgery is sufficient.

Behind the choice of femininity on the part of men lies their fascination with playing the subordinate role of "woman" for the sexual satisfactions of masochism that this offers. For large and rapidly growing numbers of men, to judge by the pornography, websites, shops and services that serve them, the behaviours and appurtenances of femininity are a kind of sex toy. In this chapter I look at these Internet resources to show that men's practices of femininity are not about being "women" but about adopting the socially prescribed behaviours of a subordinate group in order to enjoy the sexual satisfaction of masochism. I argue here that transgenderism on the part of men needs to be understood as originating in socially constructed sexual fantasy rather than constituting a biological condition. Transvestism, transsexualism and transgenderism can be seen as being sexual practices rather than making those reared as "men" into "women". Indeed being reared as "men" may be a necessary precondition of men's practice of femininity. They pursue "femininity" because it represents the subordinate opposite of masculinity and offers the delights of masochism. This pursuit can only have meaning for men who understand that their masochistic pleasures are in contradiction to their masculine status. Manhood produces men's "feminine" behaviour rather than being in contradiction to it.

There is some support from the medical profession for understanding men's practice of femininity as sexual fantasy. Ray Blanchard, a psychologist at the Clarke Institute in Toronto, which is one of only two places which carry out transsexual surgery in Canada, coined the term "autogynephilia" to describe "a male's propensity to be sexually aroused by the thought of himself as a female" (Blanchard, 1989, p. 616). Blanchard carried out research on males who came to the clinic reporting gender dysphoria and seeking transsexual surgery. He, somewhat arbitrarily, divides these men into heterosexual and homosexual dysphorics according to the primary object of their sexual interest. Heterosexual dysphorics are men who seek to remain with wives or female partners and are likely to define themselves as "lesbians" if they have transsexual surgery. Homosexual or androphilic gender dysphorics are those who are sexually attracted to men and remain so if they have transsexual surgery. The men he identifies as heterosexual are placed in his category of "autogynephiles". Those seeking transsexual surgery are exhibiting the most extreme form of autogynephilic behaviour. They are sexually excited by the fantasy of themselves with women's bodies.

In less extreme forms, autogynephiles get sexually excited by such things as wearing "women's" clothing, or engaging in "women's" activities. In one case that Blanchard describes the man had "early masturbation fantasies" of "helping the maid clean the house or that he was sitting in a girls' class at school . . . his current masturbation fantasies were knitting in the company of other women and being at the hairdresser's with other women" (Blanchard, 1991, p. 236). Another patient "was sexually aroused by shaving his legs and then contemplating the result" (p. 237). The endless stream of autobiographical accounts of their motivations by proud crossdressers that have been published in the last few years make it clear that sexual excitement is what motivates them (McCloskey, 1999; Anders, 2002; Miller, 1996). The heterosexual crossdresser "Rachel Miller" writes "If men perceive something as sexy on a woman, why couldn't they see it as sexy on themselves? It seems reasonable to me" (Miller, 1996, p. 55). It seems reasonable to me too, that men can either project the clothing and behaviour that represents subordination onto women for their excitement, or shortcircuit the process by just adopting it themselves. He understands women to represent "sex" and what is "sexy", asking "Is wanting to be sexy exclusively for women?" (p. 55).

But this understanding, that men's interest in the accoutrements of women's subordinate position is a sexual one, is controversial. Many male to female transsexuals and their medical practitioners reject it because they consider it disrespectful of their experience. The medical profession has encouraged transsexuals to develop complicated stories about how they have always known they are females trapped in male bodies. The required oral histories are modelled on the stories given by male homosexuals to sexologists in the late nineteenth century and early twentieth century (Weeks, 1977). The "inverts" interviewed by Havelock Ellis, for instance, were identified as persons who, by some mysterious process, had women's brains trapped in male bodies (Ellis, 1913). At that time homosexuality was understood to be biologically determined by a fault in sexual development. Male homosexuals were seen as essentially feminine and lesbians as essentially masculine. Transsexual surgery was not available. When such surgery became available in the 1950s, stories of having a woman's soul in a male body were interpreted as the criteria for diagnosing a new breed of person constructed by medical science, the transsexual.

Aspirants for transsexual surgery in the present have to give the correct story, such as having felt they were "really" female since they were small children, in order to be seen as deserving surgery: to be seen as "real" ones (Jeffreys, 1990). However some men are becoming impatient with the gatekeeping of the medical profession. They want surgery on demand and not to have to make up stories to deserve it. Donald (Deirdre) McCloskey says he had to "lie" to doctors, making himself fit the required case history so that he could have surgery. But he is contemptuous of the attempts by the medical profession to retain control. His attitude was "Oh, yes, Doctor, whatever your dopey list says" (McCloskey, 1999, p. 145). He cites in support of this contempt Pat (now Patrick) Califia's statement that surgery should be an "inalienable right" and transsexuals should not have to recite a catalogue of symptoms (2002, p. 144).

Neither the doctors who believe there are "real" ones, nor the transsexuals themselves who want surgery have wanted to see transsexualism as simply a form of sexual deviation stemming from the desire for masochistic sexual excitement. In some countries transsexual surgery is available on state or private medical insurance schemes on the grounds that it is necessary as treatment for the illness of having a mind differently sexed from the body in which it resides. If transsexualism is understood to be a form of sexual fantasy then the insurance schemes are unlikely to pay up. As a result many transsexuals and their activist groupings reject the notion that transsexualism is about anything other than men "really" being women.

Blanchard's research has split the international transsexual network. One influential male-to-constructed-female, Anne Lawrence, psychotherapist, believes that Blanchard's concept of autogynephilia characterizes his experience very well, and also that of hundreds of other MTFs, many of whose stories are on his website (Lawrence, accessed 2002). Lawrence sees himself as one of the heterosexual group "who are attracted to women, who have been fairly successful as men, and who do not appear remarkably feminine". What force, he asks, could be powerful enough to drive such men to "give up our place in the world"; that is, dominant male status. It is, he agrees with Blanchard, "sexual desire – our sexual desire to feminize our bodies". Other MTFs have been less sanguine about autogynephilia. "Dr Becky" says that the concept could be used to support the idea that transsexuals are just involved in a lifestyle choice and that would "deny our validity" and create "more doubt and guilt". If the concept of autogynephilia was accepted it might be harder to get the surgery as transsexuals would be viewed with "more skepticism". There might be less chance of legislative protection of transgender rights and it might be harder to get health insurers to cover the transition process (Dr Becky, 1998).

Many transsexuals, like Dr Becky, stress that their decision to be surgically mutilated was not the result of a sexual urge but of a biological condition, or at least something more significant than just sexual excitement. Lawrence responds to this point by saying that certainly the vast majority of heterosexual transsexuals start out with powerful sexual excitement about being women though by the time they get as far as surgery this may have quietened down into something that just feels natural and no longer so urgently exciting. Donald McCloskey gives support to this notion by stating that by the time he had decided he was not just a heterosexual crossdresser but wanted to "transition", "The sexual part started to fade, something new in his crossdressing, though he didn't notice" (McCloskey, 1999, p. 20). Lawrence also points out that quite large percentages, up to a third, of those men classified by Blanchard as androphiles (i.e. they relate to men sexually before and after surgery) also have histories of finding women's attire and the idea of having a woman's body sexually exciting. The creation of strict boundaries between "heterosexual" and "androphilic" transsexuals may be a losing battle in itself. The autobiographies of crossdressers and their websites certainly suggest that many are interested in men as well as women, or interested in men while they are wearing women's clothes, at any rate.

The enthusiasm for femininity in gay male culture may require further explanation. The pursuit of masochistic sexual excitement by practising the behaviours of the subordinate class of women is likely to be one driving force, but male homosexuality has been associated with femininity in sexology throughout the history of that science. Homosexual men in the nineteenth and twentieth centuries were likely to consider themselves as in some way "feminine" because of their disloyalty to heterosexual masculinity. This was interrupted in the 1960s by the butch shift, inspired by the successes of gay liberation, which allowed gay men to escape the stereotype of effeminacy and aspire to enter the status category of "real" men through the employment of masculine behaviour and styles (Jeffreys, 2003). This butch shift is clearest in the development of the practice of gay sadomasochism, described by both critics and adherents (Levine, 1998; Preston, 1993) as a "theatre of initiation" in which gay men can gain admission to manhood. Since effeminacy is no longer required of men who love men, the pursuit of effeminacy in transvestism and transsexualism needs to be explained. The harm caused by child sexual abuse and prostitution is one explanation. This may cause some boys to seek to exit the bodies in which they were abused or possibly to fall back into the default category of femininity once their road to male power has been blocked by being subordinated to male perpetrators (Webb, 1996). Another explanation is that the bullying and harassment to which some young men suspected of being insufficiently masculine are subjected in school and in childhood, damage their chances of entering the superior political status of manhood and may cause them to resort to its supposed opposite (Plummer, 1999). Within gay culture, as within heterosexual culture, the idea that there is an alternative to either the gender of dominance or the gender of subordination is still not well understood.

The industries that have grown up to service transvestites/transsexuals, whether straight or gay identified – such as specially designed clothes and shoes, makeovers, training in movement and voice, all of which are designed to train and accoutre men in traditional femininity – suggest that the "femininity" they aspire to is a social construction. There are no similar industries for women who aspire to masculinity. The phenomenon of female-to-constructed-male transsexualism, which has grown considerably in the 1990s thanks to the Internet, does not seem to be about sexual fantasy but has rather different causes. FTMs are overwhelmingly lesbians before they seek surgery. The phenomenon of women transsexing and wanting to remain with their husbands who then have to reclassify themselves as homosexual, does not seem to exist. The causes of female-to-male transsexualism do not seem to lie in the excitement involved in wearing "men's" clothes. As I have explained elsewhere, the causes lie in the oppression of women and lesbians (Jeffreys, 2003). The first cause seems to be the inability to happily love women while having a woman's body, as a result of an internalized hatred of lesbianism imbibed from a womanhating and lesbianhating culture. Another cause lies in histories of sexual and physical abuse by men which make women want to exit the body they associate with victimhood, and gain safety by identifying with the abuser. Some FTMs want to access the privileges that men are born into by virtue of their male dominant status. Some seek to transition on reaching the menopause, which can be a traumatic event for lesbians who are so desperate to avoid becoming socially despised older women that they choose to become surgically altered "men" (Devor, 1999). The makeover industry is not aimed at FTMs.

THE MAKEOVER INDUSTRY AND ITS CLIENTS

The emporia which exist specifically to service men make no bones about stating that they will fulfil their clients' fantasies. They do not see themselves as servicing a biologically determined condition but servicing men's sexual fantasies as brothels and lapdancing clubs do, and these are frequently run by ex-prostituted women who are seeking to exit prostitution but still use the skills of servicing men's sexual demands that they have acquired. Some are run by the wives of MTFs who have been trained to understand and support the sexual interests of their husbands and other similarly minded men. Others are run by transvestites themselves.

The makeover industry is a growth market. The Internet offers hundreds of makeover studios for aspiring transvestites/transsexuals to choose from. One such is "Hidden Woman" in Reno (Hidden Woman, 2002). This makeover store and salon, like the many other specialist real-world and web stores, sells all the paraphernalia that men require in makeovers: lingerie, wigs, breastforms to stuff down bras and adhesive to keep them in place, equipment to hide their penises, and fetish footwear. The fantasy woman that transvestite men have in mind, according to the photos on these sites and what is available in the emporia, embodies the exaggerated, extreme femininity of pornography. The high-heel shoes are likely to make walking impossible. Extremely pointed and ridiculously high, they look like, and are doubtless designed to be, torture implements. The stiletto heels go up to 6 inches. The profits to be made in the makeover industry are indicated by the price tag of $1,725 attached to the all-day session offered by Veronica Vera in her studio (Miss Vera, 2002). Veronica Vera has been a prostitutes' rights activist and spokeswoman.

The ABGender.com website describes itself as "America's Most Popular Transgender Resource and Shopping Directory" (ABGender, 2002). It features a plethora of makeover establishments with titles such as "Miss Erica's Finishing School" and "FemmeFever". "*La Maison de L'Esprit Feminine*" advertises on the site that it creates "an atmosphere where you can explore the wonderful pleasures normally available only to . . . the female gender". But these "wonderful pleasures" are likely only to be available to men who decide to embody the "female gender". Swooning masochistic sexual satisfaction derived from the accoutrements of femininity is not the usual experience of women who will often find beauty practices a chore and a bore. *La Maison* says it will make "fantasy a reality" and thus enable the men the sexual satisfaction of "dressing" in a safe environment. "A Woman's Touch" will train men to "walk and carry yourself with the poise of the woman you have truly become". At "Awesome Makeovers" they will create "The Sexy Secretary Look" that many of their clients are "quite pleased with". "Transformation in the UK" sells:

> Realistic breasts, silicone breasts, hourglass figure shapers, sexy lingerie, realistic vaginas, wigs, feminine footwear, slinky and kinky clothing, stockings, French knickers, make-up, beard cover, Make-overs, jewelry, pre-painted fingernails, false eyelashes,

> gloves, evening bags, magazines, transformation videos, kinky TV/TS [transvestite/transsexual] videos, kinky fun, feminizing hormones, breast development, combination hormone treatments, Feminine speech therapy home-study course.

The supply of hormones does suggest that there is not a rigid demarcation between crossdressers and transsexuals as once there was. Men can acquire feminine body parts as accessories as well as clothes. Though it is crucially necessary for many transvestites/transsexuals to see themselves as quite distinct from drag queens, who are identified as homosexual, the distinction is not always clear. The list of makeover establishments includes Drag Queen Makeover Software to make a man into a "Drag Queen for a day".

Another aspect of the industry that has developed to service crossdressers is laser hair removal. "Rocky Mountain Laser Clinic" offers "Permanent Hair Removal for Trans-Genders" with before and after photos (Rocky Mountain Laser Clinic, 2002). The suppliers to the transgender industry also offer "Beard Shadow Cover", "Personal Transgender Identification Card", and larger size wigs (Tgnow, 2002). "Fredericks of Hollywood", the famous mail order lacy underwear company, advertises on the Tgnow site as "Crossdresser Friendly" and says, "A very high percentage of Frederick's customers are Crossdressers!" (Tgnow, 2002). Fredericks offers men crotchless panties, "shear [sic] babydolls", high heels and wigs and much more. It is clear that if women's desire to get out of the degrading costume of femininity posed a threat to the profits of such purveyors of fetishistic femininity as Fredericks, the demand by men might easily compensate.

The opportunities to profit from this sexual interest of men are increasingly varied. A profitable sideline for one cosmetic surgeon is operating on the faces of transsexuals to make them more feminine. Douglas Ousterhout of San Francisco tells his potential clients "Looking feminine is, of course, extremely important to you. First impressions are often based just upon your face" (Ousterhout, 1995). He not only does the usual run of brow lifts and fat removal but also changes facial contours by modifying bone structure, and will operate on the bones in brow, chin, nose, cheek and jaw, and Adam's apple. He also does hair and breast implants.

The feminine fantasies that the Internet transvestites/transsexuals tend to experience hark back to the 1950s or to the sex industry. Crossdressers often deliberately wear clothes that they associate with prostituted women. These are the sexiest clothes they can imagine. Charles Anders tells us that "Newly minted gals gravitate toward the sex bomb look for all sorts of reasons . . . Or maybe they associate dressing up with a sexual turn-on, so they want to wear clothes that scream 'nasty girl'" (Anders, 2002, p. 85). The feminine fantasies incorporate extremely traditional and rather insulting ideas of what being a woman might consist of. Vicky Valentine, for instance, on the "Transgendered Galaxy" website is Miss September 2002. His personal ad is as follows: "I am an outgoing, fun early 30s t-girl living and going out in London. I like to dress as feminine as I can, and love high heels and stockings, classy dresses as well as looking like a trollop at times too!" (tggalaxy.com, 2002). The Transgendered Galaxy site is strongly sex industry related and offers a number of links where its male consumers can access men and boys in pornography and prostitution. The site seems to specialize in racial sexual stereotyping offering "Brazilian transsexuals" or "www.black-tgirls" or "ladyboy", which features "shemales from Asia" and is illustrated by the skinny naked bottom of an Asian youth who is looking back over his shoulder at the viewer. The image of femininity that some transvestites adopt is gleaned from pornography. Thus the website "Transvestite Transformation" offers "Back to School", in which the transvestite is dressed in a girl's school uniform. The man sits on a stool with legs spread wide showing his knickers in one frame and in another bends over so that his knickers are clearly on view (Transformation, 2002). This image represents the common heterosexual male pornographic fantasy of sexually using a young girl but transposed in this case onto a man's body.

The website "Transsexual Magic" offers a definition of the transsexual person which many women would reject as a definition of womanhood: "She grows her hair long and wears sexy, beautiful clothing, shaves her legs and plucks her brows. In day-to-day life, she wears makeup and speaks in a feminine voice" (Transsexual Magic, 2002). This website seems to be directed at those men who look resolutely male even when dressed as women. It advises such men to develop feminine auras that cause them to be perceived as women despite their appearance. They can acquire the auras with affirmations and candle rituals, "Begin to affirm that 'I am perfect. I am a woman. I am beautiful.' And people will begin to see you in the same light." It says, "Most male adults cannot 'pass' as women. Even if most of us could afford the sexual reassignment surgery and survived, we would not ravish the world with radiant beauty." The autogynephilia of this transvestite is clear in his admiration of himself in the mirror. He gets a great deal of satisfaction from gazing at his "majestic pair of legs" and remarks, "Decked out in a pair of sexy high heel shoes, you will glorify the Divine creator of all that is beautiful." To get "shapely and feminine" legs he shaves them "smooth and clean". On some websites men exchange their beauty tips with relish, since for them these practices deliver sexual excitement. On the "Transgender Forum" website a man writes, "I reapply lipstick constantly throughout the day", and, "It takes me about 10 minutes to apply all of my makeup", and, "I also find that applying liquid makeup to my legs and arms when wearing a dress helps to hide imperfections" (Transgender Forum, 2002). He says, "I use red polish on my toenails which I find very sexy."

Most of the transvestites/transsexuals who access these websites are heterosexual in that they seek to remain with their wives and call themselves lesbians. Wives are not always pleased when their husbands embark on femininity as sexual fantasy and the websites address this. A new term for transvestites who seek to remain with their wives is t-girls. On Renee Reyes' website he provides a "T-Girls survival guide" – that is, how to retain wives and get them to accept the crossdressing practice (Reyes, 2002). He says that the "happiest and most balanced t-girls I've known over the years have been married to genetic females" in "traditional" marriages. He provides a list of the benefits to women of a "transgender male" partner in order to gain compliance from wives. One of the "most compelling benefits" is that t-girls "come to appreciate the inner beauty of femininity – often times even better than their female counterparts". There is some truth in this. Many women see no inner beauty in the extreme practices of femininity that these men engage in. They may see the very high heels, the short skirts and makeup as degrading and time-wasting. Transvestites/transsexuals are invested in an old-fashioned, uncomfortable and degrading idea of femininity that many women reject in the present. They represent an archive of arcane practices and are likely, unfortunately, to sustain a fossilized femininity into the future because this is what arouses them.

Reyes' idea of femininity is that it means a trivial obsession with shopping and new dresses, a rather 1950s vision. Thus "little bonuses" are that transvestite/transsexual husbands will spend time shopping with their wives and "the wife gets a new dress – every time 'she' gets one". Wives are advised to "get involved" in "playtime" with tv/ts husbands in which the couple will travel interstate to a place where transvestites get together to dress in privacy. Alternatively the wife can send her husband out to crossdress while she remains home. Wives must indulge their husbands' crossdressing, they are told, because these men do not choose this behaviour and cannot help themselves, so whether a wife likes it or not "nature will take its course". Women should get involved or their husbands will do "something silly that will result in embarrassment for the family unit", or "return home with a deadly venereal disease" or "develop a new loving relationship with someone accepting of his transgenderism". These are all threats designed to gain enforced cooperation from wives. Wives are told that the husbands will go ahead anyway and will embarrass, infect or leave them if they are not compliant.

The Internet has created a new class of transsexuals. They credit the net with inspiring their desire to transition. Donald (Deirdre) McCloskey is a conservative American professor of economics. He saw himself as a heterosexual crossdressing man and had "dressed" from the age of 11. He was married with two children (McCloskey, 1999). When he was 53 he found the resources available to transvestites/transsexuals on the Internet and decided that he was really a woman: "Here was a library expressly designed for sexual arousal of crossdressers, and aroused he was" (1999, p. 20). He explains it thus: "There seem to be two patterns: either you've always known you were of the wrong gender or you've constructed a psychological dam against the realization, which suddenly breaks, usually in mature adulthood" (p. 79). Donald considers that he had such a dam. He is not prepared to see himself as simply making a choice. His wife could not cope so he told her she was a "failure as a wife" and did not "know what love means", while being comforted by his "red-painted toenails" (p. 61). He had already reached the pinnacle of achievement as a professor and his decision to identify as a "woman" did not damage his career, he was simply redefined as a woman and is likely to have won extra equal opportunity points for his university since there are few women professors in economics. For men like McCloskey, having transsexual surgery is a privilege of his class and gender status. Many men who transsex have achieved prosperity and security through male privilege and fancy something a little different.

The heterosexual transvestites/transsexuals can be pillars of the establishment. A newspaper article about the makeover studio "Rebecca's Girls School" tells us that the clients are mostly from the lobby group Trans-Gender Education Association (TGEA), which represents the interests of crossdressers, drag queens and pre- and postoperative transsexuals (Vitzhum, 1999). At the Halloween party of TGEA in the studio one-third of the men sit next to their compliant wives and girlfriends. They are described as a "conservative bunch". "Debbie", for instance, is a retired colonel. Many of these mainstream men seem to take up an interest in femininity as a hobby for their retirement. Several of the men were in the police force. The status of these men in the malestream power structure of male dominance might explain why their vision of femininity is such a conservative one. It might also explain why they have the remarkable power and influence that the transgender lobby has achieved in western countries. They have the influence to change laws to protect their hobby, and legal systems in many countries now incorporate the protection of transgender rights – that is, to be accepted as women and not discriminated against. Indeed one of the transgender lobby groups in the USA, GenderPAC, which holds conferences on "gender" each year, has a mission statement that says "GenderPAC believes that gender ought to be protected as a basic civil right" (GenderPAC, n.d.). This is quite a problem for feminists who wish to eliminate gender rather than protect it.

TRANSFEMININITY AS MASOCHISM

The Internet has greatly facilitated the pursuit of this hobby. Some men, it seems, now become transsexual because they find out how exciting it is to pretend to be women in sex chat rooms. Thus Peter says that he, "Like many transsexuals these days", had a "conversion experience in cyberspace". He started having cybersex as Trina or Gina, and found that, "The male–female ratio was favorable, and being pursued by men was as thrilling as Peter had dreamed. In 1996, he began using the Internet to research hormones and sex-reassignment surgery" (Vitzhum, 1999). Peter calls himself a "lesbian". He is quite open about the fact that being a woman means masochism to him, and says:

> We haven't even talked about the masochism of it all. I think, sexually, there's a desire to be punished, and part of that is the illusion of what women are. That they're there to be the sexual object and there to be the punished object. It all kind of goes together . . . There's a degradation aspect of it, of giving up control. Part of the whole transsexual experience is to live that fantasy of spreading your legs and being fucked.
>
> (Vitzhum, 1999)

The crossdressing author Charles Anders notes:

> It may be politically incorrect, but I'm guessing a lot of guys associate wearing slips and hose with a passive, receptive role in sex . . . For some guys, becoming feminine could be part of a fantasy of submission, where someone else ties them up and spanks them, or dresses them up as a French maid named Fifi and makes them serve cannolis on their knees.
>
> (Anders, 2002, p. 10)

Transgender pornography suggests forcefully that the excitement of tv/ts is masochism. The Transgender.Magazines.co.uk site sells 17 magazines, of which 11 have clear masochistic themes, to judge by the one-line descriptions. Titles include "Enforced Feminisation", "TV Maid Servant", "Enforced Sex Swop", "Humiliated TV", "Transvestite Sex Slave", "Enslaved Transvestites" (Transgender Magazines, 2002). One constant theme in transgender porn is that of men having makeup and feminine clothing placed on them by force. The editors of *Best Transgender Erotica* (Blank and Kaldera, 2002) say that they specifically searched for something different to put in their anthology which was not just about men being forced to don "feminine" clothes and makeup by others: "In our call for submissions, we actively discouraged writers from submitting any exemplars of the time-honored forced-feminization story . . . Mom forcibly feminizes son, Aunt forcibly feminizes nephew . . . and so on" (p. 10).

The masochism that lies at the root of crossdressing is clear on the numerous men's lipstick fetishism websites too, because in the cosmology of men's fetishism lipstick is associated with sadomasochism. Lipstick is an important part of the armoury of the sex industry dominatrixes that cater to this aspect of male sexuality. But, more importantly, a crucial part of this lipstick sadomasochism is that the male clients are forced to wear lipstick, and this symbolizes their submission and humiliation. A site called "Bomis: The Lipstick Fetish Ring" has links to sites such as "the Lips and Lipstick Lover's Lounge, Buster's Lipstick Fetish Forum, Angels Lipstick/ Panty Fetish Site, Lipstick Blowjobs, Lipstick and Makeup Sex, Heavy Painted Bombshells, Teen face shots (Closeup head pics of teenage girls in makeup)", and many more (Bomis: The Lipstick Fetish Ring, 2004). The "Lipstick and Leather Bookstore" (in association with Amazon.com) delivers the sound of a whip cracking when you enter the site and whenever you select an item (Lipstick and Leather Books, 2002). This site provides photos of a large number of dominatrixes, who are wearing a good deal of lipstick and applying it. Each "mistress" has a website to be visited and they have lists of recommended SM reading material which link to Amazon. On one page there is the instruction "for another kiss of the whip please click on the lipsticked lips". The male customers clearly require a great deal of detail about lipstick since each mistress identifies her favourite lipstick and they are shown in full colour on pouting lips.

On the same site is a page called "Goddess Tika's Lipsticked Luvs" (Goddess Tika's Lipsticked Luvs, 2002). Tika is a dominatrix. This contains stories designed to stimulate ejaculation in the male customers and gives a good indication of what the submissive male customers require of mistresses when they visit brothels. The stories have two basic ingredients. The dominatrix gets the male submissive to drool as she applies lipstick, or he is forced by a woman or women to apply lipstick to himself, or to submit to being lipsticked. This is the moment of greatest humiliation and, presumably, ejaculation. In a story entitled "The 'lip powers' of a Goddess!" the dominatrix writes, "I am a 'Cruel Goddess', as I torture my Slaves with my lips", and, "I sometimes put my lipstick on in front of my slaves while they watch. I order them to watch Goddess's lips and imagine that they were 'Man enough' to touch those full soft lips." In a story entitled "Makeup Counter" a male submissive describes his feelings of being made up by women: "You continued to outline my mouth heavily. I knew it was now a very bright red. My cock began to throb . . . Waves of emotion went up and down my neck and into my head . . . wavered back and forth between admiration and terror" (Goddess Tika's Lipsticked Luvs, 2002). He then gets treated to the application of blusher and mascara and says, "I was so humiliated that I wanted all of this so badly I could ache from it that I could hardly breathe", and then he has more waves of emotion. He ends up "wearing more makeup than the saleswoman!" In another story in the section "4 stories of submission" a male narrator writes that the mistress "begins to tease my lips with her lipstick case . . . I can hardly control myself". This page contains a lipstick personality test in which men can look at eight diagrams of the shape into which lipsticks are worn as they are used, and work out which personality fits their own use profile. It is hard to imagine women who wear lipstick because it is mandated by a workplace, or out of habit ingrained in childhood, getting so enthralled by detail, but then lipstick fetishists are not women. Women's role is to give pleasure to the male fetishist by wearing the fetish or by applying it to male clients in brothels. The fact that lipstick wearing is deliciously "humiliating" for men makes it clear that lipstick represents, for them, women's inferior status. Lipstick does not elevate the status of women, unless they are in the sex industry as dominants, but symbolizes subordination.

For conservative men who want to gain the sexual excitements of masochism it may seem impossible to remain "men" because they associate manhood with dominance. But women and lesbians do not base their self-definition on sexual masochism. This is not the very core of our understanding of ourselves as it is for autogynephiles like Peter from TGEA. There is an arrogance in the assumption on the part of such men that their sexual interest in subordination makes them women, and in the concomitant campaigning to amend sex discrimination legislation so that their peculiar understanding of themselves as women is protected by the law as constituting womanhood.

THE CONSERVATISM OF CROSSDRESSERS

When men are "dressed" the naked reality of male dominance becomes clear. This male behaviour arises from men's power and privilege and creates grave problems for wives. The wives of crossdressers find the men's behaviour deeply disturbing and struggle to keep their marriages going because ending the marriage and becoming poor, lone women appears, to many, a worse alternative. As crossdressing men tend to be conservative in their values, so, it seems, are their wives. The wives feel betrayed and usurped when their husbands suddenly start doing femininity. Peggy Rudd is the author of *My Husbnd Wears My Clothes* (1999), which is an instruction manual for the unhappy wives as to how they can repress their misgivings and their own interests and selflessly service their husband's excitement. She says that crossdressers are likely to be high achieving and traditional males. Peggy has absorbed the ideology of the transgender movement that this particular sexual interest of men is transgressive and revolutionary. She says "I believe crossdressers are a generation ahead of society in the evolution of the true gender identity" (Rudd, 1999, p. 25).

They are ahead, apparently, because they can do femininity as well as masculinity. But their practice does not look very world-changing when closely examined.

Rudd tells us that crossdressers, "By day . . . may command a corporation with hundreds of employees. By night they may see the positive feminine traits emerge" (1999, p. 43). These men retain the status that male dominance provides for them and are able to enjoy the excitements of masochism by adopting "women's" clothes when they get home. Women are not in the position to be so "ahead". They are unlikely to be running corporations in the first place, and do not have adoring husbands who will fondly attend to their secret bedroom practice of masculinity. Rudd describes a crossdresser at a weekend transvestite activity: "After a weekend of dressing as a woman, her feet were killing her and she seemed anxious to get back home to the routine of wearing a business suit, starched shirt and comfortable shoes" (1999, p. 111). Peggy explains that, "Many crossdressers are very successful as men" and women can help them in their success, as wives have traditionally done: "I know crossdressers who are pilots, accountants, physicians, psychologists and geophysicists. Many are highly successful professionals . . . The wife can assist her husband by being supportive of his career and the demands that the career may make upon him" (p. 120). "For many crossdressers," she says, "being feminine is a good release from the pressures felt on the job. Because of this, being enfemme helps him be more successful as a man" (p. 120). Wives can even, she says, help their husbands to fulfil leadership roles in crossdressing support organizations. Peggy, and the wives she advises, do not seem to have careers of their own, successful or otherwise. They are traditional wives who support their husbands' careers.

Rachel Miller, who identifies as a heterosexual crossdresser and a happily married, Christian, family man, proudly asserts the conservatism of crossdressers, "I found well-educated, bright, considerate, spiritual, family-orientated men who shared similar feelings. There were so many of us who were solid citizens by any reasonable definition, that it was inconceivable that we could all be perverts" (Miller, 1996, p. 54). He, like many crossdressers, is keen not to be seen as transsexual or homosexual. He is not a pervert. It is a puzzle that the practices of these men have been interpreted as transgressive and revolutionary by a transgender movement when they are so middle American. Peggy Rudd estimates the numbers of men crossdressing in the USA at 15 million. If this is correct then this is not a minority activity but an ordinary part of traditional American family values. Women are relegated to being feminine but men can be masculine in order to have money and status, and feminine at home where their wives service their sexual fantasies of masochism and provide an audience. Men's practice of femininity maintains the system of two genders and thus firmly locks male dominance into place rather than undermining it.

THE EFFECT ON WIVES

Peggy uses her Christian faith to enable her to sacrifice her interests to the service of her husband's sexual excitement. In self-abnegation she says "I knew it was wrong to judge my husband" (Rudd, 1999, p. 54). However her motivation seems to be the lack of any alternative for a middle-aged woman whose interests have always been subordinated to her husband's. The advice she gives in her "Open letter to a crossdresser's wife" makes it clear why it is hard for a woman to simply leave: "Let me tell you emphatically that the grass is not greener on the other side of the fence. It is a man's world out there . . . Life is not easy for a woman alone" (Rudd, 1999, p. 69). Women's opportunities in the world outside their marriages are restricted by male dominance but it is a man's world inside their marriages too, in which they are required to service their husbands' sexual interests however disturbing they find them.

Wives find it very difficult that their husbands, after "coming out" as crossdressers, will only engage in lovemaking while wearing women's clothes and expect their wives to relate to them as women. Wives do not necessarily want to be "lesbians" as they call it, although the actual experience of lesbianism is rather different from being forced to relate to a man in a frock. Wives are required to abandon their own sexual desires, which are likely to eroticize female subordination and be responsive to male dominance since that is the way in which women are trained to be sexual and these women are conservative in their tastes (see Jeffreys, 1990). Their husbands no longer do male dominance in the bedroom or in wooing their wives but expect them to adjust to servicing their new "femininity". A letter to Peggy shows the lengths to which a woman can be prepared to go to overcome her own interests and continue to service her husband:

> I am doing everything possible to help him. For example when he comes home from the office after a tiring day his feminine clothes are already laid out for him . . . I know in my heart there's still room to improve my attitude . . . He needs some kind of prop in order to be sexually aroused . . . he needs to be wearing some kind of feminine clothing when we make love . . . I am not a lesbian. I don't like being made to feel like one.
>
> (Rudd, 1999, p. 59)

Peggy herself found the reversed sexual role expected of her by her husband's new persona very difficult. "Wives", she says, "have said that they feel betrayed sexually. In our relationship this was true. Once Melanie moved in there has been no love making with Mel . . . Discovering that I would be making love to Melanie was what the big shock actually was all about" (1999, p. 118). Crossdressers whose wives are not compliant are likely, it seems, to shout and hit their wives. Peggy cautions husbands against these behaviours if they want their wives to accept their practices (p. 81) – she guilt trips the wives by telling them "that if she resists her husband's desire to crossdress he may experience insurmountable pain. The desire to crossdress will not go away. There is no cure!" (p. 81). Thus wives must accept.

The female role under male dominance requires many varieties of servicing of men; that is, domestic labour and the labour of childrearing, emotional labour and sexual servicing, as well as the performance of femininity for the men's excitement. The crossdressers only want to do the "femininity" part of the female role and they do not do it for women's delight, quite the reverse. Thus wives complain that their husbands will spend hours primping while they do the housework as usual. Peggy gives what she says is a paraphrased comment from wives that she frequently hears: "He says he wants to be feminine and beautiful, so he primps in front of the mirror while I clean the house. He steps out of the bedroom vanity looking like Miss America and I look like a woman appearing in an Ajax commercial" (Rudd, 1990, p. 76).

Another big difficulty the wives have to face is the fact that their husbands have usurped their role. The wives will have been trained since childhood to do femininity and may well feel that they have mistressed this behaviour quite well. They expect the rewards that go with it, such as being treated romantically by a "masculine" husband. This is, after all, how traditional heterosexuality is supposed to work. But when the husband begins to crossdress she is in danger of losing her sense of self and role in life. Peggy explains, "I have heard about wives who do not want their husbands to look pretty. The wife has been on a pedestal all alone, and she doesn't want to share the vaulted position. Some wives feel envy when the husband walks out of the closet looking as pretty as she does" (Rudd, 1999, p. 122). Charles Anders says that one of his female partners had "wanted to be 'the girl in our relationship' and feared I'd usurp her place" (Anders, 2002, p. 132). "Femininity" may be a chore and a bore but it is likely to be, after a lifetime's work, the basis of a woman's identity and feelings of self-worth. When her husband does it better she loses the meaning of her existence. She is rendered superfluous, and the practice of femininity she has engaged in all her life may seem hollow at best. After 50 years of femininity she may wonder what it was all about. The rewards that femininity are supposed to bring disappear as, "She can picture life with no more romantic dinner dances and no more nights out with the man of her life" (Rudd, 1999, p. 119). Some wives, according to Peggy, suffer the extra humiliation of seeing their husbands continue to do the masculine role in relation to other women in their social or professional lives while the wife has to relate to the Fredericks of Hollywood knickers. This can seem very unfair.

TRANSFEMININITY – TRANSGRESSING GENDER OR MAINTAINING IT?

Women are not, like men, in a position to "choose" femininity. Femininity is enforced upon women and is a mark of women's low status. It is not a sex toy for women but the way in which they are required to model their bodies, their emotions and their lives. It is not easier or more "natural" for women to learn the beauty practices of femininity than it is for men. Girls learn that they must engage in these practices as, usually in their early teens, they understand that they must be "feminine" and give up tomboy activities in favour of sitting decorously and concealing their muscles. Carole Bouquet, the French face of Chanel in the late 1990s and a film actress, describes the onset of "femininity" as something difficult that suddenly just happened and interrupted her career as a tomboy, "She was a tomboy with short hair. Her femininity only showed through, she says, in the teens, and then she was gauche about it – a mass of self-consciousness and nerves" (Swain, 1998, p. 6). The femininity is represented as something natural that protruded through the artificial veneer of tomboyhood. The result of her undergoing this transition is that she gets described by men like the male writer of this profile as exerting "magnetism" over men and "she can be wild and sophisticated, ostentatious and austere". In order to be "magnetic" she had to stop climbing trees and riding her bicycle.

Many lesbians report having been tomboys in their youth, but so do the great majority of women who go on to be heterosexual (Rottnek, 1999). The process of transitioning from the condition in which a girl may play with boys, use her strong body in physical activities and give no thought to how she looks, to "femininity" in which she must learn to walk in crippling shoes and constraining clothes and constantly paint and check her face to ensure that her mask is intact, is a harsh one and likely to cause, as it did for Bouquet, "self-consciousness and nerves". Their mothers, girls' and women's magazines, and their friends, train them and there is much to learn. Girls have makeover studios too, but these are likely to be the bedrooms of relatives and friends rather than commercial premises accessed via the Internet. Girls have to practise femininity until it feels "natural" in order to create "sexual difference".

Although the naked reality of male dominance may seem to be clearly revealed by an examination of transfemininity, the practice has been supported and even proclaimed progressive in the last decade by the heavyweights of queer theory. The major difference between the queer gender project and the feminist one lies in what is to be done with gender after the revolution. Feminist theorists such as Monique Wittig (1996), Janice Raymond (1994), Catharine MacKinnon (1989) expect that gender will be abolished, or simply be unimaginable in the egalitarian future. The stars of queer theory, on the other hand, seek to retain gender as an aid to sexual excitement. One such is the queer theorist Judith Halberstam.

Judith Halberstam promotes the value of "female masculinity" and the right of women to access this, as she sees it, social good. Halberstam does not have a political analysis which would enable her to see that masculinity is the product of male dominance, indeed she repudiates that notion and says that women can, do, and have historically done it just as well as men. She hates femininity, however, and is very aware of how young women's lives are reduced and constrained by its acquisition. The only purpose she can envisage for femininity is sexual: "It seems to me that at least early on in life, girls should avoid femininity. Perhaps femininity and its accessories should be chosen later on, like a sex toy or a hairstyle" (Halberstam, 1998, p. 268). Pat Califia is another exponent of female masculinity who argues that "gender" should be retained as a sex toy (Califia, 1994). Califia's practice of masculinity began in sadomasochism but has now extended into transsexualism and she has renamed herself Patrick. The transgender theorist and activist Kate Bornstein argues that sadomasochism is itself the most extreme and exciting way to act out the power difference of gender (Bornstein, 1994).

Queer theory has, understandably, been enlisted to support men's practice of femininity. After all both queer theorists who promote transgenderism and the men who access transvestite porn on the Internet have a similar interest in "gender". They are all interested in milking the performance of gendered behaviour for its sadomasochistic excitements. Femininity is exciting because it is the behaviour of subordination, and it is precisely because it is the behaviour of subordination that it cannot be preserved.

At the end of this chapter it is fitting to return to the thoughts of Janice Raymond who provided the tools for feminist analysis of transsexualism in *The Transsexual Empire* (1994). She explains why the analysis of transgenderism is so useful for feminists, saying that it places gender "stereotypes on stage . . . for all to see and examine in an alien body" (Raymond, 1994, p. 184). But, she says, it is possible to overlook the fact "that these stereotypes, behaviors, and gender dissatisfactions are lived out every day in 'native' bodies . . . they should be confronted in the 'normal' society that spawned the problem of transsexualism to begin with" (p. 185). The rest of this volume concerns itself with the problem of femininity in what Raymond calls the "native" bodies of women.

4

PORNOCHIC

Prostitution constructs beauty

In the late twentieth century the industry of pornography became highly profitable and respectable. As it burgeoned in size, so it began to have considerable social influence in the construction of beauty practices. In the 1960s and 1970s in western countries censorship controls on pornography were progressively relaxed under the influence of the "sexual revolution". I have argued elsewhere that this sexual revolution enshrined as positive social values men's sexual desires for access to women, particularly through pornography and prostitution (Jeffreys, 1990, 1997b). But historians of sexuality have understood the "sexual revolution" to be about women's sexual freedom. Certainly women made some gains. Women's right to some form of sexual response and to have sexual relationships outside marriage became much more accepted, but the main beneficiary of this "revolution", I suggest, is the international sex industry. The sex industry was able to expand in an economic and social climate of laissez-faire, free market capitalism. New technologies of the videotape and the Internet were extremely well suited to this industry and were the immediate source of new pornography practices. The values of pornography, and its practices, extended outwards from magazines and movies to become the dominating values of fashion and beauty advertising, and the advertising of many other products and services. There has been a pornographization of culture. In this chapter I look at the way in which pornographic practices have influenced the fashion and beauty industries.

PORNOGRAPHY BECOMES RESPECTABLE

The sex industry increased hugely in size, social acceptability and influence on malestream politics in the 1980s and 1990s. The normalization of the industry coincided with its period of greatest expansion in the 1990s as a result of the policy of the Clinton administration in the USA not to prosecute porn (*Adult Video News*, 2002a). *Adult Video News* (AVN), the online magazine of the US pornography industry, speculates that Clinton liked porn and had a special stock on his airplane Air Force One (2002a). AVN says that Clinton was a libertine and that during his presidency porn production companies doubled and porn made inroads into many areas of American society.

The US industry went to great efforts to gain acceptance. It hired lobbyists, participated in charity and campaigned for condom use to prevent HIV infection. It learnt from another very damaging industry, tobacco, which though it has lost social standing now, at one time used lobbyists and people to front for the industry very well. For instance, male smokers who epitomized masculinity were used to promote the industry, until they died of its effects. The American porn industry created sex industry exhibitions, now held in several countries, and several states in Australia yearly. It invented the awards ceremony. This was started by *Adult Video News* in 1983. As AVN (2002a) puts it:

> With more and more mainstream media attention focused on the Awards Show every year, the extravaganza has also served to considerably raise the profile of the industry throughout the nation and indeed, the world. And they're not called the adult equivalent of the Academy Awards for nothing. Like the Oscars, a Best Film or Best Video Feature statuette can significantly boost that production's sales and rentals.

The American industry has employed the tactic of making celebrities out of a few leading porn stars who then crossover to be used in the promotion of mainstream pop culture. Now porn stars are respectable enough to be on US radio shows like *Howard Stern* or the Disney-owned ABC Radio's *Porn Stars are People Too*. Porn stars are appearing in mainstream TV shows. Porn performers dance on stage at music award shows.

One example of the degree of social acceptance that the porn industry has achieved is the success of Richard Desmond, the famous UK pornographer who publishes such top-shelf titles as *Big Ones* and *Horny Housewives* and a "live" sex website. In February 2001 the British Labour government approved Desmond's takeover of the tabloid newspapers the *Daily Express* and the *Daily Star*. Eight days later the British Labour Party banked a £100,000 donation towards election expenses (Maguire, 2002). Despite some critical reaction to what looked like a decision to hand two major UK newspapers to a porno king in return for a donation, in May 2002 Desmond was invited for tea at Downing Street to meet with Tony Blair. It is hard to imagine this degree of social acceptance of pornography and the sex industry as completely reasonable sergeants in arms to the Labour Party in the 1970s, when pornography still had a disreputable air about it. The profits of the porno industry are now so large that it is able to command considerable political obedience.

One motor force in the normalizing of what has come to be seen as softcore porn is the development of extreme hardcore porn in the 1990s. In that decade US pornography, which dominates the world market in this form of sexual exploitation, became much more violent and degrading towards the women used in it. *Adult Video News* describes the move towards "hardcore" porn thus:

> There was the requisite "spit and gape" maneuver, where a guy would stretch his partner's asshole as wide as it would go, and then hock up a good-sized loog into it. Anal and d.p. became a requirement; soon it became the "airtight" trick (a cock in every hole), the ultimate-in-homoerotic-denial position (double-anal), mega-gangbangs, choke-fucking, peeing, bukkake . . . even vomit for a brief, unsavory period. We can only wonder what'll hit next.
>
> (Adult Video News, 2002a)

This kind of porn, which has progressively increased in popularity, is, according to AVN, directed at young men who like locker room humour. As some areas of porn have become more and more extreme in the violence directed at women, others have become normalized and have been able to make their way seamlessly into respectable fashion and "art".

THE ECONOMICS OF PORNOGRAPHY

In the 1990s the sex industry began to be covered seriously in the business pages of newspapers. Pornography companies began to be listed on the Stock Exchange. The exact profits being made from the industry are hard to gauge, partly because there is such a diversity of forms of sexual exploitation, and because some companies are not keen for their involvement in pornography to be known. There are some estimates available, however, for the USA. Bill Asher, President of the porn video company Vivid, estimates that the industry in 2001 was worth $4 billion including video, DVDs, TV, Internet, strip clubs and magazines but says that was already twice what it had been worth only 3 years previously. Denis Hof, an associate of Larry Flynt of *Hustler*, confirms that the industry is increasing in size very fast. He says that whereas only 8 years previously 1,000 porn videos per year were produced in the USA, the figure was 10,000 in 2001. The size of the industry on the Internet in 2002 was indicated by the existence of 200,000 porn websites (Confessore, 2002). A report from an IT research company in 2002 forecast that profits from pornographic materials transmitted to mobile phones in the USA would reach an annual US$4 billion by 2006, out of a "total porn spend of US$70 billion" (Nicholson, 2002). For the industry outside the USA it is hard to get estimates. However, a report by the EU Women's Committee on the impact of the sex industry in Europe in 2004 estimated that "70% of the £252 million that European Internet users spent on the net" (i.e. one particular pornographic medium) "during 2001 went to various porn sites" (Eriksson, 2004, p. 11).

In the 1990s pornography was embraced by the corporate world in the USA. Very large, mainstream companies started to take considerable profits from the industry. The big companies make their profits from distributing porn. AT&T in 2003 was distributing it through its cable television network. Later in that year it announced the intention to drop all adult programming (Brady and Figler, 2003). The major hotel chains Marriott, Westin and Hilton profit from pay-per-view porn in the rooms. General Motors, the world's largest company, owns DirecTV, which channels porn into millions of US homes. General Motors now sells more graphic sex films every year than does Larry Flynt (Egan, 2001).

Adult Video News claims that porn videos are worth more than the legitimate Hollywood film industry and often use the same personnel (*Adult Video News*, 2002a). The industry is centred in Hollywood and creates, according to AVN, more employment for Hollywood's army of film technicians and set personnel than mainstream production. The porn industry uses similar methods and language, for instance porn production companies now have "contract girls" who are under contract to work for the company, as film actresses used to be in the regular industry. There are more and more crossovers between the regular and porn genres. Mainstream movies are made about the industry, enabling men to see strip and sexual acts in their local movie cinema. The regular industry becomes more and more pornographized, showing ever more graphic sexual activity. Another aspect of the normalization that is taking place is the way the music industry is becoming intertwined with the porn industry. Whole genres of pop music now converge with the respectable porn industry, with porn actors doing signings at Tower Records, for instance. They market to the same consumers, young men.

PORNOGRAPHIC ADVERTISING

In the early twenty-first century the ubiquity of porn in advertising has led to some disquiet being expressed in the quality press. A piece by Jessica Davies in *The Times* comments on the explicitness of the pornographic imagery in *Vogue*:

> First is a Dior advertisement in which a young model, slathered in oil and ostensibly playing air guitar, strums her crotch with her legs splayed wide. Next is a YSL perfume ad featuring a naked girl

> standing beside two gay-looking men. Then there is a Kurt Geiger promotion for shoes which features a couple having sex against a wall, the woman (naturally) exposing an acre of flank. And an Emanuel Ungaro ad in which a skimpily clad girl masturbates while kneeling on a wooden floor.
>
> (Davies, 2001)

Davies asked the *Vogue* editor, Alexandra Shulman, for her thoughts on this and reported that, "she acknowledges that 'fashion erotica' as she calls it, is being used more", but she has, "'no problem with such imagery'". Shulman said, "I take the view that it's positive rather than negative . . . It certainly doesn't offend me – and the magazine is selling well." But she did say to Davies that the "trend for more explicit shots may have gone too far". It is unlikely, however, that she will have any say in deciding what is "too far". An advertising director at another publishing house told Davies that "my personal views would probably upset a lot of my clients" and though she dislikes much of what goes into her magazine she is "in hock to the powerful fashion and beauty houses that fund it" (2001).

Jonathan Freedland, in the *Guardian*, expresses his concern that pornographic advertising has spread beyond fashion, even to the humble Pot Noodle. As Freedland describes it, "They show a man at the mercy of a prostitute in dominatrix gear, while he drools over an especially spicy Pot Noodle. He begs for the snack to do its worst, ending with the slogan: 'Hurt me, you slag'" (Freedland, 2002). The Pot Noodle ad is symptomatic of a trend within fashion advertising in which not only are the women stripped of their clothes and placed in suggestive positions learnt from pornography, but they are now frequently represented as prostitutes.

One way in which fashion advertising is following pornography is that nakedness is becoming de rigeur. Breasts are now routinely exposed, either completely or behind filmy drapery that is entirely seethrough. The designers and photographers use nakedness precisely to get media attention. It is unlikely that the revealing clothes will find much of a market among women but that does not matter in a time when fashion labels are so desperate for custom that any attention which might boost their perfume and handbag lines is worth having. One such fashion photo covering one quarter of the back page of *The Age* newspaper in Melbourne showed a woman wearing only part sleeves and a low-slung skirt in a non-seethrough fabric. The model was otherwise naked except for an apron of transparent cloth covering her upper body. The commentary under the picture runs, "A model shows off an outfit by New Designer Toni Maticevski at the Melbourne Fashion Festival yesterday. Maticevski's feminine collection features unorthodox cutting and draping, pleating and asymmetric hemlines" (Express, 2002). It is not the hemlines that lead to the photo being included and women are unlikely to race to buy the apron.

Bruce LaBruce, a Canadian gay pornographer, comments on what he calls the "ever-narrowing gap between pornography and fashion" and that he has heard of "at least five new magazines coming out that make the distinction decidedly academic" (LaBruce, 2001). LaBruce describes a photo shoot he has done "just to be ahead of the curves" with a Russian male "porno star" and a male "Brazilian hustler type", "A stylist friend of mine outfits the Russian in a $45,000 reversible black mink Gucci coat and several Helmut Lang suits. I photograph him picking up the rent boy while shopping at Bed, Bath and Beyond in Chelsea before taking them to a '70s-style apartment, where I continue the shoot as they have sex. It's kind of a joke" (LaBruce, 2001). LaBruce has some ambivalence about his chosen profession and says in an article he wrote for the *Guardian*, "As I stood on the set of my first 'legitimate' porn movie and found myself obliged to walk over and wipe the ass of one of the performers who was experiencing a little anal leakage, I didn't feel particularly glamorous" (LaBruce, 2000). Unglamorous pornography gains a glamorous edge through its association with fashion, however.

The closer and closer integration of porn and fashion photography in relation to adult women does not seem to have attracted much outrage. Adult women, it seems, are fair game for sexual exploitation. But children are seen as innocent and to be protected, so the move in fashion towards kiddy porn has caused serious outbursts of negative criticism. The US Media Awareness Network documents the journey into pornography of the bisexual designer Calvin Klein (Media Awareness Network, 2002). Klein gained notoriety and sales in 1980 when he used the 15-year-old Brooke Shields as a model and had her saying things such as, "Nothing comes between me and my Calvins". He contributed signficantly in that decade to the overt sexualization of fashion advertising. In the 1990s he went much further. In a 1995 campaign he used pubescent models in provocative poses:

> In one of these ads, the camera focused on the face of a young man, as an off camera male voice cajoled him into ripping off his shirt, saying "You got a real nice look. How old are you? Are you strong? You think you could rip that shirt off of you? That's a real nice body. You work out? I can tell." In another, a young girl is told that she's pretty and not to be nervous, as she begins to unbutton her clothes.
>
> (Media Awareness Network, 2002)

According to Media Awareness, Klein insisted that the campaign was not pornographic and that the ads intended to, "convey the idea that glamour is an inner quality that can be found in regular people in the most ordinary setting; it is not something exclusive to movie stars and models".

It does seem unlikely, however, that Klein would be innocent of the precise similarity between his ads and child porn. As a man active in the sexual subculture of gay men in New York in the 1970s/1980s (Gaines and Churcher, 1994) he is likely to have been familiar with pornography, considering its great importance in gay male culture (Jeffreys, 2003). In 1999 Klein went further with an ad campaign for a children's underwear line that featured young children in their knickers smiling for the camera on a huge billboard in Times Square, as well as in full page ads in the *New York Post*. The ads were withdrawn after only 24 hours.

The outrage that was voiced at the kiddy porn campaign has not discouraged designers from using sexualized child images for their shock value. In 2001 models as young as 9 were used to show Stella Cadente's collection in Paris wearing "plunging necklines and high hemlines" (Fitzmaurice, 2001). The "modesty" of the "heavily made-up children", we are told, "was barely covered up by a tiny ruffle of material" (2001). It is probably not coincidental that this kiddy porn show comes "amid one of the leanest years in memory for the French fashion industry" (2001). Pornography and prostitution are industries of last resort when economic times get tough. Child models were used to model adult women's clothes by Italian designer Mila Schon in 1999 and Vivienne Westwood in 1997 (Fitzmaurice, 2001).

Another indication of the way that the sex industry is being integrated into more and more areas of social life is the craze for pole dancing as a fitness routine (Tom, 2002). The craze started in New York and took over from aerobics with women installing poles in their homes for exercise. According to *The Australian*'s columnist Emma Tom, "Pole dancing, aka 'cardio strip' classes, are all the rage in New York and Los Angeles gyms with celebrities such as Heather Graham and Kate Moss receiving private tuition. Well-known fitness fanatics Pamela Anderson and Goldie Hawn have even installed poles in their bedrooms" (Tom, 2002). Pole dancing is being used in fashion shows too. Supermodel Elle MacPherson hired strippers to launch a lingerie range at a strip club in Sydney in 2002. The models posed twined around poles (Tom, 2002).

The distinction between fashion shows and sex industry performances is sometimes very difficult to draw. The Australian model Pania Rose has described her discomfort at having to perform a pornographic scenario in a fashion show (Rose, 2003). On arrival at the fashion show venue she discovered the show was called "Jeremy Scott's Sexibition. Live peep shows". That immediately made her feel uncomfortable because she did not want to pole dance. She found that her outfit was, "very revealing. I think my corset is actually a mini saddle". She had to "kneel in hay and try to be 'provocative' . . . But 15 minutes into the hour-long show I just feel degraded. My knees are bleeding, my top isn't staying up and I feel ridiculous" (Rose, 2003, p. 18).

Elle MacPherson is portrayed naked but for a strategically placed towel in one shot, or sticky tape over nipples in another, and naked but wound in what looks like clingfilm in another, on a hot-supermodels website (Hot Supermodels, 2002). There are many websites dedicated to showing supermodels naked. The Elle MacPherson site carries the advertisement: "Enlarge your penis! All natural penis enlargement pills. Doctor tested and Approved! No Pumps! No Surgery!" It is likely that the sites function as a kind of softcore porn for the punters. For male consumers, the men involved in the fashion industry, the male-dominated media, fashion modelling and pornography are part of the same continuum of the sexual objectification of women for male excitement. There are distinctions beginning to develop between hard- and softcore fashion advertisements which reflect the distinctions between hard- and softcore porn.

The symbiotic relationship between fashion photography and pornography is becoming so close that it does seem likely that the arty fashion magazines which already display fashion on women who are almost naked and in just raped poses, will soon expect models to engage in actual sexual acts for fashion shots. Such a development is presaged in the work of one of the most famous fashion photographers of the moment, Terry Richardson, who is compared to Helmut Newton in his status but recognized to be even more sexually explicit in his approach. Richardson gained fame for sexualized fashion spreads in the 1990s and for epitomizing porn chic. His fashion shots for the label Katherine Hamnett, for instance, included ones "where the models' pubic hair was visible beneath their short skirts", and Sisley, where, memorably, "the model Josie Moran squeezed milk from a cow's udder into her mouth" and he has "made Kate Moss, minus her knickers, look like a world-weary call girl" (O'Hagan, 2004).

Richardson has expanded into the production of his own personalized pornography in which he is photographed engaging in sexual acts with models and other young hopefuls. An *Observer* journalist interviewed him about an exhibition in Manhattan and the publication of two glossy volumes of hundreds of these photographs. A sample of photographs is described thus: "Terry being serviced by two babes who could be, may well be, fashion models. Here he is receiving a blow job from a girl who, for some reason, is trussed up in a suitcase, just her head – and open mouth – protruding. And here he is being fellated by another girl crammed into a dustbin" (O'Hagan, 2004). Richardson professes not to use porn and says, "I don't like to exploit anybody" (O'Hagan, 2004). Apparently "girls . . . come knocking on the door" of his studio to be photographed in sex acts with him. Richardson explains his motivations thus: "I was a shy kid, and now I'm this powerful guy with his boner, dominating all these girls" (O'Hagan, 2004). It is likely that his reputation is so considerable that young women expect to gain some advantage and perhaps become models or famous through grappling with his "boner". Where once young women had to sexually service men to gain jobs in the fashion and entertainment industries, there is now an extra spin. They might have to be photographed and exhibited as well. As men like Richardson increase the sexual explicitness in fashion shoots it may not be too long before the advertisements which already exist on billboards and in magazines in which women kneel in front of men as if about to service them sexually will feature actual fellation.

The pornographizing of fashion photography in its most extreme forms may not have much effect on what women wear since not many will choose to be half-naked in their social or professional lives. However, there are ways in which it has a negative impact on women in general. It popularizes the "slut" and prostitute look, very short skirt, boots, piercings for young women. It makes looking as if you are in the sex industry chic and thereby helps sex industrialists by normalizing their business of the international traffic in women. The sex industry sells clothes and the fashion industry sells prostitution and pornography.

MADONNA AS ROLE MODEL

The cult created around the singer Madonna was an important element in normalizing the prostitute look as high fashion. In the late 1980s the cult of Madonna as "transgressive" heroine united liberal feminists, camp makeup artists, anti-feminists, and postmodern cultural studies theorists. Madonna dressed up in the clothing more usually associated with the sadomasochist brothel and kept grabbing her crotch on stage. She created the *Sex* book, which is full of pornographic and prostitution imagery and has made videos which are directly about prostitution (O'Brien, 1992). When criticized for the scene in which she is chained to the bed in *Express Yourself* and crawling on hands and knees across the floor she says "Okay, I have chained myself, though, okay? . . . I'm in charge, okay? Degradation is when somebody else is making you do something against your wishes, okay?" (quoted in Schulze *et al.*, 1993, p. 28). Madonna's analysis of how the forces of male domination work lacks sophistication.

Camille Paglia chooses to celebrate Madonna specifically because she, Paglia, is "radically pro-pornography and pro-prostitution" and sees, "Madonna's strutting sexual exhibitionism not as cheapness or triviality but as the full, florid expression of the whore's ancient rule over men" (Paglia, 1992, p. 11). While many Madonna fans defend her against accusations from detractors that she represents herself as a prostitute, Paglia says that she certainly does this, and it is what makes her powerful. Prostitutes, in Paglia's vision, are dominant over men. That would probably be news to the millions of women suffering in the international sex industry, the vast majority of whom would like to get out but cannot

(Jeffreys, 1997b; Barry, 1995). Madonna's performances make it seem that prostitution gives women power over men. She represents woman's occupancy of what Monique Wittig calls the category of sex (Wittig, 1996) as powerful, and appears to gleefully embrace the performance of the sexual corvée allotted to women. Her defenders, who wax lyrical about her powerfulness, are unable to distinguish between an actor presenting a prostitute as having power over men and the exercise of power in the real world, including in the brothel.

Postmodern theorists of cultural studies elevated Madonna to cult status with a slew of scholarly books in postmodern language and a whole academic area of study devoted to her at American universities (Lloyd, 1994; Schwichtenberg, 1993a). Those who wished to argue that popular culture could lead to women's empowerment rather than playing a role in women's oppression, chose Madonna as their symbol. They promoted Madonna as the very model of women's agency and transgression and as a role model for a new generation of empowered women. In the course of their eulogies they pilloried what they considered old-fashioned, anti-sex feminism – the kind that criticized popular culture for its womanhating values.

Postmodern approaches are more subtle than that of Camille Paglia, though, I would argue, the basic message is the same; that is, Madonna as transgressive role model for young women. As Ann Kaplan puts it in a collection issuing from the new Madonna studies: "According to the British cultural studies approach, Madonna, especially in her early phases, has been a useful role model for adolescent women in her self-generating, self-promoting image, in her autonomy and independence, and in her determined creativity" (Kaplan, 1993, p. 162). Cathy Schwichtenberg, editor of *The Madonna Connection* (1993a), lauds Madonna for exemplifying that practice so beloved of postmodern feminists "gender performance" – that is, she acts out an exaggerated femininity and thus shows that femininity is actually a social construction, "Madonna bares the devices of femininity, thereby asserting that femininity is a device. Madonna takes simulation to its limit in a deconstructive maneuver that plays femininity off against itself – a metafemininity that reduces gender to the overplay of style" (Schwichtenberg, 1993b, p. 134). The idea seems to be that those for whom Madonna was a role model, usually young teenage girls, would recognize from this performance that they did not need to do femininity. They would have the sophistication to understand, as presumably her fans in cultural studies departments did, the way that "pastiche" worked, that is:

> Gender play is the mix and match of styles that flirt with the signifiers of sexual difference, cut loose from their moorings. Such inconstancy underscores the fragility of gender itself as pure artifice. Thus, gender play takes shape in a postmodern pastiche of

> multiple styles: masculinity and femininity fractured and refracted in erotic tension.
>
> (Schwichtenberg, 1993b, p. 134)

Madonna is seen by postmodern theorists as transgressive in "crossing the established boundaries of appropriate gender roles and sexuality drawn by patriarchy and heterosexism" (Schulze *et al.*, 1993, p. 23). But, postmodern theorists point out, many critics of Madonna cannot see that she is posing a "radical threat" (Schulze *et al.*, 1993, p. 23) and tend to characterize her as representing the prostitute instead. What is the nature of the "threat" that Madonna enthusiasts consider that she poses? Madonna takes men's sadomasochist and prostitution fantasies out of brothels and pornography into the malestream entertainment industry. She markets the practice of prostitution to young women as a form of women's empowerment. The effect is that she has contributed significantly to normalizing prostitution and making it publicly acceptable to portray women as prostitutes in fashion and advertising generally. Cheryl Overs, spokesperson of the pro-prostitution organization, Network of Sex Work Projects, credits Madonna with making their work very much easier in the 1980s (Doezema, 1998). She understands Madonna to have aided in the normalization of prostitution in malestream culture.

Madonna became disappointingly unrevolutionary as soon as she stepped down from the limelight. She chose marriage and motherhood. As the *Daily Mail* newspaper reported: "She's a sweet girl and will be an excellent mum say boyfriend's parents" (quoted in Smith, 2000). However, with the encouragement of an entertainment industry that knows that porn sells, and the desire to make a splash, she chose to represent prostitution while she made her fortune. The damage she wrought is that young girls' fashion is now more firmly attuned to servicing male sexuality. The prostitute or "slut" look continues to be chic. In making this critique I am aware that I will be dismissed by cultural studies feminists in the way in which they write off women in Madonna's audiences who don't appreciate her performance, "When the hater is a woman, one might speculate that the rejection is manifestation of a barely displaced 'abjection of self,' a self-loathing resulting from the interiorization of the patriarchal feminine" (Schulze *et al.*, 1993, p. 31). This is an example of what the radical feminist philosopher Mary Daly calls "patriarchal reversal" – that is, feminists are accused of representing precisely the values and practices that they criticize (Daly, 1979).

PORNOGRAPHIC BEAUTY PRACTICES

The women in pornography have their bodies transformed to suit the fetishistic interests of the male consumers. They have breast implants, as well as other forms of cosmetic surgery, Brazilian waxing and labiaplasty. *Adult Video News* demonstrates, in an interview with a porn star, Tabitha Stevens, just how severe the mutilation required of those who wish to be successful can be. The television programme *Entertainment Tonight* chronicled and partly paid for her US$30,000 plastic surgery. The surgeon was, by her account, viciously incompetent:

> "I had cheek implants put in, one of them he put in crooked, he put them in the wrong way" she explains. "He put them in through my eye; they were supposed to go in through my mouth. Well, one of them shifted, it was coming out of my eye. He had fixed it, but it was shifting again, and it was very uncomfortable. So I went back to him again. And he wanted to charge me to do it again. And I said, 'You can kiss my ass'."
>
> (Adult Video News, 2002b)

Tabitha has had five breast jobs and wants to have liposuction done on her "pinky" toe so that she can sell the fat taken from the toe on the Internet.

There are other examples of the practice of selling off flesh taken from the bodies of porn models. The porn star Houston sold off the parts of her labia that had been removed in labiaplasty surgery. *Adult Video News* (2000) explained that the "World gangbang queen" had a "double multi-hour procedure to reduce labia and replace breast implants. 'I've never liked my labia,' Houston said. 'They're always falling out of my bikini.'" She is reported to have had "a centimeter of pussy trimmed off the inner labia". A photographer recorded the operation. AVN explained that "It took some time for Houston to feel well enough to perform" (*Adult Video News*, 2000), and said she subsequently auctioned off "a pile of her labia trimmings on the on-line XXX auction Internet site, Eroticbid.com."

As the pornography industry has grown and become normalized to the extent that women are being exposed to it in their homes by male partners, it has spawned new "beauty" practices of its very own. The upsurge in the requirement that women should have large breasts, and the concomitant profits of the breast implant industry, owe a great deal to pornography but I deal with this issue in a later chapter. Here I concentrate on the impact of porn on women's genitals. Pornography has created a new area of women's bodies on which they must lavish anxiety, money and painful procedures. Where once women barely glanced at their genitals they are now being required to give them as much attention as they previously reserved for their faces.

SHAVING AND WAXING WOMEN'S GENITALS

The prostituted women in pornography have their pubic hair removed: "the vast majority of women in porn have smooth-shaven vulvas, or close to it" (Castleman, 2000). This has, apparently, not always been the practice in porn. In the 1970s there were "full bushes" and then from 1980 a "trend towards hairlessness" (Castleman, 2000). There is little information available on why this change took place. It might be due to an increasing demand on the part of male buyers to be able to look into women's genitals in "split beaver" shots unimpaired by hairiness. The craze for tabletop dancing clubs in the 1990s might be another response to this demand since they enable male buyers to stare for considerable periods of time into the shaved genitals and anuses of women. There are other reasons why men might have difficulties with hair. It makes women look grown up. Many men prefer women to look prepubescent and thus hairless. Men are trained by porn to see hairlessness in women as "natural" and to find the hairiness of their girlfriends distasteful or less than exciting.

There are problems associated with shaving the genitals, though this is the practice that porn stars employ (Castleman, 2000). Shaving has to take place every day to keep hair under control and it causes "razor bumps". The shaved area can become very itchy as the hair grows back, or women can get ingrown hair of the genitals that is very painful. Porn stars explained to Michael Castleman on the Salon.com website how they deal with having to be hairless. They shave daily and wear "loose underwear and clothing", because, "A shaved vulva chafes more easily than one covered with a soft cushion of pubic hair" (Castleman, 2000). One porn star says that many women on porn sets do have the razor bumps and ingrown hairs that are the telltale signs of painful damage, but the cameras cannot pick it up so the women look "smoother than they really are" (Castleman, 2000). Rome told Castleman (2000) that she gave up shaving as soon as she got out of porn and did not have to do it any more: "It was part of getting ready for work."

Though, as we have seen, porn stars have to shave their genitals because they must be hairless everyday, it is the practice of Brazilian waxing that has caught on among women outside porn in order to create hairlessness for their men. Waxing is not useful for day-to-day hairlessness because it only works on hair of a certain length, so women have to wait until hair regrows before they can undertake the procedure again. It is an extension of bikini waxing; that is, the waxing of the bikini line that became necessary as the fashion industry mandated that women should have to wear tiny bits of material to render them more exciting to male observers. The tiny bikinis did not cover enough of a woman's body to conceal pubic hair and they were expected to wax since visible hair on women was considered disgusting. Two forces worked together, the requirement that women perform their sexual corvée on the beach and the cultural fear and hatred of women's body hair.

The practice of Brazilian waxing is supposed to have originated with seven Brazilian sisters in New York City who "pioneered and perfected the

Brazilian method in the US and have a long celebrity (Gwyneth, Naomi) client list. According to Jonice, 'In Brazil, with bikinis so small, waxing is part of our culture'" (Fashion Icon, 2002). Brazilian waxing removes all hair from the pubic area: "The Brazilian wax basically takes it ALL away, leaving just a tiny strip of closely-shorn hair in the front (referred to by some regulars as an 'airstrip', a 'thong wax' or a 'Playboy wax')" (Fashion Icon, 2002). For some women it is just an extension of the bikini wax: "Many women request a Brazilian because it gives a clean, close wax and the freedom to wear even the most revealing swimwear and lingerie" (iVillage, 2001). The procedure is carried out thus:

> a paper thong might be provided, but most likely, you'll be in the buff. First the hair is snipped with scissors so the wax can reach the follicles. Then, using a wooden stick, a technician places warm wax on the area a little bit at a time . . . A traditional Brazilian includes the labia and the area that reaches into the buttocks. If there are stray hairs after waxing the technician may also tweeze the area.
>
> (iVillage, 2001)

The website explains that it is painful: "Do not expect a picnic. It hurts and there's no way around this! . . . The ones who have to keep going over and over a spot are the worst – and simply prolong the agony . . . The torture is not everlasting. A Brazilian bikini . . . should not take longer than a half hour" (iVillage, 2001). The problem of ingrown hairs still exists and would doubtless be excruciating in the genital area but, apparently, Brazilian waxers can be less scrupulous about trying to find and tweeze them out than regular waxers. Salons use antiseptic soothing lotion after waxing to try to alleviate the discomfort.

The main reason women wax their genitals appears to be the desire to please the kind of male partners who find the look of pornography and prostitution sexually exciting. An Australian Brazilian waxer in *Cosmopolitan* (McCouch, 2002) explains that when she first got herself waxed it "hurt like hell", but, "The best was when my boyfriend saw it. He'd never been with a totally 'bald' woman before and said, 'My God, you're so hot!'" She waxed her sister, and her husband ended her sister's misgivings by saying "Come on, try it. It sounds sexy" (McCouch, 2002, p. 92). She says that clients can become dangerous as they try to deal with the pain: "A few of my clients are even dangerous. One thrashes around so violently from the pain that I'm afraid she's going to break the table and spill hot wax over both of us" (McCouch, 2002, p. 94). An insert panel within the article is entitled, "No Pain, No Gain. Guys wax on about why they love it when you take grooming to the extreme". The message is clearly that waxing is for men's satisfaction. No other motivation is mentioned. The "guys" express how much they like women to wax their genitals. Rodney, a 28-year-old accountant, says, "A Brazilian is just the right balance of slutty and sexy, bad girl and sweet. That she would go through the pain and lavish so much attention on herself down there is so cool – and the fact that it's partly on my behalf is very exciting" (McCouch, 2002, p. 94). John, a 24-year-old chef, says "It shows she really cares – and believe me, we notice!" Dan, 27, a pilot, says "The Brazilian wax turns me on in so many ways – seeing more than I normally do is unbelievably stimulating. Plus, I feel like I'm with a bit of a naughty girl." Greg, 32, an advertising executive, says "If a woman gets a Brazilian wax, it means she likes to look after herself and has a sexy side." Thus women learn that the pain, indignity and expense (about US$45 per session) of Brazilian waxing may improve their chances of pleasing a male partner.

The requirement of some men that women be shaved is now an ordinary topic of advertisements in my local paper in Melbourne. A waxing studio ad makes it clear that a Brazilian is necessary if women are to be acceptable to men sexually: "People whose lifestyles progress beyond the missionary discover the advantages of being more carefully groomed. Intimate coiffure? Perhaps" (Ready for Brazilian Waxing?, 2004, p. 15). The accompanying photo is of a young pouting woman with a long fringe covering half of her face. Across this in small print it says, "Not everyone likes hair in their face". This is an example of how the beauty industry has been pornographized. It also shows the kind of blackmail that is used to force women into the waxing studio.

Shaving is a significant aspect of men's pornographic imagination and practice. There are discussion sites on the web where men can indulge in pornotalk about shaving their female partners and themselves. One man writes to the "Shaving" section of the Lovers' Feedback Forum: "Found this excellent link on genitals, detailed shaving pictures and methods, etc." (Lloyd, 2002). The men in the discussion have very specific requirements of women: "I love it when women keep their pussy smooth and clean. But I do mean smooth. It is definitely not nice when she has stuble [sic] from not waxing, plucking or shaving on a regular basis" (Lloyd, 2002). Another says, "I enjoy giving my wife oral sex, but those hairs just get in the way . . . Now I shave her every few months" (Lloyd, 2002). The existence of shaving as a porn genre for men is clear from the instruction on the AskMen site on how to get a female partner to shave: "Try to find a movie with a shaving scene, since this will really give you a better chance at making your partner *bald and beautiful*" (Strovny, 2002). This is a good example of the way that porn can be used by men as an instruction manual for their female partners: teaching what is required to sexually service men. The author suggests more coercive measures too, however: "jokingly tell her that you will not give her oral sex until she shaves herself for you . . . If she still does not want to do it for you, switch sex partners" (Strovny, 2002). He recommends taking a woman by surprise if she will not agree: "Her knowing, or rather not knowing what you're about to do to her will add to the already kinky element of grooming foreplay." But he says shaving is hard work. Men should practise on a woman's legs first so as not to damage her genitals when they get round to them. Strovny recommends that when men ask women if they can shave them they should "use a prankster tone; this gives you an escape plan if she reacts sourly", or, "Another straightforward way of asking her is by pulling out a razor and shaving cream during foreplay."

Now that hairlessness is the rule for porn, a genre of porn has developed for men who like to see women with hair. This is called, on one website, "bearded clams" (Shave My Pussy, 2002). This name implies that women's genitals are dangerous, as in the toothed vagina idea, and, perhaps, that they smell. Women are, of course, called "fish" in parts of male gay and heterosexual culture because of this supposed smelliness (Jeffreys, 2003).

As a result of Brazilian waxing women became more aware of their labia because they were now visible in a way they had not been before. In pornography women's labia are frequently airbrushed so that they are uniform. The women do not have obviously unequally sized labia or particularly long labia because they are tidied up in the airbrushing so that men will not be offended, and be able to purchase a uniform product. But airbrushing is not enough and women in porn regularly employ labiaplasty, in which the labia are cut to shape, to create the regulation look. This pornographic practice has an impact on women outside the industry when boyfriends pressure women to look like hairless porn stars. Women, already trained in male dominant cultures to dislike their genitals, notice their genitalia more. They may worry that they are not like those on the women in porn, or their male partners may make this clear to them. They then graduate to the cosmetic surgeons who already have a nice little earner in tidying up porn stars. The influence of pornography is openly admitted by the surgeons themselves. Thus Dr Alter, a leading exponent of labiaplasty, calls the demand for the procedure the "Penthouse effect" (Alter, 2002). He explains that *Playboy* caused the demand for breast enlargements in the 1960s/1970s, then "crotch shots in magazines and porn flicks have heightened women's awareness of their down-theres" (Alter, 2002).

Labiaplasty is called by *Cosmopolitan* magazine "sexual-enhancement surgery" (Loy, 2000) and includes:

> vaginal tightening (similar to the husband's knot – the stitching up of the torn or stretched vagina after child birth), the liposuction and lifting of lips that have begun to lose the battle with gravity, the "repair" of the hymen, the clipping of elongated or asymmetrical inner lips, unhooding the clitoris for more friction, and injecting fat (taken from the inner thigh) into lips thought too thin.
>
> (Loy, 2000)

Aya Zawadi (2000) in a piece called "Mutilation by Choice" in the US *Soul Magazine*, compares labiaplasty with female genital mutilation. She interviewed women about the reasons why they were considering labiaplasty and these revealed anxiety and self-consciousness about the supposed ugliness of their labia. One woman said, "Long lips are so ugly and disgusting, I feel so self-conscious about them, I'd consider getting it done." Another explained, "Mine protrude past my outer labia, I'm planning to get the surgery done as a birthday present to myself" (Zawadi, 2000). The after-effects that her interviewees suffered were unpleasant. "Betty" still had pain 6 weeks after the surgery. She had little scarring but said other women who had it done at the same time as she did have: "Awful scarring. I couldn't look. I just know she [the woman who shared the room with her] was horrified and terribly depressed" (Zawadi, 2000). This woman ended up going to counselling to deal with the experience. As "Rhonda" said, "You may think you are doing it for your own self-esteem, to feel more desirable, but in the end you're really doing it for the men." Other after-effects include "a lot of pain and a wait of up to two months before you can have sex. Not to mention very swollen lips." Risks after labiaplasty include loss of sensation, over-tightening of the vaginal opening, discomfort from clothing and an unnatural look to the genitals rather than a positive change. Zawadi's (2000) conclusion is that "We've fought too long and hard against what still goes on in other parts of the world to now volunteer ourselves to mutilation in a doctor's office."

One reason that heterosexual women may feel their genitals require surgery is that they do not know what other women's genitals look like. A leading Australian plastic surgeon said that in the early 1990s there was no demand for female genital plastic surgery, but now he was seeing two per month and demand was growing (Fyfe, 2001). He attributed the rise in demand to "men's magazines", and stated that 90 per cent of women who come to him for genital plastic surgery falsely believe that something is wrong with them. The portrayal of women's genitals in "unrestricted publications" (i.e. those available without plastic wrapping on newsagent shelves) in Australia is prohibited under guidelines determined in 1999. This means that porn magazines that want to avoid plastic wrapping digitally alter pictures of women's genitals so that they are not "realistic". Women who do see other women's genitals in pornography are therefore unable to make a realistic comparison with their own. Elizabeth Haiken, author of *Venus Envy: A History of Cosmetic Surgery* (1997) supports this view of the origins of the popular demand for labiaplasty: "Before crotch shots were published nobody was interested in this, but now everyone knows what labia are *supposed* to look like" (Leibovich, 1998).

Victoria's story in *Marie Claire* suggests that women's pursuit of labiaplasty arose from the revelation of labia through the practice of Brazilian waxing:

> When it became all the rage to get heavy bikini waxes and have almost no pubic hair, my prominent labia really started to bother me. When I was naked, I could see my labia hanging down at least an inch. I felt like it looked as if I had testicles. It was like a betrayal of my body. I always hated that moment when the guy was putting the condom on, hovering over your open legs. If I thought that he'd seen it, I couldn't get it out of my mind during sex. And sometimes during sex, it could get pushed inside, which wasn't agonizing, just annoying. I was really self-conscious – to the point where if my boyfriend would come in the shower with me, I would cringe. I even felt self-conscious when I went to the gynecologist.
>
> (Hudepohl, 2000)

The after-effects Victoria suffered were very painful: "The area was very swollen, maybe five times the size it had been before, and the stitches were more extensive than I thought. I had to lie down a lot with an ice pack between my legs, and on the third day, when I went for a short walk, it started throbbing, so I had to go home and reapply the ice." But she considers they were worth suffering because she now feels less self-conscious: "Now I feel so comfortable with my body when I'm naked, sitting in front of my boyfriend. I feel sexier and am less inhibited. I can hardly see the scar. The thing I like the most is looking at myself straight-on in the mirror and not seeing anything hanging" (Hudepohl, 2000). She does not suggest that her boyfriend influenced her decision. In this case Victoria sought painful and debilating surgery because she was culturally induced to see her perfectly ordinary genitals as unsightly. Her surgeon profits from societal womanhatred.

When labiaplasty surgeons advertise their wares they play on the notion that the practice is in women's interests rather than just making women more sexually acceptable to men. On the website LabiaplastySurgeon.com, on which a cosmetic surgeon touts for hire, the procedure is described thus:

> Labiaplasty is a surgical procedure that will reduce and/or reshape the labia minora – the skin that covers the female clitoris and vaginal opening. In some instances, women with large labia can experience pain during intercourse, or feel discomfort during everyday activities or when wearing tight-fitting clothing. Others may feel unattractive, or wish to enhance their sexual experiences by removing some of the skin that covers the clitoris. The purpose of a labiaplasty is to better define the inner labia.
>
> (LabiaplastySurgeon.com, 2002)

The "best candidates" are, "Women who are either experiencing sexual dysfunction or embarrassment because their labia . . . are oversized or asymmetrical. Also women who dislike the large size or shape of their labia, which may cause inelegance or awkwardness with a sexual partner" (LabiaplastySurgeon.com, 2002). Before and after photos on the site show the genitals of some unfortunate woman. "Before" she has identifiable labia minora that may be about 1 centimetre long, "after" she has none that can be seen. Another surgeon, Dr Robert S. Stubbs, offers a greater variety of surgical procedures on women's genitals, including making the outer labia bigger, "labia majora augmentation", and "clitoral unhooding" or general "genital enhancement". Before and after photos of all these procedures are available on the web in a Surgical Art Gallery (Psurg, 2002).

Labiaplasty surgeons also offer other "genital surgeries". Women can have the "urethral opening redefined" and "necessary improvements to the vagina" can be made at the same time (LabiaplastySurgeon.com, 2002). The surgery on the vagina is called "vaginal rejuvenation" and it is described as being: "For women who've experienced multiple childbirths", whose vaginal muscles may have experienced "enlargement" during delivery so that they then have "loose, weak, vaginal muscles". The surgery, "can usually correct the problem of stretched vaginal muscles resulting from childbirth(s), and is a direct means of enhancing one's sexual life once again". The question of whose sex life will be enhanced here, that of the woman or her disgruntled male partner, is not quite clear. The technique can be performed on an "outpatient basis" and "tightens muscles and surrounding soft tissues, by reducing excess vaginal mucosa (vaginal lining)" (LabiaplastySurgeon.com, 2002). Other forms of surgery are available for women concerned about the effects of age on their genitals. Thus the labiaplasty surgeon Dr Gary Alter explains that the female genitals change shape as women age and women might need to reverse this, "As we age, gravity causes all parts of our body to descend. Therefore, the pubic hair, mons, and vaginal region also descend, causing an aged appearance. This area is elevated by performing the opposite of an abdominoplasty or tummy tuck; excess skin above the pubic hair is excised, raising the pubis. This procedure is often combined with an abdominoplasty" (Alter, 2002).

Labiaplasty surgeons now routinely offer hymen repair to women from cultures where virginity is required of them on marriage. Liberty Women's Health Care of Queens, New York, for instance, offers a variety of genital surgeries including "Hymen Repair Surgery, Restoration, Hymenoplasty, Hymenorraphy of Hymenal Ring" (Liberty Women's Health, 2002). They explain the need for these procedures thus: "The hymenal ring normally gets disrupted after a woman has had sexual intercourse or even after strenuous physical activity or tampon use. Sometimes, for cultural or other personal reasons (for example, an upcoming marriage), a woman would like to restore a more intact, tighter hymenal ring." When this is the case they offer a special surgical technique that can "repair and tighten the hymen to a more intact, virgin-like state in most patients". The surgery is "virtually undetectable". The practice which the clinic is offering is common in countries such as Turkey where a woman's virginity is a necessary part of the marriage contract (Cindoglu, 1997). In such countries women are subject to traditional patriarchal codes of morality. Girls and women are surgically remade into "virgins" so that a better price can be achieved for them, or a better class of husband. Immigrants from these countries are now creating a lucrative market for surgeons prepared to perform the surgery in western countries such as the USA and the Netherlands (Saharso, 2003).

Liberty Women's Health piously assert they would never "provide or condone any form of female circumcision or genital mutilation, regardless of one's cultural beliefs". They will perform surgery to make women conform to both pornographic western demands and traditional Islamic ones, by cutting them up, however. This is evenhanded, but surely not easily distinguished from the mutilation they reject. Labiaplasty surgeons also profit from reversing female genital mutilation. There is a good profit for doctors from inscribing the cruel requirements of culture in hymen repair or labiaplasty onto women's bodies as well as in repairing the damage that results from such requirements.

The surgery being carried out on women's genitals to satisfy men's pornographic desires is a good example of the way in which the medical profession can act as a handmaiden to male dominance. Medicine is now in the practice of carving the genitals of pornography on women's bodies. As Dilek Cindoglu says of the practice of surgeons in Turkey who do hymen repair surgery: "Physicians as professionals and medicine as an institution are not independent of the social environment in which they exist" and their surgeries need to be seen as "interventions of medicine in the social fabric in a very patriarchal manner" (Cindoglu, 1997, p. 260). Western surgeons who perform culturally required labiaplasty and other "sexual enhancement" surgeries are deeply involved in the pornographizing of women.

The result of the normalization of pornography in the 1980s and 1990s, through the cult of Madonna and the Internet, is that the image of what is beautiful for young women and girls has become inextricably intertwined with the sex industry. Looking like Madonna has morphed in the twenty-first century into looking like Britney Spears but the impulse, to represent prostitution, is the same. On the catwalk the values and practices of prostitution and pornography now dominate. Male designers are selling the look of sadomasochist prostitution in particular, to the rich and fashionable. In the next chapter I take a critical look at what passes for fashion and the men who create it.

5

FASHION AND MISOGYNY

It has become unpopular since the 1980s, when post-structuralist thinking began to dominate in universities, to point out that fashion reflects and serves to maintain female subordination. In work of a postmodern persuasion fashion tends to fly free from its material, political underpinnings. The political forces that affect what constitutes fashion at any time, such as sexism, capitalism, classism and racism, disappear. Instead fashion is celebrated as a free spirit, something that enables everyone, and particularly women, to exercise choice and creativity, to express their identities, transgress boundaries. Thus even feminists who write about fashion seem to fail to notice that whatever changes take place in fashion there are always differences written into what women and men may wear. These differences enable the sex class of women to be distinguished from that of men and, in recent decades, turn a full one-half of the human race into toys to create sexual excitement in the other half. In this chapter I argue that fashion design in the late twentieth century became particularly misogynist through the incorporation of pornographic and sadomasochist imagery, nakedness, corsets, black leather and vinyl, even blood and injury. I ask why fashion designers are so predominantly male and gay, and examine their role in this process.

CREATING THE DIFFERENCE

The creation of sexual difference/deference in fashion is carried out in several ways. These include the display of skin, use of skirts versus trousers, the use of bright or pastel colours for women while men are restricted to greys and browns, and the placing of the stigmata of prostitution and sadomasochism on women's bodies. They also include the placing of zip fasteners and buttons so that they open to the left or right in order to display sex, and the rule that women's clothes should not have functional pockets, necessitating the carriage of a handbag.

The requirement that women should display skin while men should not, does not seem to be limited to western cultures. Joanne Eicher has written most interestingly of this issue among the Kalabari in Africa. She prefaces her work on the Kalabari with a wonderful quotation from the nineteenth-century US feminist Elizabeth Cady Stanton: "Why is it that at balls and parties, when man comes dressed in his usual style, *fashion requires woman to display her person, to bare her arms and neck*? Why must she attract man's admiration? Why must she secure his physical love?" (quoted in Eicher, 2001, p. 233, emphasis in the original). Stanton's answer to this question is that women must secure men because marriage is their only career, and this is best achieved by using methods perfected by prostitutes of showing off their bodies to arouse men's appetites.

Among the Kalabari, where, Eicher points out, men are in control economically and politically, "adult males appear in public for everyday or ceremonial purposes with the upper and lower body as well as the head, and usually the feet, covered. Although a man may choose to dress casually with only a wrapper around his waist and a bare chest within the confines of his compound, he will not leave his domestic space with his chest bare or legs uncovered" (2001, p. 240). This is in sharp distinction to the behaviour of women, where "the bare shoulders, breasts, and legs of a Kalabari woman may be displayed when she is dressed to participate in any part of an *iria* ceremony, even though these parts of an adult woman's body are not visible when she is dressed for everyday activities" (Eicher, 2001, p. 241). Eicher suggests that readers consider the Hollywood Academy Awards ceremony to see how similar ways of distinguishing the dominant class of men from the subordinate class of women are replicated in the west. In this ceremony, she says, women are in "gowns that display various parts of their bodies" while men are in suits which conceal their body shapes (2001, p. 243). Eicher's chapter ends with two photos by James Hamilton that show much better than words can, the absurdity of the clothes that "fashion" routinely expects women to wear, when worn by men. In one a man is wearing a half-suit and in the other an off-shoulder shirt. Both look ridiculous, because the men have been divested of their social status through the medium of inappropriate nakedness.

The casual observer wandering through the areas devoted to male and female fashion in a department store will notice that fashion is overwhelmingly, and before all else, gendered. This gendering is so dramatic that it seems surprising that any book on fashion would be able to ignore or deride this fact. It hardly needs to be said that the men's department generally offers clothes that are not full of holes to show the body, there are no skirts or dresses, clothes are not skintight, they tend to be functional and look as if they are well suited to a number of activities. They are not devoted to revealing the male body as a sex object to the female viewer. They also tend to be made of superior materials and made to last though they are, however, restricted to drab colours. The "women's" clothes, on the other hand, often resemble dolls' clothes – tiny, in garish colours and shoddy materials, and revealing much of the body.

This distinction is particularly clear in the phenomenon of the suit. Anne Hollander, in her homage to the suit (1994) makes it clear that she considers the suit the best ever clothing invention. She explains that the suit came into being for men around 1800 and that nothing similarly wonderful has ever been invented in the world of women's fashion. She describes at great length the superior qualities of the suit over anything women were prescribed, but a brief quotation will suffice here:

> This ideal offers a complete envelope for the body that is nevertheless made in separate, layered, detached pieces. Arms, legs and trunk are visibly indicated but not tightly fitted, so that large movements of the trunk or limbs don't put awkward strain on seams or fastenings, and the lumps and bumps of the individual body's surface are harmoniously glossed over, never emphatically modeled.
>
> (Hollander, 1994, p. 8)

The suit performs the function of covering the body comfortably, allowing considerable movement without rucking up, and conceals imperfections of the body. Hence it is a form of clothing that allows human dignity, and thus it was denied to women. When extended to working women in the 1980s, the suit tended to become restrictive and take the form of short skirts, shoulder pads and, once again, tightness. However, Hollander's book, like the vast majority of literature on fashion does not comment on the implications of the masculine form of the suit for the power difference between women and men. Instead she says, "In general, people have always worn what they wanted to wear; fashion exists to keep fulfilling that desire" (1994, p. 141). This might be true if women's ideas about suitable clothes were truly free of all social influences, but women and men are restricted to what is available in their own socially constructed imaginations and, most importantly, to what is in the shops.

The extent of the sexual distinction that exists in clothing in the twenty-first century derives, historians tell us, from the great shift in men's clothing at the end of the eighteenth century. Before that time upper-class men could engage in personal adornment as women did. The French revolution resulted in a shift in western culture. Men gave up the rich adornment that had established differences in social status between the rich and the poor in favour of a more democratic model in which all men were able to establish brotherhood by wearing similar clothing. This clothing was sober and dark and represented the values of the world of capitalist work that these men were joining. The clothing of women had never been the same as that of men, however. They had worn skirts in order to distinguish them. From the French revolution onwards the extreme differences noticeable presently in formal wear between women and men developed.

J.C. Flugel, author of the much quoted book, *The Psychology of Clothes*, first published in 1930, seeks to explain why only men gained this new and democratic form of clothing. He argues that the distinction in clothing between men and women is based on the need for the excitement of sexual imagination. He rejects the feminist critique of the degrading costume imposed on women which, interestingly, must have been well known at the time he was writing, as "the sexual delusions of old maids" (Flugel, 1950, p. 109). He says that some women state that it is at men's insistence that they engage in "the decorations and exposures of female dress" (1950, p. 108). Such women argued, as many feminist commentators have in recent times, that, "it is only in response to an insistent male demand that women consent (as they pretend, reluctantly) to expose their persons. The charge of immodesty is admitted, but the real guilt is thrown back upon the other sex" (Flugel, 1950, p. 109). But these annoying women are, he says, "women who, in virtue of inferior personal attractiveness, are likely, themselves, to receive less than the usual amount of male attention" and they are likely to be "unsatisfied women" and "old maids" who, in his masculine understanding would be unsympathetic to sexual seductiveness on the part of women. I have written elsewhere about how the scientists of sex, among whom male psychoanalysts like Flugel figured in great number, attacked the feminists who sought to criticize the sexual power relations between men and women in the early part of the twentieth century. They were routinely accused of being elderly spinsters or sexual deviates who could not be expected to understand normal heterosexuality or might even be hostile to it (Jeffreys, 1985/1997).

Despite his rejection of the spinster feminist perspective, Flugel's own words suggest that it is quite reasonable. In considering the idea that the sexes might dress alike he argues that this would not appeal to "us" (presumably men) precisely because "we" want to experience the sexual excitement afforded by dress distinction. He says that there is "no escape", from "the view that the fundamental purpose of adopting a distinctive dress for the two sexes is to stimulate the sexual instinct" (Flugel, 1950, p. 201). In this most famous of works on the psychology of fashion the relegation of different clothing to women is unambiguously identified as serving the function of men's sexual excitement.

In the last quarter of the twentieth century, fashion for women was explicitly pornographized so that the role of women's clothing in creating men's sexual satisfaction became very clear. Fashion photographers and designers created images and clothes based upon the fetishes of men's pornography, such as corsets, black vinyl, and women's nakedness. Though there might once have been assumed to be a separation between pornography, in which women are packaged for men's sexual excitement, and fashion, in which clothes are marketed to women to make them feel "beautiful", this separation has broken down entirely.

FASHIONABLE SADOMASOCHISM

Women's fashion has come to follow the codes of sadomasochist pornography in particular. Within pornography the genre of sadomasochism has become more and more important (Russell, 1993). This is true of prostitution too. In SM pornography and prostitution women are beaten, tied up, fistfucked, burnt, cut, by the male customers. But women perform the role of dominatrix to men too, because that is a way that men can gain the excitement of submission in an environment that they control. As fashion photography has incorporated men's sexual interest in sadomasochism both these two sex industry roles on the part of women are represented for men's sexual excitement.

Historian of fashion, Valerie Steele, documents the trend towards fashion designers incorporating SM in her *Fetish, Fashion, Sex and Power* (1996). She explains (p. 4):

> Corsets, bizarre shoes and boots, leather and rubber, and underwear as outerwear (to say nothing of tattoos and body-piercing) have become almost as common on catwalks as in fetish clubs . . . fashion designers as diverse and important as Azzedine Alaia, Dolce and Gabbana, John Galliano, Jean-Paul Gaultier, Thierry Mugler, John Richmond, Anna Sui, Gianni Versace, and Vivienne Westwood frequently copy "the style, if not the spirit, of fetishism".

The majority of the designers Steele mentions are gay and I argue here that the stigmata of gay male sadomasochism underlie their designs. They project onto women gay male SM interests (Jeffreys, 2003). She does point out that these SM interests are specifically male, and says that men to whom she spoke of her book were enthusiastic whereas women were likely to think the subject disgusting or depressing unless they were women "in the arts, with an interest in pornography" (Steele, 1996, p. 14).

Steele explains this phenomenon as arising from the inevitable and biologically constructed form of male sexuality: "Human males, therefore, seem to have evolved highly visually oriented patterns of sexual arousal as a result of being continually alert to the possibility of mating with any 'attractive' (i.e. apparently reproductively fit) female who might happen by" (1996, p. 23). She says that fetishes such as the corset fit this sociobiological model because they exaggerate the reproductive shape of women. The sexual revolution of the 1960s, she considers, led to a "reassessment of sexual deviations" (p. 33). Punks contributed to making fetishism fashionable, she says, and then Helmut Newton, the fashion photographer, "made fetishism chic" in the 1970s (p. 38). Steele also comments that "perversions" became more popular with men who used women in prostitution so that women in brothels had to incorporate them in their repertoire. The spread of sadomasochistic imagery from the brothel to fashion shows the importance of prostitution in constructing cultural expectations of women in general. But in the world of fashion the sadomasochistic fetish costume is being promoted by gay fashion designers in particular.

An important aspect of sadomasochist costume that the designers promoted is the corset. The corset is important to male sadists because it represents the torture of women in that not too distant period of the nineteenth to early twentieth centuries. It speaks of constriction, pain and the destruction of women's health. Interestingly there have been scholarly controversies over whether the nineteenth-century corset really was oppressive to women or not. These are well covered in Leigh Summers' fascinating volume *Bound to Please* (2001). She argues, however, with a wealth of evidence, that the corset was profoundly harmful to women. Steele lists the fashion designers who have promoted the corset as Jacques Fath, Jean-Paul Gaultier, whose perfume is packaged in bottles shaped like one of his corsets, Thierry Mugler, Azzadine Alaia, Christian Lacroix, Ungaro, Valentino and Karl Lagerfeld (Steele, 1996, p. 88). Gaultier is open about his personal interest in corsets. He says that he has "loved corsets since I was small" (Hirschberg, 2001, p. 13). He has made corsets for men, but when asked whether he has ever tried on a corset himself he responded, "No. Oh, no. I am shy. That's why I like the people who wear my clothes to be brave" (Steele, 1996, p. 88). Steele comments on the extent of the influence of gay fashion designers: "The spread of 'downtown' gay male style has also become increasingly conspicuous at the highest levels of fashion: from Versace's bondage gladiator boots to Chanel's triple-buckled leather combat boots, which resemble the ones worn by motorcycle cops" (1996, p. 113).

The interest of gay sadomasochists in both the wearing and the production of corsets is illustrated in the career of the doyenne of body modification, Fakir Musafar. Musafar, a self-mutilating former US advertising executive who changed his name, has been very influential in promoting "body art" and other practices of sadomasochism through the gay and heterosexual communities in the 1980s and 1990s (see Jeffreys, 2000). He set up a corset business in the 1950s when he had reduced his own waist from 29 to 19 inches. He sold the business when it was unsuccessful. Now it might be more profitable.

Steele's book gives a number of examples which demonstrate that the renewed interest in the corseting of women in recent times for the sexual excitement it affords to men, is harmful and oppressive to the women victims. Steele interviewed a woman victim from a previous generation of men's corset enthusiasms, Cathie J. whose body has been permanently affected by wearing her corset 24 hours a day. Her corset wearing seems clearly to be at her husband's behest since he "has had a lifelong interest in corsets" and had a corset custom made for her wedding (Steele, 1996, p. 83). Cathie says that her husband is sexually stimulated by the sight of women wearing corsets whereas she does not get any sensual feeling from it. She says that, on the contrary, "My interest is to please my husband", and estimates that, "ninety-nine percent of the time, women wear a corset because their husband or significant other likes it. At least that's true of my generation" (Steele, 1996, p. 85). The corset wearing takes its toll on her body such that it is hard to spend time without wearing it. There is discomfort, "When you try to get smaller there is some discomfort, I don't know if you would call it 'pain'," she says. There is more of a problem with "chafing sensitive skin," occasionally to the point of causing "a blister or minor wound" (p. 85). Cathie did not like the dizziness that results from rapid lacing. Restricting women's ability to breathe seems to be an important aim of heterosexual male corset fetishists. Steele includes the story of Ethel Granger, a woman famous among male fetishists for the degree of mutilation that her husband had inflicted on her body. Will Granger would, "lace Ethel occasionally in front of visitors so tightly and so rapidly that she blacked out" (1996, p. 85).

Gay fashion designers have been projecting other staples of gay male sadomasochism such as black leather and bondage onto the bodies of women too. Gianni Versace introduced a bondage collection in 1992. Steele comments that some women "took offence at Versace's SM clothes, describing them as exploitative and misogynistic" while other women "interpreted the dominatrix look as a positive Amazonian statement – couture Catwoman" (1996, p. 164). Versace himself insisted, Steele says, that " 'women are strong' and argued that as women have become liberated, this includes the freedom to be sexually aggressive" (p. 164). Versace's designs, Steele says, drew on a "design vocabulary associated with leather-sex . . . exploiting the charisma associated with 'radical sex' i.e. gay sado-masochism" (p. 166). Steele comments that, "The collection was less about women's issues than about rebellious, transgressive, unapologetic, pleasure-seeking, powerful in-your-face *sex*" (p. 166). But whose "transgressive" sex is she talking about? Steele explains that "The overwhelming majority of fetishists are men" (1996, p. 171) and women wear fetish costumes because they are in the sex industry or to please boyfriends and husbands. Thus fetishism is a male problem and women are simply the objects on which the designers project their interest in sadomasochism.

The designer John Galliano used the SM fetish fabric, rubber, in a 2003 collection (McCann, 2003, p. 14). The collection was called "Hard Core Romance" and included "S&M bondage". Performing in SM porno costume can be unpleasant for the models. In the show to promote this collection his "seven-inch platform heels caused one model to fall to her knees, and three near misses". Getting into the clothes was difficult. In this case the models "were dusted with talcum powder before easing on their tight-fitting rubber".

Steele points out that other fetish costumes of gay male sexual culture and pornography were projected onto women too:

> Both the motorcyclist and the cowboy are important gay male icons. Women's fashion designers (many of whom are gay men) have also frequently been inspired by the clothing of the cowboy and the biker. The fashionable cowgirl copies every element in the macho wardrobe of the cowboy, from his big hat to his polished boots, and all his leather gear. She is almost a caricature of the Phallic Woman.
>
> (Steele, 1996, p. 179)

These idealized forms of masculinity emerged from the "butch shift" in gay male culture of the 1970s, when, in a post gay liberation rejection of sissy stereotypes, exaggerated working class masculinity became the staple of gay sexual fantasy, exemplified in the Village People dance music group (see Jeffreys, 2003).

GAY FASHION MISOGYNY

There does not seem to be any academic or popular interest in the fascinating question of why the field of fashion for women is so dominated by gay men. In an article in *The Advocate*, the US gay magazine, Brendan Lemon muses, "To observe that gay men and lesbians dominate the fashion business may seem about as controversial as saying that Russians rule Moscow. But with a few exceptions (Todd Oldham, Isaac Mizrahi), the ranks of top designers who are publicly out of the closet are surprisingly thin" (Lemon, 1997). Lesbians seem few on the ground and he does not name any, but gay men abound. The fashion reporter of the *Guardian* newspaper, Charlie Porter, wrote in 2003 that the male gay domination of the industry could be expected to make it a less sexist environment for women designers, but this has not turned out to be the case: "In an industry where most of the men are gay, you would expect a more enlightened position on sexism. Not so: although there are a few female designers such as Miuccia Prada, Donatella Versace and Donna

Karen, it is men that mainly keep control" (Porter, 2003, p. 6). The question of why gay men should be so interested in creating clothes for women, who are not their sexual partners, or, probably, the focus of their erotic imaginations, is an important one. Within gay culture there is an obsession with the imitation of a particular gay male version of femininity in drag shows and in parades such as the Sydney gay Mardi Gras. Up until the 1970s and the gay liberation movement, male homosexuality was automatically assumed to be associated with femininity as a result of biology. There was a cultural assumption in this period that the innate "femininity" of gay men would make them more sympathetic to women and understanding of what women would want or need. But in fact there is no biological femaleness involved in being gay.

Homosexuality cannot be explained by genes or hormones but is a socially constructed form of behaviour (Rogers, 1999). Gay men develop an identification with "femininity" as a result of being shut out of, and often badly persecuted and harassed by masculine society (Plummer, 1999; Levine, 1998). Femininity is the default position for those excluded from the privileges of heterosexual male dominance. It is the position that relates erotically to masculinity and represents its opposite. The "femininity" that gay men adopt, therefore, is a straightforwardly subordinate form of behaviour invented by them and labelled feminine because that is the way to be subordinate under male supremacy. As a gay adventure to accommodate their position of inferiority in relation to "real" men, this femininity has not got a great deal to do with the lives of women. It is this gay designed version of femininity, I suggest, that male gay designers project onto women. With it they project that hatred and terror of the "feminine" in themselves that they learnt as they grew up gay and were harassed and attacked for not being masculine enough. Femininity, rather than being something to be loved or appreciated, represented the bottom position in sex to which they were relegated by their desire for masculine men.

In the 1970s "butch shift" gay men were able, after gay liberation politics refuted the notion that gayness somehow necessitated effeminacy, to eroticize masculinity in themselves and other gay men. In response, the exaggerated stigmata of aggressive masculinity began to take pride of place in gay culture. As in the work of the gay pornographer Tom of Finland, the ideal gay male form became that of a muscular figure wearing black leather chaps and Nazi caps (Jeffreys, 2003). Interestingly, the out gay designers who came to prominence in the 1980s and 1990s, Gaultier, McQueen and Ford, all have publicly masculine personas. But that public masculinity does not signify that their conflicts over gender and sexuality are resolved. Masculinity and femininity, the behaviours of male dominance and female subordination, cannot be imagined without each other. In gay male culture an individual man can enjoy an oscillation between "butch" masculinity and a degrading form of femininity for sexual excitement. It is not necessary to retreat into psychoanalytical theory to understand the politics of these behaviours on the part of fashion designers but the psychoanalyst Edmund Bergler is one of the few authors who has sought to do so.

Bergler (1987) remarked on the homosexuality of fashion designers in the 1950s. Bergler is no friend to women and I have written elsewhere about his diatribes against women's independence (Jeffreys, 1990). He was, however, puzzled by what he considered to be the "cruelty" of the clothing that gay male fashion designers inflicted on women and devoted a whole book to explaining it. He says that he had psychoanalysed several gay male fashion designers and considered that they had an extreme form of men's fear and hatred of women. The hostility and fear towards women is a result of the fact that the baby is spoiled in the womb and then "dependent on the maternal breast" (Bergler, 1987, p. 29). The problem is exacerbated in homosexual men because, "The normally heterosexual male protects himself against women with the hoax of the He-Man. The homosexual has no equivalent armor" (p. 49). Heterosexual men project helplessness onto women which helps them believe they are "he-men", but homosexual men cannot believe they are he-men by such a ruse and need more extreme measures. Thus gay fashion designers project their unalleviated hatred and fear onto women through cruel fashions.

It is interesting that Bergler had noticed, even in 1953, that the fashions women were required to wear were degrading, since they were tame by comparison with what was designed for women in the last decades of the twentieth century. But psychoanalysis does not convince me. It is not necessary to retreat to the content of the unconscious to explain the behaviour of men in male dominance. Psychoanalytic explanations do not offer solutions to men's abusive behaviour or womanhating because they depend on what happens in the first few years of life. The paid help of doctors is required to "remember" and interpret the experiences. The explanations are individualistic and ignore the effect of day-by-day social learning throughout the lifetimes of men and women. The very concept of the "unconscious" has been usefully criticized by the ex-psychoanalyst Jeffrey Masson (Masson, 1984). Let us look now at some more recent examples of the "cruelty" that gay male fashion designers, and the gay fashion photographers who have interpreted their designs, have inflicted on women.

In the 1980s fashion shows changed. Clothes that women might actually wear became less common and the designers used the shows to demonstrate how creative they were and to gain press attention. They sought to gain this attention through shows that reduced the models to pornography. Models had to appear almost completely naked and in things that could not easily be called clothes but which stimulated the sexual imaginations of their designers and the male-dominated media. The designers might still make wearable clothes behind the scenes but these were, apparently, providing smaller proportions of their income. Fashion was having a crisis. Design houses were more likely to make profits from perfume and handbags than through clothes. The shows were designed to make the name of the fashion house known.

The work of the out gay designer Alexander McQueen is the best example of this development. His graduation show from his MA in fashion and design in 1992 in the UK was based on, "Jack the Ripper and Victorian prostitutes who sold their hair to be made into locks which were bought by people to give to their lovers: he stitched locks of human hair under blood-red linings" (Evans, 2001, p. 201). Caroline Evans also comments that, "Here, as in so much of McQueen's subsequent work, the themes of sex, death and commerce intertwined" (p. 201). In his first show after graduation, "The models were inadequately wrapped in cling-film and were styled to look bruised and battered" (Evans, 2001, p. 202). His second show, *Nihilism*, "featured Edwardian jackets in corroded gilt, over tops apparently splattered with blood or dirt to create the impression of bloody, post-operative breasts under the sheer muslin" (p. 202). His fourth show, *The Birds*, featured "very hard tailoring which was based around the idea of road kill. The models at the show were bound in sellotape and streaked with oily tyre marks; these tyre marks were also printed on some of the jackets to look as if the model had been driven over". His fifth show, *Highland Rape*, featured a runway strewn with heather bracken on which, "McQueen's staggering and blood-spattered models appeared wild and distraught, their breasts and bottoms exposed by tattered laces and torn suedes, jackets with missing sleeves, and skin-tight rubber trousers and skirts cut so low at the hip they seemed to defy gravity" (Evans, 2001, p. 202). In his 1996 catwalk show for his collection *La Poupee*, "the black model Debra Shaw walked contorted in a metal frame fixed to her wrists and ankles by manacles" (p. 203).

Evans points out that much press coverage of the shows did mention that McQueen could be accused of misogyny but she does not consider this a reasonable response. McQueen explains a piece for his collection *It's a Jungle Out There* by holding up to the camera during an interview, "a piece of cloth with blond hair trailing from it like a pelt" and saying, "The idea is that this wild beast has eaten this really lovely blond girl and she's trying to get out" (2001, p. 204). This might appear cruel, says Evans, but, "The cruelty inherent in McQueen's representations of women was part of the designer's wider vision of the cruelty of the world, and although his view was undoubtedly a bleak one it was not, I would argue, a misogynist one" (p. 204). In this view McQueen just used women as a canvas on which to project the violence of the world and women should not take this personally. Moreover McQueen was actually portraying women as strong and terrifying and this was good for women. He had a "fascination with an uncompromising and aggressive sexuality, a sexuality which came to resemble that of the fin-de-siecle femme fatale, the woman whose sexuality was dangerous, even deathly, and for whom, therefore, male desire would always be tinged with dread" (Evans, 2001, p. 204). McQueen said that critics who labelled him misogynist were wrong because they did not realize that most of his models were lesbians. If the lesbianism was not apparent to the audience it is hard to see what difference it could make. McQueen says that a lot of his friends are strong lesbians and he designs with them in mind, but there is no reason why misogyny is automatically lessened if employed on the bodies of lesbians, or designed for lesbians.

McQueen, then, is cleared of misogyny because he makes women into femmes fatales and so imbues them with a power over men. The idea that women gain power over men by being clothed as prostitutes or dominatrixes, is a pernicious myth. It is even echoed by the supposedly feminist fashion theorist Elizabeth Wilson who says, "To the extent that fetish fashion is popular with women, in large part this is because it adds the idea of *power* to femininity. Another word for *power* is *freedom* . . . What *Vogue* calls the 'strong and sexy' look has become the paradigm of contemporary fashion. This is a direct result of women's liberation" (Wilson, 1985, p. 184, emphasis in the original). In Wilson's view it is the wish of newly liberated women to look like prostitutes that underpins the newly pornographic fashion. But this ignores the creative influence of the gay fashion designers and the fashion industry. The myth that women in prostitution or through sexual wiles were powerful over men has served male supremacy well, but it has not served women. Research on the experience of women in prostitution shows the serious harms they suffer in damage to reproductive health, in post-traumatic stress disorder and in suicide attempts, and it shows that the vast majority want to be out of prostitution (Farley *et al.*, 1998; Giobbe, 1991; Parriott, 1994). In a world in which women cannot gain reasonable pay or promotion, and in which violence and harassment against them are rife, dressing up sexily may seem like a way to some kind of power but only a very few, such as Madonna, are able to make big money and gain social influence out of this.

McQueen's models, like those of most of the major designers since the mid-1980s, show a great deal of their bodies including their breasts and buttocks, but there is considerable egregious cruelty on top of this nakedness such as, in the 1996 show, a woman wearing a crown of thorns, women with apparent piercings by large objects in their faces, women trapped in boxes, and the ubiquitous corset but worn over clothing. He included "bumster" jeans in the 1996 show for which he became famous. The jeans end halfway up the buttocks showing considerable buttock cleavage.

The 1995 show included women in plaster casts over half of their upper body, and women whose faces were encased in material with no eyeholes and covered in a skeletal hand. McQueen is said to be keen on animals and frequently makes women into living or dead ones. As my research assistant pointed out to me, the model in one image, with nipples showing and something like a bird's skull covering her face, had clearly been crying. One model in the 1995 show has her bare breasts buckled into a leather belt beneath a suit jacket. One 1996 model has a large horn protruding from her forehead, another has a set of antlers on her head.

The show for spring/summer 2002 had a bullfighting theme. Models were dressed up as toreadors, albeit in very high heels. Sarah Mower expresses the theme thus: "It opened with billowing smoke, the deafening sound of a flamenco-dancer's stamping feet, and a video projection of a bullfight, spliced with extracts from a pornographic movie" (Mower, 2002, p. 45). McQueen is clearly not shy about showing the interrelationship between his "fashion" and pornography. Mower seems not too keen on the impaling of one model but is enthusiastic about the collection overall: "There was one violent moment, when a model came out wearing a dress impaled with picador's daggers, but there were plenty of McQueen's great black signature pants-suits to keep the collection tipped towards what he wanted to show: real clothes" (2002, p. 45). It is hard to know how this expresses the McQueen philosophy of showing strong sexually aggressive women since it would be quite hard to be sexually anything but dead in such a costume. McQueen was voted British designer of the year in 1996 and in two subsequent years. In 2001 he was voted international designer of the year and gained a CBE from the Queen.

The work of the gay designer Gianni Versace contains similar themes but it is not so blatantly misogynist. A collection of photographs of his designs by the photographer Richard Avedon starts on the opening page with camp hyperbole, "This is a glimpse of the impassioned shameless opulent titillating sewmanship of that daredevil magician of art and artifice who was and will always be Gianni Versace" (Avedon, 1998, p. 1). His interest in gay male crossdressing is clear in an image in which a naked, muscular black man is crouched side view but looking at the camera with a hard stare and wearing two items of Versace apparel. One is an above the knee boot with a very high thin heel, which is worn on his forearm and hand as if it is a glove. The other is a leather belt with a tiny bag worn as an ammunition belt over one shoulder (Avedon, 1998, p. 30). There are plenty of images of muscular men to appeal to the male homoerotic imagination, including one with a naked penis, but with a swathe of Versace designed cloth around the upper part of his body and concealing his face. One way in which fashion designers presently seek to create outrageous images that will appeal to men's pornographic imagination is depicting the models as lesbians. In one image a woman holds another recumbent woman's legs apart as if she is about to climb onto her (Avedon, 1998, p. 14). In another a woman in high heels attacks another woman with the heel of a shoe. In yet another image there are two naked breasted women in a pose where one makes an orgasmic facial expression while the other makes as if to kiss her with black gloved hands on her breasts. Naked men are frequently shown with clothed women but they are muscular men in stark contrast to the skeletal forms of most of the women.

Another common element of fashion, as of pornography, is the representation of women as children for men's sexual excitement. Thus the Versace collection contains an image from 1994 of five women in bobby sox and high heels, with short skirts, touching themselves. They touch the edges of their skirts or ruck them up at the crotch in postures of masturbation. One lifts her skirt to examine her naked buttock, one sucks a finger. The representations of women masturbating and sucking fingers are staples of pornography and in this case it is kiddy porn (Avedon, 1998, p. 126).

The designer Thierry Mugler expresses a more extreme misogyny in his work in which women are portrayed as insects covered in black vinyl. His designs on women are illustrated in a book of his photographs entitled *Fashion, Fetish, Fantasy* (Mugler, 1998). The opening photo of the book makes it clear from the beginning that the theme will be women as fetish objects for men's sexual excitement. There is a woman in a full body suit of tight black latex with incorporated very high heels that appear to be rubber. She is standing hands on hips as a dominatrix with a man seated on the floor looking up at her crotch. The book contains vacuous and sunny aphorisms by Mugler and others that are often very much at odds with the photos they are matched with. The opening one to go with the dominatrix picture is "Life is a beauty contest. I love the language of the body, the different ways of being seductive" (1998, p. 2). The head to toe black vinyl appears as a refrain throughout the book. For instance, in one image women are encased in black vinyl suits and gloves with insect head coverings, and insect eye styled shades, all in black (1998, pp. 12–13). Many other images in the book represent women as insects.

An interesting aspect of Mugler's work is the incorporation of transvestites such as Ru Paul into his fashion shows and photography, proving that he did not require real, live women to project his "feminine" sexual fantasies upon. Men would do just as well. A page of photos of women in corsets is accompanied by the words of someone called Polly Mellen, who makes light of the harm these torture implements cause, "Who needs to breathe anyway" (Mugler, 1998, p. 18). In another photo there is a woman seated on the edge of an office chair in tight latex leggings and high heels with black top and gloves and headpiece, again representing an insect. The accompanying text reads, "Comfort, what is comfort? What about confidence?" (p. 21). Meanwhile we are informed of Mugler that, "His sense of creativity is a beautiful twinkling of an eye in the dreamboat of eternity" (p. 27).

Mugler is excited by getting women to reveal nakedness in his shows. He remarks, "I find a woman more beautiful and at the best when she shows her inner passion – when she is wearing a suit. A very strict suit. But then when she moves, the skirt opens up high on her thigh . . . or you may find out that she is naked under her jacket" (1998, p. 41). This motto is accompanied by dominatrix photos and on the opposite page a photo of a woman in an insect mask. A later bon mot by Mugler reads, "Fashion . . . It's wonderful and very cruel . . . A very demanding mistress" (p. 49) as if "fashion" has a life of its own and this dominatrix prescription for women comes from somewhere other than the head of a cruel and demanding man.

There are other remarks by Mugler which indicate his philosophy. He says that he seeks to make women powerful, "I only like women who have power. I put women on top of the world" (1998, p. 85). This sounds very like the sentiments of McQueen above. It is hard to accept unless we believe that dominatrix prostitutes really have power in the world. Women who seek power are more likely to want to enter the media, or IT or some other aspect of the corporate world rather than dealing with men's body fluids in brothels for their economic survival. He tells us that, "The Mugler woman is a conqueror who controls her looks and her life. She is free, self-confident, and she's having fun" (1998, p. 102). The women covered in black vinyl and insect paraphernalia don't look as if they are having a tremendously good time, however. He continues, "Every woman has a goddess within. I like to bring her out" (p. 110). But why a goddess would be dressed in the stigmata of sadomasochism is not clear. Mugler explains his porno vinyl look by stating, "Black leather, vinyl, nothing's more classic than that" (1998, p. 138). Black vinyl does have a history, but not in women's everyday fashion. It has a history in men's fetish clothing stores. It is a classic of pornography. Mugler opines that, "Elegance is courage and audacity, and an animal instinct that shows in every movement. It is harmony and oneness, and enjoying one's body" (p. 164). This is opposite a photo of a woman with material draped across her torso and held up by nipple rings. Elegance is not the first word that comes to mind. At the end of the book Mugler explains to us why he represents women as insects: "Insects have always fascinated me for what they are, not only for their appearance. The insect/woman is both a fragile being and an armored predator – frightening and awe-inspiring at the same time" (1998, p. 180).

Tom Ford is an out gay fashion designer who designs for Gucci and was recognized by fashion critics as one of the three most influential designers of the mid-1990s. He too goes in for representing women as dominatrixes. One collection features, "80s-inflected leather suits with armorlike shoulders and killer high heels, a silhouette by which Ford not only celebrates feminine forcefulness but also holds a mirror to what he sees as today's 'very violent' beauty ideal. 'Powerful women exuding a hint of aggression can be a real turn-on,' he says. 'You don't have to be a dominatrix to know that'" (Lemon, 1997). Ford dares to suggest that men are better at designing for women than women would be because they, "can be slightly more objective about what looks good on a woman, at least in terms of drape and fit" (Lemon, 1997). Ford is concerned to enforce on women that instrument of torture the high-heeled shoe, because it excites men sexually. "'Do you know the thing about the baboons?' he asks. 'Female baboons, when they're sexually aroused, walk around on their tiptoes.' He pauses. 'Men find women in high heels incredibly sexy'" (Lemon, 1997). What is more he forces the female staff in his offices to wear them too: "staff keep stiletto heels in their drawers to wobble around in when he comes into the office" (*Hint Fashion Magazine*, 2001).

Those who produce and photograph the work of the gay fashion designers form a network of men with common interests in sadomasochism and mutilation of themselves and others. Simon Costin, for instance, McQueen's art director, has a strong interest in self-mutilation:

> His work consists of digitized photographs of himself which he mutilates, transforms and disfigures using computer art packages such as Photoshop. Using this software he covers his skin in burns, removes his own tongue and fingers, or infects his penis and riddles it with scabs. As he has said himself, "I use myself as a model because no-one would allow me to set them on fire."
>
> (BBC, 1997)

His work as a jewellery designer places his body fluids into women's faces as, "the jewel in the crown of our Simon's show was a necklace hung with small glass phials. These were filled with his, er, seminal fluid" (Mackay, 2001).

Another member of this fashion network is photographer David LaChapelle, who has worked for several designers. LaChapelle has talked much of how his school years were ruined by the homophobic harassment he received from other boys: "I couldn't go into the lunch room because food and milk cartons would come at me from every angle" (Saban, 2002, p. 33). His private creative efforts, when not photographing for famous designers, concentrate on what one commentator calls "freaks" – "that breed of gaunt, blemishless human built and enslaved by heavy makeup, lighting and the glorifying voodoo of photographic attention, e.g., models, transsexuals and Leonardo DiCaprio" (Wilson, 1999). Cintra Wilson (1999) describes an opening of a LaChapelle photo exhibition thus: "The work is utterly devoid of connective energy or human feeling, it just fucks you slickly in the eye hole; it left me feeling empty and used." Another commentator, writing a positive piece about LaChapelle said that his "more 'interesting' images include: naked, wheelchair-bound, fat ladies with oxygen tanks; the nude, transsexual Amanda Lepore (his muse) with a succulent slice of watermelon in her lap; and a topless Angelina Jolie being nuzzled by a horse" (Saban, 2002, p. 30).

LaChapelle has worked with an English fashion victim Isabella Blow to create what she calls "a porno couture shoot" (Blow and LaChapelle, 1998, p. 2). As LaChapelle puts it, "Isabelle wanted it to be borderline pornographic. She loves erotica, loves being naughty" (p. 3). Isabella Blow "discovered" and funded Alexander McQueen. LaChapelle's connections with the pornography industry seem to be close. One photo shoot was of, "a nude session he'd orchestrated in the same suburban house with all seven of Hugh Hefner's girlfriends, a muscleman, a female body builder and Amanda Lepore" (Saban, 2002, p. 30).

LaChapelle has the pornographer's talent and imperative to get his subjects to take off their clothes. As one commentator remarks, "It would seem that LaChapelle has never met a subject he couldn't get naked, so his celebrity portraits are often controversial. 'Most of the time they want to [get naked] anyway,' he says. . . . [Drew] Barrymore not only shed her clothes, she remained that way for the entire day. 'She was even eating lunch naked,' LaChapelle remembers" (Saban, 2002, p. 31). LaChapelle spent a year in London in the early 1980s where he modelled for Leigh Bowery in his fashion shows. "'My first week in London,' says LaChapelle, 'I was modelling for Leigh Bowery in his fashion shows and taking pictures of Trojan and Leigh and the whole BodyMap scene'" (Saban, 2002, p. 31). Trojan died of an overdose, and Bowery of AIDS-related conditions in 1994 at the age of 33.

Bowery, from Sunshine in Melbourne, which is not a suburb full of Bohemians, was a gay icon for his adventures in self-mutilation. Before his early death, he performed in public in outrageous drag and with various forms of self-mutilation. He was well connected to the male gay fashion network from the first and British designer John Galliano used Bowery in his runway shows. He was tall, bald and fat and his performances often seemed to be about disgust at himself, his body and femininity. He used plastic plugs in his cheek piercings when he was not using them in performance. In one famous performance he, "'gave birth' to his wife Nicola Bateman Bowery in a mess of nudity, sausages, petroleum jelly and fake blood" (Low, 2003). In one of his last performances he "hung upside down wearing only stockings and high heels before smashing through a plate of glass" (Low, 2003). In one stage show Bowery is reputed to have sprayed the audience with "the results of a self-administered enema" (Gottschalk, 1995). But Bowery chose mainly to place the inventions of his tortured, self-hating imagination on his own body rather than, as gay male fashion designers do, projecting them onto women. A former drag queen, Laurent Mercier, explains that he entered the fashion industry so that he could dress "real" women rather than just himself. He was appointed in 2002 as designer for the Parisian house of Balmain. He commented, "Dressing up was always a fashion experiment for me. I really went the whole hog with the drag queen thing. [Now], instead of projecting my fantasies onto myself, I project them onto real girls" (Burns, 2003).

The gay US magazine *The Advocate* profiled one niche in the gay fashion network, the magazine *Visionaire*. It was started by a makeup artist, Stephen Gan, his former boyfriend, James Kaliardos and a female model friend. Gan had been the art director of advertising campaigns for Calvin Klein. David LaChapelle, along with many others, contributed without pay to the magazine, exploring whatever theme the founders dreamt up. The themes included the worship of the penis and male sexuality by gay fashion designers. Two examples are as follows: "'Erotica' (before Madonna, thank you), which showed men in corsets and a watercolor couple engaged in oral sex. The $450 'Light' issue – a battery-box with viewable transparencies guest-edited by Gucci designer Tom Ford – offered an Alexander McQueen photo of an erect ejaculating penis" (Bahr, 1998, p. 59).

Gay men can have problematic relationships with femininity and with women as a result of their situation under heterosexual male dominance. Bullying and persecution at school from playmates, teachers, rugby coaches, fathers, from police and gaybashers, and the anti-gay propaganda of politicians and rightwing commentators, all inculcate the notion that boys and men attracted to other men lack the masculinity appropriate to the status of manhood (Plummer, 1999; Levine, 1998). Femininity is the default position and can become eroticized in masochistic gay male sexuality, but it signifies the subordinate position into which they are cast in relation to heterosexual men. Thus their relationship to femininity and to women themselves can be troubled and uncomfortable. One result can be a clear misogyny as expressed in what has been called the "ick factor". As I have discussed elsewhere (Jeffreys, 2003), this term is employed in gay male writings to describe the extreme revulsion experienced by some gay men at the thought or sight of women's naked bodies.

The US queer theorist and activist Eric Rofes, for instance, explains that though he is very lesbian and feminist identified he experiences the "ick factor" which consists of "a visceral response ranging from dislike to disgust when confronted with lesbian sex and bodies" and is greatly troubled by it (Rofes, 1998, p. 46). He estimates that one-third of gay men suffer from the "ick factor" and offers in evidence what he has witnessed over 25 years in gay male culture. He has heard "many men express their revulsion at lesbian sex and women's bodies" and "countless 'tuna' jokes" which arise from the habit among some gay men of calling women "fish" after what they consider to be the repulsive smell of their genitals. He has seen "men's faces turn sour when lesbian sex appears in movies, and watched gay men huddle together in small groups voicing disgust at topless women in political demonstrations" (Rofes, 1998, p. 46). Rofes quotes one man as saying he could not become physically close to lesbians "because of the odors he believed their bodies emitted" (1998, p. 47). The clothes created by gay fashion designers that I have described suggest that some of them may be fellow sufferers with Rofes of the "ick factor".

For women this is very problematic. It can mean that those least qualified to clothe women in comfortable, attractive, dignified and functional ways, because they are themselves so deeply conflicted about the notion of "femininity" they have invented out of their own oppression, are creating the "fashion" that real live women are supposed to follow. As they do so fashion becomes more and more pornographic in the catwalk shows and photography, and in what young women actually wear. Thus Gaultier's use of piercing on the catwalk ushered in the wave of piercing enthusiasm in which chains of piercing shops were opened to mutilate women's navels, noses, tongues and genitals (Strong, 1998; Jeffreys, 2000). While gay misogynists remain so influential within the fashion industry there is little chance that it will offer dignity to women.

FASHION THEORY

I have suggested in this chapter that fashion is based on sexual difference and that the misogyny expressed in fashion has been escalating in the late twentieth and early twenty-first centuries. But this is not the understanding of academic feminist fashion theorists. Elizabeth Wilson (1985) and Joanne Finkelstein (1991) are two writers on fashion with reputations for being "feminist" who take little account of what fashion does to women. Wilson defines fashion as "dress in which the key feature is rapid and continual changing of clothes. Fashion, in a sense is change, and in modern western societies no clothes are outside fashion" (1985, p. 3). In her book *Adorned in Dreams* she says she will look at fashion as "a cultural phenomenon, as an aesthetic medium for the expression of ideas, desires and beliefs circulating in society" (1985, p. 9). Surprisingly, for a well-known feminist writer, Wilson does not mention in her definition the role of "fashion" in relation to male dominance. Rather, on the only occasion in the book where feminism is mentioned, she specifically repudiates the idea that feminist analysis might have any special role in understanding fashion. She characterizes the feminist approach as assuming fashionable dressing to "have confined them [women] to the status of the ornamental or the sexual chattel" and counters that "it has also been one of the ways in which women have been able to achieve self expression, and feminism has been as simplistic – and as moralistic – as most other theories in its denigration of fashion" (Wilson, 1985, p. 13). And she argues that rather than fashion and cosmetics use being "expressions of subordination" they are not specifically about women because "men have been as much implicated in fashion, as much 'fashion victims' as women" (p. 13). Wilson is someone who is seriously enthusiastic about fashion and argues, "to discuss fashion as simply a feminist moral problem is to miss the richness of its cultural and political meanings. The political subordination of women is an inappropriate point of departure if, as I believe, the most important thing about fashion is *not* that it oppresses women" (1985, p. 13).

Wilson remarks that: "The scholarly discourse on fashion has, in fact, increasingly suggested that adornment is intrinsically human, frequently pleasurable, and potentially subversive" (Wilson, 1985, p. 186). She is not referring here, of course, to feminist critiques of fashion that make very different arguments, such as the work of Sandra Bartky (1990). Influenced by fashionable postmodern theory, Wilson considers that there are no consistent meanings to be inferred from fashion because, "in the world of fashion, cultural signs have no fixed meaning; they change continually" (1985, p. 188). This would indeed make it hard to form any political critique of fashion if it were true, but of course some meanings do not change. Overwhelmingly members of the two sex classes, women and men, are identified through "fashion" by wearing quite different clothes with very different sets of meanings and these do not seem to change much over time.

Joanne Finkelstein also ignores the significance of sexual difference. She defines fashion as, "the shaping and adorning of the body" that has "become a way for the individual to present his or her desired self-image to others" (1991, p. 5). In Finkelstein's book *The Fashioned Self* there is an authorial "we", and the gender of the "we" is not at all clear, as in, "What does it say of our understanding of identity or human character that we have fused together the capacity for conspicuous consumption with the presentation of personality" (1991, p. 5). "We" does not seem to mean women. In Finkelstein's book too the way that fashion works to maintain the subordination of women is left out of consideration.

While fashion is dedicated to the creation and maintenance of sexual difference it requires political analysis. Fashion criticism should not be left to postmodern theorists concerned with playfulness, creativity, and agency. Fashion is no trivial matter and requires the serious attention of political theorists because it is crucial to creating the difference/deference and underpins women's subordination. If the difference was not inscribed on women's bodies (i.e. if clothing was ungendered) men would be unable to establish the sexual status of those they encountered on the street or in the workplace. They would have to forgo the sexual pleasures they are accustomed to extract from women's enactment of their subordination. But clothing is not the only means by which the difference is created. The wearing of makeup is very important too. In the following chapter I examine the everyday beauty practices such as lipstick wearing and depilation that contribute to the demonstration of women's difference/deference.

6

MAKING UP IS HARD TO DO

Everyday beauty practices, such as the use of makeup or hair removal, were central to the feminist critique of beauty launched by Andrea Dworkin (1974) and Sandra Bartky in the 1970s (1990, collection of earlier writings). In the 1990s something very odd happened. Suddenly, in the writings of popular liberal feminists and in the writings of some feminists who adopted a postmodern approach, those very same practices gained a whole new credibility. They were promoted as "empowering" to women, the proof of the new power to choose that was the legacy of feminism (Lehrman, 1997; Walter, 1999; Frost, 1999). But the practices themselves did not change. In this chapter I consider whether everyday beauty practices deserve to be the subject of this new enthusiasm, and critically examine the claim that these everyday beauty practices are good and useful aspects of women's lives.

There is little research on the reasons why women wear makeup, or engage in other forms of "grooming", the effects that these practices have on women's feelings about themselves and others, and their interactions with the public world (Dellinger and Williams, 1997). This is a puzzle since the wearing of lipstick, for example, could be seen as a very strange practice in which women smear toxic substances on their lips several times a day, particularly before they encounter the public world, and take into their bodies an estimated 3 to 4.5 kilos in a lifetime's use (Erickson, 2002; Farrow, 2002). Lipstick wearing, like the other practices we look at in this chapter, consumes women's time, money and emotional space. The absence of interest in examining it suggests that it is seen as "natural" for women and therefore unworthy of examination. More extreme forms of beauty practice which endanger women's lives such as eating disorders (Fallon *et al.*, 1994), or require serious surgery such as breast implants (Davis, 1995), have been studied, perhaps because they are seen as less "natural", and so harder to understand. But I suggest here that the everyday grooming practices that women engage in – lipstick wearing, depilation, hair dyeing and perming – do need explanation and that they can be best explained by understanding them as harmful cultural practices. They fulfil the criteria of emerging from the subordination of women and being for the benefit of men, of creating gender stereotypes; that is, making a difference. They are justified by tradition as in being seen as natural to women, and it may be that they need to be recognized as harmful to the health of women and girls. Certainly, as we shall see, the chemicals and human and animal body products involved pose risks to physical health.

When beauty practices are carried to extremes they are the subject of research, however, as a form of mental illness. Thus 30 years after the publication of Andrea Dworkin's work (Dworkin, 1974) the anxious and obsessive beauty practices that she describes so well have been identified as symptomatic of a newly discovered and labelled mental health problem called "body dysmorphic disorder" or BDD. Katharine Phillips, an expert in the field, tells us that clues to the disorder are, "frequent mirror checking, excessive grooming, face picking, and reassurance seeking" (Phillips, 1998, p. 48). When she describes the clues in more detail they turn out to resemble quite precisely the ordinary everyday practices of femininity:

> Do you often check your appearance in mirrors or other reflecting surfaces, such as windows? Or do you frequently check your appearance without using a mirror, by looking directly at the disliked body part? . . . Do you spend a lot of time grooming – for example, combing or arranging your hair, applying makeup, or shaving? Do you spend too much time getting ready in the morning, or do you groom yourself frequently during the day? Do others complain that you spend too much time in the bathroom? . . . Do you often change your clothes, trying to find an outfit that covers or improves disliked aspects of your appearance? Do you take a long time selecting your outfit for the day, trying to find one that makes you look better?
>
> (Phillips, 1998, p. 49)

Phillips provides 27 clues which denote anxiety about appearance, none of which seem exceptional in terms of women's daily lives.

In Susan Brownmiller's book *Femininity* (1984) she describes very similar practices as simply the ordinary coming of age rituals of girls:

> At what age does a girl child begin to review her assets and count her deficient parts? When does she close the bedroom door and begin to gaze privately into the mirror at contortionist angles to get a view from the rear, the left profile, the right, to check the curve of her calf muscle, the shape of her thighs, to ponder her shoulder blades and wonder is she is going to have a waistline? And pull in her stomach . . . making a mental note of what

> needs to be worked on, what had better develop, stay contained, or else?
>
> (Brownmiller, 1984, p. 9)

But, interestingly, Phillips says that the patients that are referred to her include an equal number of men and women. The men are overwhelmingly concerned with not being sufficiently masculine and worried about having small penises. It seems very odd that a concern so ordinary among women, anxiety about appearance, should, in its extreme forms, be equally manifest among men. The explanation may be that something so normal for women would mostly go unnoticed, whereas a concern with appearance that is abnormal among men would lead to them coming to the attention of a psychiatrist more easily. The only distinction between women's ordinary concern with appearance and that which leads to a diagnosis of Body Dysmorphic Disorder does seem to be the extremity of the symptoms. Applying excessive makeup, for instance, is a sign of BDD, as is buying excessive numbers of hair products. But it might be hard to work out what was normal and what was excessive in women's behaviour in a beauty culture. Phillips explains that, "Hair removal may also be done to excess. People concerned about excessive body hair may spend lots of time tweezing it, removing it from their face, their arms, or other parts of their body . . . Eyebrows may be repeatedly plucked to create the right shape" (Phillips, 1998, p. 108). But how much time is "lots"? "Other people" she says, "apply and reapply makeup", and one of her patients remarks, "I use a lot of makeup, and I take a long time to put on my eyeliner and lipstick . . . I'm in agony if I can't do this. I need my fix!" (p. 108). But what is a "lot" of makeup, or excessive time in its application? "Most people with BDD", Phillips says, "actively think about their appearance problem for at least an hour a day" (1998, p. 76). Thus those who think about the defects of their appearance for half an hour might just be the victims of the construction of ordinary everyday beauty, and not representative of the syndrome.

Whether women engage in beauty practices for 30 minutes or for 1 hour, the practices are not "natural" but culturally prescribed and it is important to understand where beauty practices come from. The history of makeup, the fact that there have been times and places in which women were not required to be obsessed with makeup, makes it clear that this practice is peculiar to a time and place and most definitely cultural rather than emanating from any natural "femininity".

THE HISTORY OF MAKEUP

The work of the historian Kathy Peiss explains when and how the practice of making up originated (Peiss, 1998). Peiss is a historian of commerce and points out that writers on beauty rarely pay much attention to the industry that creates and profits from beauty practices (Peiss, 2001). She explains that the beauty industry as we understand it today developed in the first decades of the twentieth century, particularly in the 1920s: "Between 1909 and 1929 the number of American perfume and cosmetics manufacturers nearly doubled, and the factory value of their products rose tenfold, from $14.2 million to nearly $141 million" (Peiss, 1998, p. 97). In the nineteenth century there was no mass market of beauty products. Women might make some limited range of beauty aids at home according to traditional recipes, and some could be bought. There was no expectation, however, that women would paint their faces. Makeup was called "paint" and associated with prostitution and the theatre. It was not respectable. Peiss opens her book with the story of this most important change in social attitudes, in which the practice of prostitution was transformed into an expected part of feminine grooming. She gives as an example of the change the fact that a cosmetics firm in 1938 introduced two new lipsticks named "Lady" and "Hussy". She explains:

> For nineteenth-century Americans, lady and hussy were polar opposites – the best and worst of womanhood – and the presence or absence of cosmetics marked the divide. Reddened cheeks and darkened eyelids were signs of female vice, and the "painted woman" provoked disgust and censure from the virtuous. But by the 1930s, lady and hussy had become "types" and "moods".
>
> (Peiss, 1998, p. 3)

Language changed and consumerism won out so that, "Where 'paint' implied a concealing mask, the term 'makeup,' in common usage by the 1920s, connoted a medium of self-expression in a consumer society where identity had become a purchasable style . . . apparently Hussy outsold Lady five to one!" (Peiss, 1998, p. 4).

Lipstick is a beauty practice that seems to have strong historical links with prostitution. The sexologists Harry Benjamin and R.E.L. Masters describe in the book they wrote to justify and normalize prostitution in the early stages of the "sexual revolution" (1964) what they understand to be the origins of lipstick wearing. They say that it originated from prostituted women in the ancient middle east who used it to show that they would do oral sex: "lipstick was supposed to make the mouth resemble the vulva, and it was first worn by those females who specialized in oral stimulation of the penis" (Benjamin and Masters, 1964, p. 58).

As a historian of commerce Peiss is enthusiastic about the opportunities that the newly developing beauty industry offered women. As the industry developed between the 1890s and the 1920s it was largely in the hands of women entrepreneurs, "women formulated and organized 'beauty culture' to a remarkable extent" (Peiss, 1998, p. 4). Women founded "salons, beauty schools, correspondence courses, and mail-order companies". They did not need to advertise but used the "patterns of women's social life – their old customs of visiting, conversation, and religious observance, as well as their presence in shops, clubs and theaters". Many of these women were "immigrant, working-class or black" and they "played a surprisingly central role in redefining mainstream ideals of beauty and femininity in the twentieth century . . . they made the pursuit of beauty visible and respectable" (Peiss, 1998, p. 5). The history of these women, Peiss states, "flatly contradicts the view that the beauty industry worked only *against* women's interests", because they, "created job opportunities for women, addressed the politics of appearance, and committed their profits to their community". But the fact that women were involved in the development of beauty practices does not in any way contradict the notion that such practices are harmful. As Mary Daly points out in *Gyn/Ecology* (1979), women are frequently those who are responsible for carrying out what she calls "sado-rituals" on girls and women, as in the practices of female genital mutilation and footbinding. Women carry out the dictates of male dominance even to the extent of mutilating female children. Men and male dominance escape indictment or responsibility because they are nowhere to be seen. The practices appear to originate with and be done by women alone. Industries which offer employment to women are not always beneficial: the sex industry being one example (Jeffreys, 1997b). Industries that employ women can arise directly from and serve to maintain women's subordination.

Peiss explains the rise of the beauty industry as resulting from a change in the way women thought of themselves as they moved into the public world in the 1920s. In the nineteenth century public women were understood to be prostituted women and they did paint their faces. In the late nineteenth century there was an opening up of public space to respectable women. The development of the department store was one example of this, and Judith Walkowitz has written interestingly on the way in which shopping enabled respectable middle-class Victorian women in London to come out onto the street (Walkowitz, 1992). In the same period the job market opened up to middle-class women with the birth of white-collar occupations such as office work and teaching. Peiss associates the new enthusiasm for cosmetics among women with this movement of women into the public world.

She says that "beauty culture" should be "understood not only as a type of commerce but as a system of meaning that helped women navigate the changing conditions of modern social experience" (Peiss, 1998, p. 6). Women, she says, were getting jobs in offices, stores and occupations where they had to engage in face-to-face interactions. There was a more public marriage market with the development of the dance hall and a new sense of sexual freedom: "Moving into public life, they staked a claim to public attention, demanded that others look. This was not a fashion dictated by Parisian or other authorities, but a new mode of feminine self-presentation, a tiny yet resonant sign of a larger cultural contest over women's identity" (1998, p. 55). But none of this precisely explains why women had to "put their face on" to be in the public world. Why did they need to wear masks, when men did not? There is an interesting similarity here between the adoption of makeup by women entering the public world in the 1920s in the west and the adoption of the veil by women entering the public world in some Muslim cultures in the 1980s/1990s. Research on the readoption of the veil by a new generation of women in Muslim countries suggests that women feel safer and freer to engage in occupations and movement in the public world through covering up (Abu-Odeh, 1995). It could be that the wearing of makeup signifies that women have no automatic right to venture out in public in the west on equal grounds with men. Makeup, like the veil, ensures that they are masked and not having the effrontery to show themselves as the real and equal citizens that they should be in theory. Makeup and the veil might show women's lack of entitlement.

Peiss acknowledges that big business, usually run by men, took over from the small locally owned salons which were producing their own products in the 1930s. The massive cosmetics corporations of today began to build their empires. The industry could no longer be defended as one that allowed women new opportunities of entrepreneurship, but Peiss remains upbeat. She says that the power of corporations, advertising and mass media in peddling makeup to women should be criticized but that the critics may have, "overlooked the web of intimate rituals, social relationships, and female institutions that gave form to American beauty culture" (Peiss, 1998, p. 7). Women created "intimacy", she argues, by sharing beauty secrets and experienced "pleasure, and community". This is another way in which the proponents of makeup have defended it against feminist criticism. Makeup, they say, gives women a shared and pleasurable women's culture. But there are other harmful practices in which women develop rituals, share secrets and create supportive networks. Female genital mutilation and Chinese footbinding have been said to offer similar satisfactions (Ping, 2000).

When male-run big business took over, promises were made to women which were clearly exploitative and duplicitous:

> In little more than a decade, an aesthetic of women's freedom and modernity had narrowed and turned in upon itself. *Vogue* could claim without irony that bright fingernails offered "a minor adventure" and a facial "doesn't stop at giving you a new face – it gives you a whole new point of view on life".
>
> (Peiss, 1998, p. 158)

By 1920, Peiss asserts, "the beauty industry had succeeded in delivering its message to women, that the fulfillment of individuality and femininity required the purchase of cosmetics" (1998, p. 167). In the interwar period the beauty industry became oppressive rather than liberatory apparently, and took the shape that we are familiar with in the present. By 1930 beauty contests had become normalized and were even being held in high schools, "employment tests appraised bodily appearance and guidance counsellors at Smith College routinely noted graduating students' 'attractiveness' in their records" (Peiss, 1998, p. 193). Commercial colleges and YWCAs began to offer "self-development" courses with instructions on skin care, makeup, manicuring, and hair styling to young women about to enter the workforce. Makeup had become a requirement that women could not escape instead of a sign of liberation. The message of advertising, Peiss explains, "was reinforced and refined in the workplace and in school, at home and at leisure, as women experienced growing pressure to adjust their looks to new norms of feminine appearance" (1998, p. 200).

BEAUTY STANDARDS CONSTRUCTED FROM WHITE DOMINANCE

The "choice" to wear makeup and engage in other grooming practices is not made in a political vacuum. There are very real material forces involved in constructing this "choice" for women. Peiss writes positively about the opportunities offered to black women in the interwar period to set up beauty salons and become entrepreneurs before big business took over the industry. By the 1960s it was clear that the beauty practices that black women were taught were aimed at emulating a white ideal. African-American women have written eloquently on the racism of beauty standards in the USA that not only have white women bleaching their faces and their hair, but create impossible goals of emulating whiteness for black women. This has led to an industry of hair straighteners, and face whiteners, and other products designed to enable black women to approximate to a white ideal. Since it is unlikely that black women are somehow naturally excluded from the province of essential beauty, it is clear that what is beautiful is constructed politically and incorporates race, class and sex prejudices. When black women are chosen for their "beauty" to be models, such as Iman from Somalia, or Waris Dirie, their faces and bodies are likely to conform to white ideals and not to resemble the commonest features of African-American women's faces (Young, 1999).

In the days of the black power movement of the 1960s black women rejected the requirement that they should use white beauty practices. They rejected the hair straightening that was virtually compulsory for black women in the 1950s and early 1960s in favour of a more "natural" look. Michelle Wallace explains that "Being feminine *meant* being white to us" (Walker, 2001, p. 256, emphasis in the original), and in protest she repudiated, "makeup, high heels, stockings, garter belts", and supportive underwear in favour of "T-shirts and dungarees, or loose African print dresses" (2001, p. 263). As part of this protest the Afro was born. But it was hard for black women to remain outside the dictates of fashion, the Afro itself became commoditized (p. 263).

MAKEUP AND MALE DOMINANCE

Though the wearing of makeup is a pervasive aspect of the construction of femininity, there is surprisingly little research that fits makeup wearing into the political context of male domination. Quite comprehensive anthologies of research on "gender" do not mention makeup (Jackson and Scott, 2002). The one area of makeup use that has been studied is the workplace. Dellinger and Williams' (1997) study demonstrates very well that women are constrained to wear makeup in the workplace where it can be, quite simply, a job's worth issue. They carried out in-depth interviews with a diverse group of 20 women who worked in a variety of settings. They sought to "examine the appearance rules that women confront at work and how those rules reproduced assumptions about sexuality and gender" (1997, p. 151). Fourteen of the women wore makeup every day to work, two wore it some of the time, and four never or almost never. The women said that their workplaces did not have a formal dress code policy and that wearing makeup was their "personal choice". However many experienced, or perceived that they would experience, "negative consequences if their makeup is not properly applied" (Dellinger and Williams, 1997, p. 156). They felt that women who did not wear makeup did not appear to be "healthy", "heterosexual" or "credible". Women who usually wore makeup to work reported that on days that they did not they received comments about how they looked tired or did not look "good" and that such comments would affect how they felt at work that day. One woman specifically said that she wore makeup to avoid negative comments such as, "God, what's the matter with her? Is she sick or something?" (1997, p. 157).

On the other hand the wearing of makeup in the workplace was reinforced through positive comments. Many women said they wore makeup to feel confident about themselves or that it made them feel powerful. But at the same time they talked about feeling self-conscious without it, with one woman saying, "I don't like to look at myself in the mirror when I don't have it on" (Dellinger and Williams, 1997, p. 158). Some women were not comfortable in public places without makeup. A Taiwanese respondent said she wore makeup to give her a "wide-eyed"

American look (p. 159). Women may well say makeup empowers them but the interesting question is, what disempowers them about being without their mask? The constraints imposed by sexism and racism and the political structures of male domination are likely to be responsible for women's discomfort about moving into the public world "barefaced".

Another pressure on women to wear makeup is the requirement that they should appear to be heterosexual. As Dellinger and Williams comment "makeup . . . marks women as heterosexual" (1997, p. 159). One heterosexual respondent commented that women who did not wear makeup in her workplace are thought to be "tomboys". The assumption of heterosexuality, the authors note, is "built into professionalism" and thus, "An implicit requirement for looking appropriately feminine is that women look 'pleasing' to men" (1997, p. 160). One heterosexual woman explained that men, "tend to work easier with someone who is easy to look at", thus the requirement of servicing men's sexual fantasies is translated into workplace appearance requirements for women and lesbians just don't really fit in (Dellinger and Williams, 1997, p. 160).

One lesbian respondent who did not wear makeup at home or at work said that when she started working as a social worker she got comments such as, "You need to wear a little bit of makeup", or "You need to get a perm", or "You need to get some better clothes" (Dellinger and Williams, 1997, p. 161). This lesbian passed for straight at work. Another lesbian "actively uses makeup at work as a way to smooth workplace interactions with men" (p. 163). She says she uses makeup to "mute her 'difference'" (p. 162). She is a tall woman and wearing makeup makes her male clients both less likely to think she is a lesbian and less likely to see her as a threat because of her size. Makeup, then, makes women look unthreatening. A heterosexual African-American woman says that she used makeup to "enhance her credibility in a racist society" (p. 166). She felt the need to emphasize how professional she was to lessen the effect of racism and makeup was a way to do this. This woman said she was prepared to "let the sexism" pass in favour of diluting racism.

The authors conclude that workplace pressures do construct women's choices to wear makeup and that such choices cannot be, "understood outside the context of these institutionalized workplace appearance norms" (Dellinger and Williams, 1997, p. 168). Interestingly the authors sought to address the recent suggestions in feminist scholarship that makeup wearing might not just be enforced but about "creativity and pursuit of bodily pleasure" for women and that women might even be able to use makeup in ways that resisted appearance norms. They clearly have little sympathy with these notions and their data do not support them. They consider the idea that makeup wearing is part of a women's culture that can be enjoyed by women in the workplace. Women's commenting on each other's use or absence of beauty practices could in theory be seen as a "topic of conversation that bonds women together. Women may be able to show their affection and concern for one another through compliments and advice" (1997, p. 169). But they point out that such comments can also be divisive and can, as one respondent expresses, make her feel inadequate. It does seem to be the case that harmful cultural practices are frequently carried out by and among women when the agency of men is not apparent. Women can seek to support each other through the ordeals of performing the practices, offer each other advice and shoulders to lean on. This would be a culture formed to survive oppression, however, and not unambiguously worthy of celebration.

This research does not support the idea that women can subvert the appearance norms associated with wearing makeup. The few examples that are given of such subversion are that some women said they only applied makeup once a day, or that they did not check and reapply, or that they wore the minimum they could get away with. These don't seem very revolutionary strategies. The authors reject the notion promoted by a school of queer post-structuralist theorists such as Judith Butler, who say that women can "perform" femininity and "play" with gender (Butler, 1990). They say that "resistance through bodily practices may be easier to find in studies that do not evaluate the actual constraints imposed on women by social institutions" (Dellinger and Williams, 1997, p. 169), in other words an attention to the forms of force and control in the workplace undermine the idea that makeup can be worn "playfully".

Dellinger and Williams conclude that the women in their study are not "cultural dopes" and, "act as knowledgeable agents within institutional constraints" (1997, p. 175). Thus they may be very aware of what they are doing and why but still feel it necessary to engage in the practice even if in a minimal form. The concluding paragraph conveys a point usually overlooked in writings about the joys of makeup wearing; that is, that this practice has implications for reproducing "inequality between men and women, and also between different groups of women" (1997, p. 175). Makeup wearing helps to construct inequality as well as being a reaction to it.

Sadly the 1990s witnessed a revival of the requirement of savagely differentiated dress codes for women in the workplace. As a *Vogue* article put it in 1991: "Women at work have reclaimed their sexuality . . . Dresses are back, makeup is in" (Hochswender, 1991, p. 234). The writer argues that many women executives see this as empowering them. The readoption of femininity results, she believes, from the fact that women have gained credibility in the workplace and can now use femininity to their advantage. It could represent the complete opposite, of course – the control of career women by forcing them into a feminine and nonthreatening mould. Indeed the *Vogue* article gives some useful examples of the sanctions that are employed against women who do not follow workplace femininity dress codes. In one case the accounting firm Price-Waterhouse denied a partnership to Ann Hopkins because she needed to, among other things, "walk more femininely, talk more femininely, dress more femininely, and wear makeup" (Hochswender, 1991, p. 230). She sued and won. While the tone of the article is upbeat about the delights of dressing in a feminine fashion in the workplace there are many examples that show that this is not about choice and pleasure. "Dressing for work", it states, "is a small act of daily courage" (Hochswender, 1991, p. 232). This does not sound playful and shows how women have every day to work out how to look sufficiently feminine and sexy but not too sexy and, of course, carry out their routine of beauty practices. Meanwhile, as she points out, it is not that way for men who "seem to have it a lot easier". Men can wear a uniform suit that "disguises their sexuality rather than enhances it". In other words they do not have to think how they can best dress to draw and entrance the eyes of their female workmates and, "Even the most extravagant men, the ones who wear custom clothes, can never be accused of looking like hookers" (Hochswender, 1991, p. 230). The woman has to agonize over how to look "tough but feminine, sexy but authoritative", which is a tough call.

Women's magazines may play a role in coercing women into makeup in the workplace. The magazine *Ebony* aimed at African-American women uses a hectoring tone in one article telling working women how they should dress. The opening sentence says ominously, "Wearing the proper attire for your work place – whether it is on an assembly line, at a typist's desk, in an executive suite or in a television studio – can make the difference in success or failure" (Townsel, 1996, p. 61). The article continues in a fashion likely to frighten women into compliance:

> In light of today's diverse fashion and cosmetic markets, working women have little excuse for derailing their otherwise promising careers, by committing flagrant dressing faux pas. In fact, even workers with limited time and finances can spruce up their professional image by paying close attention to their hair, nails and cosmetics, and by choosing sophisticated, business-appropriate attire for work.
>
> (Townsel, 1996, p. 61)

The *Ebony* article uses as an authority a woman who is a spokesperson for a cosmetics company. She says, not surprisingly, such things as, "Makeup is very important because your face is the first thing people see when you're in the workplace", and makeup provides the necessary, "clean, finished look" (1996, p. 62). As an example of how important appearance is in the workplace, the article features Teresa Fleming who works as a seat belt installer at a car assembly plant and, "makes deliberate efforts every day to maintain a feminine, clean-cut image in her workplace, which is typically hot and gritty" (Townsel, 1996, p. 64). She gets her hair cut and curled twice a week, applies eyeliner and lipstick daily and goes through extreme measures to maintain her long, manicured fingernails such as, "I've cut out room for two fingers in my work gloves, and I wrap my nails in tape before my shift . . . I haven't lost a nail in the last two years" (p. 64). Thus this woman is handicapped at work and has to engage in time-consuming and expensive practices. Compared with men this does seem an unfair disadvantage. The makeup company spokeswoman, probably employed in this article because her company is an important advertiser with the magazine, says that a woman's beauty regime should only take 7 minutes each morning. But the practices she recommends sound rather too complicated to be performed in such a short time. She does not allow for the thinking time involved when women adapt their makeup, as she says they should, to their day – for example, if they have any important meetings. She says women should use a toner to close pores and give a youthful appearance, a moisturizer and then, "your foundation, blush, mascara and a light lipstick – and you're out the door" (Townsel, 1996, p. 62). But, she says, nails must be clean and polished and they are not included in the 7 minutes and she does not even mention hair and clothing. All in all the beauty regimen is likely to take a long time out of the day.

There is very little research on the time that women sacrifice in beauty practices. A survey of 2,000 women by Marks and Spencer in the UK has found that the average woman takes the equivalent of 10 working days a year getting ready for work at 27 minutes per day, and 10 per cent take more than an hour per day. The majority of women spend 21 minutes getting ready for a shopping trip, 54 minutes for a night out with the girls and 59 minutes for "a romantic evening" (Hill, 2002). These are considerable amounts of time that men and the women who eschew such routines can spend on other activities.

It should be clear from these examples that makeup is not simply a matter of "choice" in the workplace but the result of a system of power relations that can require women to engage in this cultural practice. The idea that makeup is a "choice" is undermined by an examination of the tactics that cosmetics corporations employ to get children using makeup and wedded to their brands. Makeup manufacturers are targeting girls as young as 8. A market research study found that one-fourth of girls under 13 had experimented with makeup and the advertisers are keen to reach them (Cardona, 2000). Proctor and Gamble are seeking to market their Cover Girl cosmetics range to 8–10-year-old girls by making the use of makeup resemble play. Thus they have: "Peelers Polish 'peelable' nails, enamels and Pure magic Body Art, a package of body paint and stencils that comes in designs such as Halloween shapes" (Cardona, 2000, p. 15). They have kiosks in shopping malls to entice girl children in to surf their website, and display glitter and lip gloss in them rather than the more adult products in their range so that parents will not be alienated. A company called Kiss Products has licensed animated characters from Walt Disney Co. to promote their lip gloss and nail polish kits at Disney stores. The Cosrich Group has licensed Barbie to promote lip glosses and body glitter: "Disney's products for girls are packaged in boxes with pictures of Tinkerbell, Winnie-the-Pooh and other Disney characters, while Barbie makeup comes packaged with plastic charms and bracelets" (Cardona, 2000, p. 15). In the USA cosmetics industry estimates put sales to children at US$1 billion annually. One range of personal-care products is now targeting children as young as 6. The promotion of cosmetics as forms of play to children will create the "choices" of adult women. They will have been trained to understand makeup as a form of personal fulfilment and play at an age before they have had the opportunity to recognize any alternative.

Women cannot be said to make free "choices" to engage in beauty practices in a culture in which men have the power to enforce their requirements. A good example of the force of men's opinion in the creation of beauty practices lies in the way shaving is discussed on the The Carnal Knowledge Network website. The website, which is clearly run by and represents the views of men, asks the question, "Does it really matter if I'm too lazy to shave my legs?" The answer is, "The accepted norm in society today dictates that a woman shave her legs . . . Other women who do not experience these [medical] conditions SHOULD remove the hair from their legs. The facts are that the VAST majority of men prefer smooth shaven legs" (Carnal Knowledge Network, 2002). In response to the question, "Does this mean that women have to shave their legs just because most men seem to prefer this?", the response is:

> Obviously the answer is no, if you want to take the "high and mighty" attitude of it's my body and I'll do what I want to. You can grow shoulder length hair on your legs but YOU WILL be greatly limiting your chances of finding and keeping a mate by alienating yourself from the accepted norm. If you don't shave your legs and keep them clean and appealing, many guys will simply lose interest in you romantically (sorry, facts of life).
>
> (Carnal Knowledge Network, 2002)

The website's advice continues its haranguing tone. To women who might have the habit of not shaving their legs in winter when they are not wearing shorts the response is that such women will be labelled "that girl who doesn't shave her legs", and, "THIS IS WHAT WE TALK ABOUT WHEN YOU'RE NOT AROUND!!" It goes on: "most of us like a woman who takes the time to keep herself up; we're obsessed with it" (Carnal Knowledge Network, 2002).

The suggestion that women will not acquire male partners without shaving resembles the reasons given for the carrying out of harmful beauty practices in other cultures, such as female genital mutilation and the reconstructing of hymens; that is, girls have no chance of marrying without them. Though it might be expected that the pressures on young women to have male partners might be less in western cultures where they have more chance of a career that is not that of wife, they are still extreme. Feminine respectability in western culture requires attachment to a male partner.

The idea that women "choose" to engage in these practices is also undermined by an examination of just how painful and fraught they can be for the victims. The "Girl Talk" online discussion forum addresses shaving as well as other harmful beauty practices, and reveals a tortured and painful process in which young women seek to accommodate the pain and discomfort inherent in such practices. They communicate with each other in heartfelt messages about how to avoid the pain and deal with the problems that result. One problem that women who remove body hair encounter is ingrown hairs. One woman in the discussion forum describes the problem thus:

> I had a bikini wax a couple of months ago and ever since I have had horrible problems with in grown [sic] hairs. I have tried the lotions (tend skin etc.) and hot baths. I've even tried to get at them with tweezers, but that is just making the situation worse. Please let me know what else I can do!
>
> (Girl Talk, toria5, 9 July 2002)

Women respond to her with the names of other products she can use to help with the problem. Clearly cosmetics manufacturers make profits from selling both the cause of the problem and solutions for it, which is a nice little earner. Another problem that Masaki asks about is "red bumps on my legs from shaving" which prevent her from wearing shorts or skirts. She describes the problem as "terrible" (Girl Talk, masaki, 30 June 2002). Another woman writes of the problems she got from bleaching the hair on her arms. The bleaching led to "really gross, noticable roots [sic], even though I only did it a week ago", and she is considering waxing though she cannot afford it (Girl Talk, Victoria, 21 June 2002). Her questions are:

1. Does it look weird for your arms to be completely hairless?
2. In general, how fast does it grow back?
3. How can you conceal it while you're waiting for it to be long enough to wax?

4. In general, how long will it be from the time it starts to grow back until you can wax it again?
5. Approximately, how much does it cost? (Whole arm, not just forearm.)
6. Does the regrowth look or feel like stubble?

(Girl Talk, Victoria, 21 June 2002)

Another woman, Serenause, writes in about the problem of "underarm irritation" from shaving (Girl Talk, Serenause, 28 June 2002):

> I absolutely cannot shave my underarms without irritation – no matter what I do! I try to be really light and not press too hard with the razor, and I've tried to do it quickly and slowly. But I can never get a close shave, and furthermore, ALWAYS leaves red bumps . . . I've tried to put lotion there, including the . . . lotion that comes in the waxing kit for after hair removal. NOTHING works. The hair is to [sic] coarse to wax (and it's too painful!) – The result is unsightly for tanks/sleeveless shirts – what can I do? please help!

The young women engaging in these agonized exchanges could be said to be creating a women's culture around beauty practices, but it is a culture of survival designed to enable them to negotiate harmful cultural practices with slightly less pain. The exchanges suggest just how much of young women's attention, time, money and emotional energy are taken up with the practices that demonstrate their difference and enable them to play their part in the sexual corvée.

The exchanges resemble those carried out about much more damaging practices of self-mutilation on websites such as BME, Body Modification Ezine. On the BME website young women describe practices of cutting and burning their arms, breasts and other parts of their bodies (Jeffreys, 2000). They also write as if they feel compelled, but the practices are way beyond those that would be considered the ordinary requirements of beauty. On the BME site beauty practices have gone off the rails of social acceptability, but in their very obvious destruction of skin and flesh they may help us to understand the harm involved in such apparently respectable everyday practices as whole body depilation. An understanding of why young women continue with these practices requires an awareness of the very considerable force that has been required to create this result. Cynthia Enloe, in her work on international politics, *Bananas, Beaches and Bases* (1989), asks us to reflect on what forces have created situations that appear to those brought up in western culture as just facts of nature, such as treeless landscapes or all-women typing pools. These are not "natural" facts but the result of social and economic forces that favour a shortsighted destruction of natural resources or the containment and exploitation of women in cheap labour. Similarly when depilation is identified as a culturally constructed practice, rather than a fact of nature, it is possible to seek out the forces which create it.

MAKEUP AND MENTAL HEALTH

One of these forces is psychiatry. A useful example of the way in which male dominance enforces makeup use by women is the treatment of women in mental hospitals. Some hospital psychologists understand the maintenance of feminine beauty practices to signify "mental health" and enforce makeovers for women they consider recalcitrant. Resistance by women to these practices is seen as a symptom of ill health. Thus Michael Pertschuk says that the first thing medical students are taught is to observe the patient: "How is he dressed? Hair neat? Hands clean? If the patient is a woman, is she wearing makeup? How well is it applied? Has she attended to her hair and nails?" (Pertschuk, 1985, p. 217). The men are not required to wear makeup to show their mental health, but women are. "Attention to personal grooming", he says is, "a diagnostic tool" (1985, p. 218). Apparently depressives, "may not bother at all with cosmetics as the routine tasks of life become overwhelming" (p. 219). Pertschuk says that the most important thing for these depressed women to do is to accept their "female identity". Signs that they feel, "incapable of filling any aspect of this identity as they conceive it", are: "elimination of a figure through excess weight loss or gain, avoidance of cosmetics altogether and androgynous clothes selection" (1985, p. 219).

Pertschuk's big worry is that, "The woman who feels unable to meet the demands of a female identity and who grooms and dresses accordingly is indeed likely to be viewed as asexual by those around her" (1985, p. 221). The woman may desire precisely such freedom from men's gaze but Pertschuk will not allow it. He sees the solution for such women who refuse to service male sexuality as "appearance training". He explains how this cruel procedure was carried out on a 29-year-old woman with anorexia who, "In appearance . . . looked rather like a thin, frightened nine-year-old boy. She wore no makeup. Her hair was worn very short. She was dressed in nondescript slacks and a top. She was extremely diffident in her manner" (1985, p. 222). He used what he calls a "flooding procedure" on her:

> We coaxed her into the situation she feared i.e. using cosmetics, and helped her work through her anxieties. Her initial response to the occupational therapist's extremely modest application of mascara, lipstick, and powder was to say that she now looked like a prostitute. However, after repeated application of cosmetics for

> a week, she became somewhat more accepting. The occupational therapist worked with Alice to teach her to apply makeup herself. The entire staff conscientiously attempted to reinforce her with compliments about her appearance. The next phase of training involved selection of clothes . . . The goal was for her to select a few items of more becoming apparel, specifically a dress. The patient had not worn a dress in nine years. Again with much coaxing, Alice was able to do this and was lavishly reinforced for her efforts.
>
> (Pertschuk, 1985, p. 222)

This attempt at something like dog obedience training did not, as Pertschuk says, "cure Alice", but he thinks it "did help" (1985, p. 223). She now wore dresses for appointments and was letting her hair grow so he was probably able to look on her with more satisfaction. She had a "sexual identity" for him.

In the same edited collection on the psychology of "cosmetic treatments" there are comments that reveal a remarkable prejudice against women who resist beauty practices. Douglas Johnson, writing on "Appearance and the Elderly" remarks that women, "at about age 50 . . . steadily decline into sexual oblivion" (Johnson, 1985, p. 153). Gerald Adams remarks that a study he conducted found, "that unattractive women are more likely to use an undesirable influence-style that includes demanding, interrupting, opinionated, submissive, and antagonistic behavior" (Adams, 1985, p. 139). It is alarming to think that some hospitalized women's mental health is in the hands of men whose attitudes would be likely to damage the self-esteem of even the most robust of women. The relationship between makeup and depression may be rather different from that espoused by the psychologists who do makeovers on hospitalized women. Researchers have found that, "Middle-aged females who get depressed tend to subscribe to a more traditional feminine role, and the degree of their depression is significantly related to their degree of acceptance of the feminine role" (Tinsley *et al.*, 1984, p. 30). Emily Tinsley *et al.* say that their work supports the conclusion that, "women who adopt more androgynous and masculine sex roles tend to be more mentally healthy" (1984, p. 26). This completely contradicts the ideas of the makeover brigade.

MAKEUP HARMFUL TO THE HEALTH OF WOMEN AND GIRLS

Harmful cultural/traditional practices are identified in UN understandings, before all else, as those that are harmful to the health of women and girls. Makeup practices fit this criterion well because the substances that women apply to their hair, face and body in pursuit of beauty are directly dangerous to health. Hair dye, for instance, has been linked with bladder cancer. An American study of 3,000 women, half of whom had developed bladder cancer, found that, "Even after adjusting for cigarette smoking . . . women who use permanent hair dyes at least once a month for one year or longer have twice the risk of bladder cancer as non-users" (Robotham, 2001). Hairdressers exposed to dyes in the workplace are also at increased risk. The anti-bacterial agent triclosan which is used in cosmetics as well as toothpastes and other household products is under consideration for banning in Australia because a Swedish study has shown that the chemical accumulates in mothers' breast milk as well as in fish. It is likely that the chemical helps germs develop resistance to prescribed antibiotics (Strong, 2001). New products that are increasingly being developed by the bio-tech industry are being marketed as beauty aids. These products, named "cosmeceuticals", might more properly be regulated as drugs because of the active effects they are supposed to have on the body. One, for instance, which contains antioxidants, will penetrate the skin and is supposed to scavenge for free radicals. Another is supposed to banish grey hair at the roots. But these products are not being regulated with the care usually applied to drugs (King, 2001).

In *Drop-Dead Gorgeous* (2002) Kim Erickson describes what is known about the toxic effects of the chemicals in conventional cosmetics from scientific research. She points out that women doing the daily beauty ritual expose themselves to more than 200 synthetic chemicals before they have morning coffee. Many of them have been identified as toxic by the US Environmental Protection Agency. The US National Institute of Occupational Safety and Health has reported that 900 of the chemicals in cosmetics are toxic. One study, for instance, found that there were such high levels of lead in Grecian Formula and Lady Grecian Formula that researchers were unable to wash it off their hands after using the product. Another found that women who dyed their hair suffered greater chromosomal damage than women who did not use hair dyes. Allergic reactions to nail polish, which contains the most toxic array of chemicals, included lesions on the face, neck and hands of experimental subjects who were sensitive to toluene and formaldehyde (Erickson, 2002, p. 4).

Coal tar, Erickson explains, is a particularly dangerous ingredient. Coal tar colours can contain benzene, xylene, naphthalene, phenol and creosol and almost all such colours have been shown to cause cancer. This is important considering that two out of five women in the USA dye their hair. Another ingredient, formaldehyde, is found in nail polish, nail hardeners, soap, shampoos, and hair growth preparations. It is outlawed in Sweden and Japan and the EEC allows its use only in low quantities. The lead in hair dyes is a known carcinogen and hormone disrupter. Propylene glycol is the most widely used delivery vehicle and solvent used in cosmetics in the place of glycerin. Its most well known use is in antifreeze and brake fluid. It is an acknowledged neurotoxin, has been linked to contact dermatitis, kidney damage, and liver abnormalities, and the inhibition of skin cell growth, but it is used in baby lotions and mascara. Erickson points out that talc, which is commonly used not just directly but in blushers, powders and eye colours, is chemically similar to asbestos and carcinogenic in animals. Women who regularly use talcum powder in the genital area increase their risk of ovarian cancer threefold. Toluene, found in nail polish, is subject to a warning from the Environmental Protection Agency because breathing in large amounts of the chemical can cause damage to the kidneys, the liver and the heart. There are estimated to be more than 200,000 visits yearly to the emergency room in the USA related to allergic reactions to cosmetics use.

There is no requirement for testing cosmetic products in the way that food or medicines are tested in the USA. The skin, however, is a highly effective way of transmitting chemicals into the body, as in the use of skin patches for hormone replacement therapy. Thus the unregulated chemicals are absorbed into the bodies of the women who use conventional cosmetics products daily. The lack of regulation is maintained by the political influence of the immensely profitable cosmetics industry whose sales grew from $7 billion in 1970 to $28 billion in 1994 in the USA.

Apart from the damage to women's bodies directly, the chemicals used in cosmetics damage the environment in other ways. As Erickson puts it, "millions of gallons of synthetic chemicals are washed down the drain and into sewer systems every day" (2002, p. 9). The petrochemicals used in makeup pollute waterways and destroy marine life. The by-products of the chemicals as they degrade interfere with the functioning of hormones and thus sexual development. These hormone disrupters devastate wildlife. The cosmetics industry generates huge amounts of waste from product packaging, from which toxins can leach into soil and groundwater. As a form of collateral damage 10–15 million animals are tortured and killed every year in US laboratories that test the safety of cosmetic and household products.

Erickson does not, however, argue that makeup is unnecessary. Indeed she comments, apparently seriously, that "Lipstick is the finishing touch that makes your face come alive", unless the toxins kill you, of course (2002, p. 225). She accepts the inevitability of makeup use and recommends products made with natural ingredients or that women should, supposing they have a spare moment, make their own. Assuming that makeup could, as she suggests, be made from less physically harmful ingredients, this may help to alleviate one aspect of this harmful practice but would not affect others. Psychological harms may still be suffered in, for example, the everyday variety of body dysmorphic disorder, the sense of inadequacy, created by the makeup industry. Nor would it lessen the role of makeup in creating sexual difference.

A new product on the market called "Perfect Pout" in honour of its supposed effect, consists precisely of a toxic substance that causes skin irritation. It promises women luscious lips without collagen, "It gives you fuller looking lips in just 60 seconds" (Skin Doctors, 2002, p. 7). The product appears to be an irritant that causes the lips to swell. The text explains, "There isn't a man alive who doesn't get turned on by luscious, plump lips. They'll watch them moving as you speak. As you eat". The toxic substance lasts up to 5 hours but can be reapplied five times daily. In the advertisement Suzi of Newcastle is quoted as saying, "I feel so much sexier now I have a seductive pout – I see guys looking at my mouth and I know exactly what's going on in their heads."

Another health concern is the use of animal products in cosmetic production that could transmit Bovine Spongiform Encephalopathy (BSE) to humans. The British government's BSE Inquiry considered this problem and because little was known about how animal products were used an audit was conducted. There are four pages detailing the derivatives of the animal slaughter industry and the products they are used in. Cosmetics manufacture uses: brain, fat, placenta, spleen, thymus, bones in the form of tallow and gelatine, and skin/hide in the form of gelatine and collagen used in implants. As a result of concern about transmission the "Cosmetics Directive" of the European Union, which covered the materials that could be used in cosmetics manufacture, outlawed the use of certain animal derivatives such as tissues from, "the encephalon, the spinal cord and the eyes" and material from the skull, tonsils and spleens of "ovine and caprine" animals (i.e. sheep and goats) in amendments in 1997 and 1998 (Home Office, 2000). Tallow is still used despite the EU ban on other derivatives because there is, apparently, no suitable alternative. Since BSE is not confined to the EU, and the transmission is so inadequately understood, it is probably sensible for women in all countries to avoid cosmetics made with any animal parts. The use that the inquiry was particularly worried about was in anti-ageing creams where a break in the skin could facilitate transmission.

Everyday beauty practices take up women's time, energy, money and emotional space. The chemicals employed are a threat to women's health. Women can seek each other's support in the performance of these practices, particularly in finding out how to dull the pain and discomfort, but this does not form the basis of positive bonding networks between women so much as support networks of the oppressed. Though the supporters of makeup argue that it offers a realm for the exercise of women's creativity, this is rather limited. Women are not in a position to paint sunsets on their foreheads but are required to conform to strict rules in order to function in workplaces and escape criticism and discrimination. Men, and women who eschew makeup, clearly find other things to do with their time, money, creativity and emotional energies. Makeup steals years from women's lives and from the exercise of their talents in order to fulfil the requirements of the sexual corvée. In the next chapter I look at another requirement of women's sexual corvée that is more obviously harmful, the wearing of high-heeled shoes.

7

MEN'S FOOT AND SHOE FETISHISM AND THE DISABLING OF WOMEN

The wearing of high heels causes pain, disability and, often, permanent deformity for women. The continued existence of this harmful cultural practice in western societies requires explanation. William Rossi, author of the bible of men's shoe fetishism, *The Sex Life of the Foot and Shoe* (1989), tells us how important disabling shoes are to men by declaring that, "Men are still uncertain whether the greatest of all inventions was the wheel or the high heel" (Rossi, 1989, p. 119). Rossi, like other foot fetishists, from fashion designers to ordinary male habitués of brothels and consumers of pornography, is well aware that the high-heeled shoe is an instrument of torture for women. As Rossi says, "The high heel makes no practical sense whatever. It has no functional or utilitarian value. It's an unnatural fixture on a shoe. It makes standing and walking precarious and tiring. It's a safety hazard. It's blamed for a host of pedic and bodily ills" (1989, p. 119). But for foot fetishists, as we shall see in this chapter, the damage and pain are crucial parts of the sexual excitement they gain from their obsession. I look at the role that men's sexual interest in the deformed and disabled female foot has played in creating and sustaining Chinese footbinding, that signature practice of supposedly highbrow western culture, ballet, and high-heeled shoes, and seek to understand the impact of this aspect of male sexuality on women's lives.

There are other ways in which high heel wearing fulfils the dictates of male dominant culture and gives satisfaction to men. Heels are a good way to make a difference. As Rossi puts it, "There is no practical reason why boys and girls, or men and women, should wear shoes with pronounced styling differences. The *only* reason is sexual, an insignia to designate the separation of the sexes" (1989, p. 17). Women are immediately recognizable as they walk with difficulty on their toes in public places. Thus high heels enable women to complement the male sex role of masculinity, in which men look sturdy and have both feet on the ground, with clear evidence of female fragility. Men's masculinity is confirmed most strongly thereby. They may even have to help women up kerbs and out of cars because they are liable to fall and twist an ankle. The wearing of high heels is also a way of complimenting men. Men are given the opportunity of sexual satisfaction and can know that this woman cares enough to wear fetishistic shoes for them, and for all men. This is a very generous compliment. Thus high heel wearing both complements and compliments men in powerful ways.

FOOT AND SHOE FETISHISM

Sexologists, the "scientists" of sex, agree that foot and shoe fetishism is the commonest kind. The sexologist Havelock Ellis, considered by some to be the most significant "prophet of sex" in the twentieth century, identified men's foot and shoe "erotic symbolism", as he called fetishism, as the "most frequent" form of fetishism (Ellis, 1926, p. 15). Fetishism is mainly a behaviour of men, though the sexologists rarely make this plain. They explain that fetishists choose some part of a woman or article of apparel as the focus of their sexual excitement rather than a whole woman. There are various explanations for why this should be. Some say that the male child first experiences arousal while aware of this body part or item of clothing and thus associates it with sex all his life. This does not explain why women are so rarely fetishists. Another form of explanation relates fetishism to the fear of castration, in which case the fetish stands in for the penis. This might explain why fetishism is male, but only for those who want to place any credence in psychoanalysis.

Ellis, like other male commentators on fetishism, routinely uses ungendered language that conceals the fact that fetishism is male. There are clues, such as when he says, "It would seem that even for the normal lover the foot is one of the most attractive parts of the body" (1926, p. 15). Women readers will understand that they are not "normal lovers" since they are unlikely to have found their partners' feet the most attractive part of them. When he says, "In a small but not inconsiderable minority of persons, however, the foot or the boot becomes the most attractive part of a woman", we realize that by "persons" Ellis means men (1926, p. 17). In "some morbid cases", he tells us, "the woman herself is regarded as a comparatively unimportant appendage to her feet or her boots" (p. 17). Ellis says that fetishism is quite normal since, "Fetichism [sic] and the other forms of erotic symbolism are but the development and the isolation of the crystallizations which normally arise on the basis of sexual selection" (1926, p. 111). Women, by this reckoning, must be abnormal. Rossi, too, says that foot fetishism is normal because, "The human species prefers itself a little bent out of natural shape" (Rossi, 1989, p. 29). It hardly needs saying that there does not seem to have been a great demand by women for men to be bent out of shape.

Ellis goes so far as to attach very positive value to fetishism by suggesting that it is a practice of superior lovers (men). Thus he says of fetishes, "While the average insensitive person may fail to perceive them at all, for the more alert and imaginative lover they are a fascinating part of the highly charged crystallization of passion" (Ellis, 1926, p. 30). The implication is that men without the ability to fixate on women's feet are "insensitive". Ellis's enthusiasm for fetishism is likely to relate to his own practice of urolagnia, or love of watching/listening to women urinate (Jeffreys, 1985/1997). This seems to have been very important and may even have supplanted what he, along with other sexologists, tells us is normal sex – that is, sexual intercourse. He includes urolagnia in erotic symbolism, says it is "not extremely uncommon", and attributes it to men, like himself, who are superior intellectuals: "it has been noted in men of high intellectual distinction" (Ellis, 1926, p. 59). It is, he says, "within the normal limits of variation of sexual emotion". Though he tells us that "it occurs in women as well as men", there is not much evidence of this. In gay male sexual culture it is quite common, with a considerable amount of pornography and practice of what are called "water sports", but among lesbians and heterosexual women it would seem to be very unusual.

CHINESE FOOTBINDING

Sexologists, podiatrists, and writers on foot fetishism like Rossi, point out that this desire of men to see women distorted and in pain is not just an aberration of male sexual behaviour in western culture. It flourished for 1,000 years in China, crippling women in their millions. But what those who record and delight in foot fetishism also show are the considerable similarities between this practice and the wearing of high heels in the west. The majority of western women are probably unaware of the connections, but as they walk in high heels their feet are arched at a similar angle to that achieved permanently in footbinding. In Imperial China footbinding was gradually adopted by upper-class women from the eleventh century onwards until, by the nineteenth century when a protest movement arose to campaign against it, it had reached most areas of society. Binding was initiated at 6 or 7 years old and carried out by the girls' mothers. Strips of cloth were used to bind all toes except the big toe back onto the sole and to bend the arch of the foot down at such a sharp angle that the ball of the foot and the heel were pushed together so that, "The flesh often became putrescent during the binding, and portions sloughed off from the sole; sometimes one or more toes dropped off. The pain continued for about a year and then diminished, until at the end of two years the feet were practically dead and painless" (quoted in Levy, 1966, p. 26). Locomotion was difficult thereafter and women could be reduced to getting about a room on their knees, using strategically placed stools. Women of higher classes would have their feet bound until they were only 3 inches long, whereas women of lower classes, who needed to get about to some extent, would bind to 5 inches.

The reasons why men enforced this practice on women, and women's motivations for enforcing it on their daughters, are instructive towards understanding the wearing of high heels today. One reason was to create a clear difference between men and women. Levy explains that conservative thinkers saw applying rouge, putting on makeup, piercing the ears, and binding the feet, "were all necessary practices which enabled women to conform to the social dictum that they had to differ from men in every visible physical aspect" (1966, p. 31). An important reason was the sexual excitement the practice afforded to men. Men claimed that a resultant tightening of the vagina gave the same sensation as intercourse with a virgin (Levy, 1966, p. 34). They gained a satisfaction similar to that which contemporary western men gain from high heels, through the imposition of a mincing, and what men considered to be a provocative, gait, "The eye rejoiced in the tiny footstep and in the undulating motion of the buttocks" (Levy, 1966, p. 34). A Chinese man who married a footbound woman was interviewed by Levy and his comments on the attractiveness of the footbound gait make it sound very similar to the high-heeled gait of today. He repudiates the freedom of movement that Chinese women gained when footbinding was ended, "Women now all have large feet. They jump and run when walking and fail to give the onlooker a gracious feeling" (1966, p. 282). Chinese men gained sexual pleasure from playing with the disabled foot, kissing it, sucking it and placing it in their mouths or around their penis, "ate watermelon seeds and almonds placed between the toes", and drank the water the feet were washed in. One way of gaining satisfaction from footbinding, watching women "pare down their calluses" created by the disability, is similar to the satisfaction that contemporary foot fetishists take from the damage that high heels cause (Rossi, 1989). Another motivation for men to enforce footbinding was that the practice restricted women from exercising any freedom or independence and thus protected their chastity. Footbinding functioned as a kind of chastity belt.

Women were dragooned into binding their daughters' feet, despite knowing the pain it would cause, because they had no alternative for subsistence but marriage, and no man would marry them without tiny feet. The tinier the feet, the more desirable the girl would be as a wife. The same was true of prostitution. Some girls were bought from their families and brought up to be sold into prostitution. They were bound, and prostituted women with the tiniest feet were in most demand and got the best price. Thus the sale and exchange of women between men in marriage or prostitution required footbinding to continue.

A movement within China against footbinding began in the nineteenth century and continued until the 1930s when footbinding was all but abandoned. It was motivated by ideas of modernity and progress as well as by concern for women's equality. In the 1970s a new generation of feminists in the west identified footbinding as incorporating the essential elements common to the harmful beauty practices still in existence in the west such as women's dancing en pointe in ballet, and the wearing of high heels. Andrea Dworkin said footbinding was a "political institution" that "reflected and perpetuated the sociological and psychological inferiority of women" (Dworkin, 1974, p. 96). It "cemented" women into the roles of "sexual objects and breeders". Footbinding, Dworkin continued, did not so much "formalize existing differences between men and women" as create them, and thus, "One sex became male by virtue of having made the other sex some thing, something other, something completely polar to itself, something called female" (1974, p. 107). Dworkin comments that the practice shows the way in which men require that women be in pain and crippled for their satisfaction. Through the crippling of a woman a man "glories in her agony, he adores her deformity, he annihilates her freedom, he will have her as sex object, even if he must destroy the bones in her feet to do it. Brutality, sadism, and oppression emerge as the substantive core of the romantic ethos. That ethos is the warp and woof of culture as we know it" (Dworkin, 1974, p. 112).

Some contemporary male foot fetishists reject feminist arguments and are prepared to mount a defence of footbinding. J.J. Leganeur, on his foot fetishist website, tells us that footbinding resembles the wearing of high heels in that, "Both Chinese bound feet and high heels (as well as ballet shoes en pointe) give the feet an erotic or sexy look", and, "They also make the girl/woman walk in a mincing sexy gait, with buttock sticking out more and the back arched more" (Leganeur, n.d.a). He defends footbinding as being consensual, pleasurable for men and the result of women's desires.

The origins of footbinding, as is the case with many of the harmful beauty practices covered in this book, lie in prostitution. It began among dancers at the Emperor's court in the eleventh century. These dancers were available to be bought and engaged in a form of prostitution. It seems likely their practice was similar to that of geishas in Japan or the dancing girls of Pakistan described so well in Fouzia Saeed's *Taboo! The Hidden Culture of a Red Light Area* (2001). In the Pakistani practice the male customers select the girls they will buy for sexual use as they dance, and the purpose of the dancing is to attract custom. In China the practice spread from prostitutes to other women. This is but one more example of the way in which the harmful practices of prostitution become the model of "beauty" for women outside that industry. The contemporary footbinding scholar Dorothy Ko allows herself to ruminate on how this dissemination of the practice took place. She suggests that, "literati from all over the empire en route to the civil service exam came face to face with beguiling entertainers scuffing in silk slippers" in "pleasure houses"; that is, brothels (Ko, 2001, p. 42). Some bought girls, she thinks, and took them home as "household entertainers or concubines", and then Ko found herself, "picturing the legal wife watching the singing and dancing in her reception room. Enraged (or enchanted, who knows?), she retreated to the boudoir and rummaged her storage chest for remnants of brocade to make new shoes and strips of gauze to swaddle her toes" (2001, p. 42).

A similar provenance, interestingly enough, is suggested for the high-heeled shoe in the USA. William Rossi says that a new girl from France brought the high heel to a New Orleans brothel in the 1850s. The shoes were so attractive to the buyers that the madam made them compulsory in the brothel. Then other brothels took them up. The male patrons were now urging their wives to buy high heels, or ordering them themselves from Paris for their wives (Rossi, 1989, p. 127). He proclaims enthusiastically, "Thus the high heel in America owes its launching and success to the nation's whores of an earlier day" (p. 127).

The feminist scholars who write from a postmodern, cultural studies perspective about footbinding do not engage in the wholehearted condemnation that might be expected of feminists. Two Asian women scholars (Ping, 2000; Ko, 2001) in particular have abandoned the insights of earlier feminist critics such as Andrea Dworkin. Dorothy Ko, a leading scholar of the practice, has sought to rescue it from its association with women's oppression. She argues that footbinding should not be universally condemned and associated just with the oppression of women: "The unanimity of condemnation in modern times masks the multiplicity of practice and the instability of meaning that is the only salient truth about footbinding" (Ko, 1997a, p. 8). Ko says that women involved in footbinding may not have felt it to be oppressive and: "Upon scrutiny, our certainties may turn out to be dead wrong, based as they are on an uncritical imposition of modern perspectives onto a Chinese past that thrived on values and body conceptions alien to ours" (1997a, p. 8). In another piece she suggests that the motivation to see footbinding as totally negative stems from the perspective of colonizing westerners in the nineteenth and early twentieth century, though this does not seem to fit well with what we know of the wholesale critiques that emerged from the indigenous anti-footbinding movement (Ko, 1997b; Levy, 1966). In fact, Ko says, the meaning of footbinding is in the eye of the beholder. Thus footbinding was, "a practice that frustrated the foreigner because it could not be reduced to a core of absolute and timeless meanings" (Ko, 1997b, p. 24). These colonizers were: "Too busy unwrapping the binders to reveal the 'inner truth'", and thus, "the foreigner has failed to learn that the meaning of footbinding is always constructed, hence always a function of the values of the beholder". She thus adopts a cultural relativist, postmodern perspective in which it is impossible to name any practice as oppressive to women because there are just too many meanings and everyone can have a different interpretation.

Ko's book, *Every Step a Lotus. Shoes for Bound Feet* (2001), is a full colour picture book full of large, shiny photos of the shoes that were made for bound feet. There is a problem in producing picture books on bound feet and particularly the shoes made for them. Their main market is likely to be male shoe fetishists and such books could be seen to encourage interest in this form of cruelty towards women. Ko is well aware of her foot fetishist audience. Early in the book she explains that despite being a perfect target for feminist critique, a turn of phrase that does not suggest she shares that critique, "our reaction to footbinding is not entirely negative" (2001, p. 10). Who is the "we" in this sentence? It turns out to be those who admire the embroidery on the shoes in museums, those who take pleasure in, "tender scenes in erotic novels and paintings of a man fondling his lover's foot", and what she describes as, "unabashed lovers of the bound foot. Foot fetishists" (2001, p. 10). These foot fetishists, she explains, "have even invented a machine that bends the foot into an arch . . . It would be hard to find a mass market for the footbinding machine, but few would disagree that admiration for pretty feet runs deep in many cultures, including our own" (Ko, 2001, p. 10). These machines are arch stretchers, advertised on foot fetishist sites and much in vogue in foot fetishist pornography, in which women are shown stretching their arches with the contraption so that they can get into the extreme forms of high-heeled shoe that fetishists demand. Her description of bound feet as "pretty" rather than deformed is a surprising one. The purpose of her book, Ko says, is "to present a new and more nuanced picture of foot-binding by explaining its origin and spread before the nineteenth century in terms of women's culture and material culture" (Ko, 2001, p. 15). She states that the "usual explanations of 'women were victims of beauty' or 'men fetishized tiny feet' are not entirely wrong, but they oversimplify" (p. 15). She says she will not be "denying the very real pain involved", but wants to explain the practice by "stepping into the women's shoes".

As Ko explains, footbinding, like other harmful cultural practices, became a tradition handed down through women to young girls:

> Once footbinding became an established custom, the patina of "tradition" alone became a strong enough motivation for mothers to pass it on. Over time, a rich array of rituals evolved around the binding of feet and the exchange of shoes among relatives and friends. These rituals – concealed from men in the women's rooms – celebrated the women's skills and became a focal point of female identity.
>
> (Ko, 2001, p. 17)

The development of rituals whereby women transmit harmful practices is common to many of the practices still undertaken today in the west, such as makeup and heels. Women teach their daughters. Ko extrapolates on these women's rituals: "The daughter's first binding took place in the depths of the women's quarters under the direction of her mother, sometimes assisted by her grandmothers and aunts: no men were privy to the ceremonial process" (2001, p. 54). The absence of men does not, as Mary Daly points out in *Gyn/Ecology* (1979), mean that men are not the enforcers of these practices, but it does enable their responsibility to be obscured. Ko compares this ritual with one she considers similar in the USA, "It was a solemn occasion marking the girl's coming of age, the first step of her decade-long grooming to become a bride – a prelude to a sweet-sixteen party" (Ko, 2001, p. 54). "Sweet-sixteen" parties are not necessarily innocuous and may represent pretty savage occasions in which girls are inducted into a painful femininity in the west. But Ko seems to see them as harmless, and thus her comparison to footbinding is rather lighthearted. Her description of how a girl's foot was to fit into the lotus shoe conveys a similarly upbeat approach: "The tip of the foot – the big toe – fits snugly into the tip of the shoe, but the arch of the foot is left comfortably alone. The vamp of some styles is so shallow that if not for the loops and laces attached to the topline . . . the shoe would not have stayed on her feet" (Ko, 2001, p. 99). Wang Ping, in *Aching for Beauty* (2000), is another contemporary feminist scholar of footbinding who chooses to stress the positive aspects of the practice, which, she considers, lie in the women's world of ritual that it created. She says that over a thousand years, "Chinese women transformed footbinding and writing – the two most oppressive patriarchal codes – into a female culture. They turned the binding into a bonding among women family members, relatives and friends" (Ping, 2000, p. 227). Bonding to swap survival tips under domination, though it may be necessary, constitutes accommodation to oppression rather than an example of women's agency and creativity that is worth celebrating.

THE BALLET SHOE

The excitement of contemplating women's pain and deformity may lie behind that symbol of high culture in the west: the ballet shoe. The shape of the ballerina's foot when it is en pointe is like that of the bound foot and the foot in high heels. Yet, in ballet, the woman is supposed to dance, and survive the pain and damage that results. It does seem likely that a large part of the pleasure that a male audience gets from this important western cultural practice derives from seeing women dance with the "grace" created by severely constricted feet, similar to the restricted gait of footbound women that so fascinated Chinese men. For some a knowledge of the pain and injury will enhance their enthusiasm for the practice. The Chinese emperor who encouraged a dancer to dance with bound feet in the eleventh century is a forerunner of the male ballet afficionado of today. The idea of dancing en pointe is supposed to have originated with the ballerina Taglioni in the early nineteenth century. As the ballet dancer Toni Bentley puts it, "at her debut in 1822, Taglioni brought classical ballet onto pointe, and it has stayed there, sometimes shakily and with much pain, ever since" (Bentley, 1984, p. 88). At that time ballet shoes were even more insubstantial than they are today so the agony must have been greater. Even today the shoes are completely unsuitable for such an athletic exercise, being entirely frail and with no support. The audience wants to see the ballerina as ethereal and full of grace rather than as an athlete, so she is not permitted to have a shoe that would offer support. This sort of shoe also, of course, satisfies the male foot fetishist audience. Bentley explains that toe shoes are not made from more lasting materials, "Because leather, rubber, plastic and synthetics are loud, clumsy, painful and, most important, ugly" (1984, p. 88).

The insubstantial nature of the shoes is clear in the fact that the professional dancer requires 12 or more pairs of shoes per week (Bentley, 1984). Before the shoe can be worn it has to be beaten into shape because it is so unsuitable for its task:

> A brand-new pair of toe shoes presents itself to us as an enemy with a will of its own that must be tamed. With the combined application of door hinges, hammer, pliers, scissors, razor blade, rubbing alcohol, warm water and muscle power – followed by repeated rapping against a cement wall – we literally bend, rip, stretch, wet, flatten a new shoe out of its hard immobility into a quieter, more passive casting for our feet.
>
> (Bentley, 1984, p. 88)

Bentley describes the "symbolic figure of the ballerina" as being created out of the pain of the early pointe shoes which she likens to the practice of footbinding: "The toe shoe of the nineteenth century bound the dancer's foot as the Chinese bound their infant daughters' feet and as laced corsets bound the bodies of fashionable women" (1984, p. 88). Before the 1950s, she explains, the shoes came in only one size, and each shoe was a "long narrow tube of satin-covered leather", which, "bound and squeezed the foot into the ideal esthetic – an inhumanly shaped minuscule pointe that did not remotely resemble the naked foot that entered it". The shoes of today, she points out, are not a great improvement, though they are wider and come in different sizes.

Bentley describes a visit by her ballet company to the London makers of their shoes. Regular visits were necessary because of the problems the shoes caused the women's feet. Each dancer had an individual, always male, maker, and the shoes could be changed to meet the deformities that had been created in their feet. Changes caused by ballet include, "the metatarsal has grown wider and flatter; various lumps, bumps, corns and calluses have grown, changed or been removed. Sometimes the heel of the shoe must be cut down to virtually nothing because of sore tendons, bone spurs or sensitive nerves on the lower ankles" (Bentley, 1984, p. 88). In a *Guardian* article in 2000 some of this damage is described: "Strip away the ballerina's satin slipper and you'll find a mess of bunions, blisters, corns and crooked toes' (Mackrell, 2002). The dancer Sarah Wildor says that the worst things for her are the corns that grow between her toes, due to the pressure placed on the bones. She trims the corns to keep them under control, but she has, "a really horrible soft one, between the fourth and fifth toes", whose only effective treatment would be an operation to shave the bone (Mackrell, 2002). A physiotherapist comments on the stress fractures suffered by ballerinas as a result of point work and jumping in shoes that do not absorb shock: "a scan will show up all areas of potential or actual stress fracture to the bone and, while a normal person's should reveal none, a classical dancer's will typically reveal several" (Mackrell, 2002). Judith Mackrell explains that masochism is part of the ballerina's image and thus, "We read with awe of Taglioni being drilled by her father to fainting point in order to master the technique of toe dancing, of Anna Pavlova exiting the stage and leaving a trail of bloody footprints" (2002). Wildor says that her feet are "agony really. During a performance the pain is the last thing on my mind but when I come off stage my feet are killing me" (Mackrell, 2002).

Foot fetishists covet used shoes because they symbolize the pain the wearers have suffered. The blood and the puss from blisters excite the shoe fetishists in audiences so that, "the most enthusiastic fans covet the worn, stained shoes in which a favorite dancer has performed" (Mackrell, 2002). This fetishism focused on the shoes was evident from the time of Taglioni. Her Russian fans allegedly cooked her slippers and ate them with a sauce (Carter, 2000, p. 81). This form of fetishistic behaviour is similar to that of devotees of lotus shoes, who would drink out of them, smell and taste them. The excitement that ballet shoes en pointe create in fetishists is evident in the fact that the most extreme "high heels" in the foot fetishists' armoury are called "ballet" heels. On the fetishist website set up by "Jenny" there is a photo of women's legs and feet in shoes whose heels present an ascending degree of difficulty. They start at 2.5 inches which is underwritten with the comment, "No problem these!", through, "Getting higher", "Practice needed", and "Fetish wear", to 8 inch "Ballet" Heels which are, "Not for me!" (Jenny, 2000). In "ballets" the foot is en pointe though there is a heel to back it up. Walking would be quite impossible, and in most of the foot fetishist pornography in which women are wearing these heels they are reclining. "Jenny's" site helpfully provides details of a variety of foot stretching machines in wood or metal that can be used to bend the arch. A woman is shown using one.

MEN'S DEMAND FOR HIGH HEELS

The reasons why men in western cultures today appreciate high heels resembles in many respects the attitudes of men in Imperial China towards footbinding. Rossi's book (1989) is a good illustration of why foot fetishists like himself demand that women wear high heels and of how they seek to enforce this through the demonization of any alternative. He says that women's shoes can be divided into four categories: sexy, sexless, neuter, and bisexual. His preferred category is "sexy" which he describes as requiring slim heels to make "the foot look smaller, the arch and instep curvier, the leg longer and shapelier, the hips and buttocks wigglier" (Rossi, 1989, p. 90). The shoes should be a skin-tight fit and have pointed or tapered toes since, "Square or round or stubby toe shapes, no matter how much in fashion, desexualize a woman's shoe and foot" (p. 90). He also sees "seminakedness" as an ingredient of the "sexy" shoe and writes of "décolleté" effects on shoes which the trade calls "throatlines". "Sexy" shoes expose what the designers and other fetishists call "toe cleavage" which replicates breast cleavage on the foot. The way in which he describes "sexless" shoes, which he clearly loathes with a passion, is representative of the hatred of "sensible" shoes in male dominant culture which forces women into disablement. Rossi says "sexless" shoes are "known by such names as 'sensible,' or 'comfort,' or 'orthopedic' shoes; or, in the trade, as 'old ladies' running shoes'" (1989, p. 93). The "sexless" shoe has "a drab, somber, lackluster look – low or flat heel, usually a mannish oxford or tie shoe, rounded or slightly bulbous toe . . . It has neither personality nor femininity. Just as a nerve is removed from a tooth to deaden it" (p. 93).

But Rossi gets himself into a confusion over who finds these shoes "sexless". On the one hand he says that the wearers are, "Mostly sexually turned-off women", who just happen to be, "women of certain religious callings or members of service organizations such as Salvation Army lassies, Mennonites and Amish; or women with serious foot ills. Then there are those women with psychosexual inhibitions or neurotic problems, who use their desexed shoes as a pedic chastity belt. Or butch-type lesbians who deliberately masculinize their appearance" (1989, p. 94). On the same page he says that "sexless" shoes are sexually stimulating to their wearers because they allow the foot "full-scale earth contact". He quotes a podiatrist to back him up with case studies and repeats this assertion elsewhere in the book. Women, it seems, feel much sexier in flat shoes and their sexual response is inhibited by the malformations created by high heels. According to this logic it is "sexually turned-off women" who wear high heels and not those who wear "sexless" shoes. The confusion is created by his identification of sexiness with his male foot fetishist sexual response to heels, which does not enable him to take seriously the damaging effects they may have on women's sexuality, health, mobility and safety. The only "sexless" shoe wearer he specifically names is Eleanor Roosevelt. Roosevelt, wife of the American president, was a strong feminist, responsible, among other achievements, for getting women's equality into the Universal Declaration of Human Rights in 1948 (Cook, 1992). She was also involved in a longterm relationship with another woman. She had her shoes specially made by an orthopaedic shoe manufacturer because comfort was important. She is a splendid role model for women, and not just in her attachment to sensible shoes. She had other things to do in her life besides providing men with sexual excitement.

Rossi's confusion over who the high heel is sexy for, continues later in the book when he asserts, with no evidence, that "Women derive a sado-masochistic pleasure in wearing them. The masochism stems from the foot distress and deformation the woman usually endures – yet a pleasurable pain in knowing the effects conveyed" (1989, p. 119). Unbeknown to them, women's high heels also represent sadism: "The sadism lies in the phallicism of the heel itself, as though the woman has taken possession of the male's genital powers" (p. 119). In fact the women are likely to be desperate to get home to take their shoes off and put their feet into a pleasurable bowl of hot water, a remedial practice that I have overheard women office workers in rush hour discussing on the London underground. Rossi says that the injuries that the shoes cause to women should, "from the woman's standpoint, more realistically be regarded as pleasure wounds or sex scars" (1989, p. 150). He is, apparently, privileged to understand the woman's viewpoint and knows that women have willingly engaged in foot deformation to give men and themselves pleasure.

On the other hand, Rossi points out, men gain a sadistic pleasure in "observing women in high heels" which comes from "viewing the insecurity and discomfort of women in these heels, forcing them to be more dependent upon masculine support" (1989, p. 121). What he calls the "erotic magic" of high heels comes from the way in which they "feminize" the gait by, "causing a shortening of the stride and a mincing step that suggests a degree of helpless bondage. This appeals to the chivalrous or machismo nature of many men" (p. 121). Moreover the male foot fetishist, but not the woman desperate to get them off, knows that the position of the foot in the high-heeled shoe, "simulates the reflex position of the foot during coitus, especially at the point of orgasm or ejaculation", and causes a "saucy backward thrust of the buttocks" (1989, p. 122). Many men,

Rossi contends, live in a weird fantasy world about the effect of these shoes on women. They believe that "high heels . . . also 'raise the sexual temperature' of a woman's genital area, and thus increase her sexuality. This, of course, has never been proven or tested" (p. 122). This is a similar degree and type of fantasy to that engaged in by male foot fetishists in China who thought that footbinding created layers in the vagina that made sexual intercourse more exciting. These sexual myths are uncannily similar east and west.

Sexual excitement from the unnatural gait that high-heeled shoes enforce on women, is one of the most important pleasures that men gain. Rossi offers considerable detail on this aspect and helpfully explains, "Just as a woman's walk can be sexualized, so also it can be desexed. The position or condition of the feet makes a huge difference in the 'sex level' of the walk; that is, whether the walk is sexually turned-on, turned-off, or merely neutral" (Rossi, 1989, p. 140). The "desexed" walk, "occurs when the feet are far apart to widen the base for more security in walking". It isn't sexy for men when women walk in a way that suggests they have two feet firmly on the ground. It is most exciting for them when women walk with their feet "very close together". This creates the "mincing step" that, Rossi tells us, is "associated with the age-old concept of female bondage" (1989, p. 142). Men have always sought to, "'confine' their women in one way or another", and this is represented in the "fetters-type walk" they have "forced" on women (p. 142). Men get excited, then, at seeing women walking like slaves in shackles. This walk can be achieved, Rossi explains, through tight skirts as well as high-heeled shoes: "The tight skirt, slit or unslit, has always been an almost universal costume, designed and worn to keep a woman's step short and delicate. Right up to the eighteenth century, bridal ankle chains or cuffs were used at wedding ceremonies, signifying the wife's traditional bondage to her husband" (1989, p. 142).

The high-heeled shoe creates another form of excitement for men by changing the posture of women and creating a new silhouette: "The body posture takes on the look of a pouter pigeon, with lots of breast and tail balanced precariously on a pair of stilts" (Rossi, 1989, p. 147). Rossi pooh-poohs the idea that the chief value of walking lies in, "exercise, mental relaxation and aesthetic enjoyment" (1989, p. 148). The "*chief* tonic value of female gait is as an erotic stimulant" for what he calls the "erotically enthralled audience" – that is, men. Women seldom walk, he says, rather, "They perform" (p. 148). He is not doing an early version of postmodern theory, that is, gender as performance (Butler, 1993) here but means that their only function in walking is to provide pleasure, in their injured and constricted gait, to men.

The most serious of foot fetishists get real pleasure specifically from the pain that women experience. Rossi says that, "Not a few men are sexually aroused to erection by observing women walk with obvious distress in tight shoes. One man confessed, 'Even when I hear a woman say her tight shoes are killing her – that's enough to bring an instant erection'" (1989, p. 155). Concern for women in the serious fetishist is conspicuous by its absence, thus one foot fetishist, who, according to Rossi, "perhaps spoke for most of his clan", said "You can cut off all the women of the world at the ankles. Give me the part from the ankles down and you can have all the rest" (1989, p. 172). This anecdote is reminiscent of the story from the history of Chinese footbinding of the rebel Zhang Xianzhong in the seventeenth century. When he occupied two provinces he, "had women's feet severed and piled them together to make 'the Peal of the Golden Lotuses'" (Ping, 2000, p. 32). One contemporary western foot fetishist had, "The big toes of [his] . . . wife . . . tattooed as an almost perfect replica of a penis. The fetishist uses these for simulated acts of fellatio" (Rossi, 1989, p. 215). He made part of his wife's body into a dildo with no concern for how this might affect her life. How would she feel on the beach? Those fetishists for whom the shoe alone is sufficient use them to ejaculate into from a distance. Such shoes are so high as to make walking impossible. Another use for the fetishist is the insertion of the heel into his anus, usually while on all fours (Finkelstein, 1996).

Men's foot fetish Internet websites are a useful source of information on the satisfactions men gain from high heels. The sites tend to be coy about the sex of their creators and contributors. In the case of J.J. Leganeur no identifying first name is used. On the site run by "Jenny" the sex of "Jenny" and those writing in the "discussion forum", despite the common use of female as well as male names, seems to be straightforwardly male. Many of the men, including Jenny and J.J., write of their own wearing of high heels as well as eulogizing about the wearing of high heels by those born female. They also write handbooks on how to train the feet to wear high heels and how to deal with the inevitable health problems attendant on this practice (Leganeur, 2000). These are apparently aimed at women but appear on close reading to be clearly aimed at men. Handbooks on how to wear heels seem to be a stock in trade of male high heel fetishists and it is hard to imagine that women would be drawn to such volumes. The writing has a similarly coy tone to that which appears on male to female transsexual sites and other transvestite sites. The detail suggests that the men who write this sort of material, and the men who read it, gain sexual satisfaction from it. For instance the reader is instructed by "Jenny", "Having found a pair of the correct height, put them on and stand up straight sideways on in front of a full length mirror. Incidentally, it is best to do this in the nude or wearing just a bra and panties. This will enable you to appreciate your body positions better. You will notice that your body weight or centre of gravity has been shifted forward" (Jenny, 2002). It does seem unlikely that women would be desperate for this advice, but men not brought up to wear heels might appreciate it, especially the detailed instructions on how to acquire the correct gait. "Jenny" specifically advises readers to buy shoes that are too small in order to prevent "toe jamming". It is precisely women's tendency to buy and wear shoes a size or half size too small that podiatrists rail against because of the damage it does to women's feet.

The high heel wearers are blamed for the problems the shoes create such as "tottering" in which, "the ankle oscillates from side to side when standing or walking. This is often the fault of the wearer, who has not developed enough strength or technique in her calves and ankles" (Jenny, 2002). Jenny tells readers that they should not consider running because this, "is a good way of breaking your ankle, heels, or both", but women may need to run. Jenny refers readers to other transvestite sites such as "Stephen at Tight Skirts Page". Male foot and shoe fetishists who get sexual excitement from what they see as "women's" accoutrements have created strong Internet networks through which they can link into thousands of sites suited to their specialized interests.

Shoe fetishism is not just a problem of heterosexual men. In the USA one homosexual men's foot and shoe fetishism organization, the Foot Fraternity, has 1,000 members. These homosexual fetishists are interested in masculine rather than feminine feet and footwear. A survey of 262 group members found that the main interests of these men were clean feet (60 per cent), boots (52 per cent), shoes (49 per cent), sneakers (47 per cent), and smelly socks (45 per cent) (Weinberg *et al.*, 1994). The researchers argue that homosexual foot fetishism resembles heterosexual foot fetishism in that it is about traditional gender differences. Heterosexual foot fetishism concentrates on the "evocation of *femininity*" through "high heels, stockings, etc." (1994, p. 618). They comment: "Thus both homosexual and heterosexual fetishism work by evoking *gender*. And it is culturally constructed gender differences that seem to lie at the base of sexual arousal in general" (p. 618). Two-thirds of the respondents had some interest in sadomasochism where the masculine footwear, "fits well into scenarios that emphasize dominance and power" (1994, p. 622).

THE HEALTH EFFECTS OF HIGH HEEL WEARING

The most important criterion for recognition of a harmful cultural practice is damage to the health of women and girls. It is this damage that justifies labelling such practices harmful, and in the case of the wearing of high heels the evidence of severe health damage is plentiful. Eight out of ten women who replied to a global shoe survey carried out by the American Academy of Orthopaedic Surgeons said their feet hurt, mainly because of high heels. The 2001 study found that 59 per cent of women wear uncomfortable shoes daily for at least an hour with "work" or "style" being given as the reason by 77 per cent. The most commonly reported sources of pain were callouses and heel pain (Ananova, 2001). Another 2001 study found that one in five women suffer painful feet because they wear shoes to please partners or employers. The study (BBC, 2001) found that one in ten would wear "uncomfortable shoes if they looked good". The results showed that although women follow fashion only one in three like wearing high heels. Over 80 per cent would not change the type of shoes they wore solely to alleviate a foot problem. One in six thought a correctly fitting shoe pressed the toes together. The British research team estimated that three out of four women may have a serious foot problem by the time they reach their 60s. The podiatrist who led the research said, "Improvements in women's foot health are only likely when healthy, well-fitting shoes become a norm for society, within or without the realms of fashion", but manufacturers, he said, did not make foot health a priority (BBC, 2001).

The serious health problems that result from the wearing of high heels, such as bunions, hammer toes, plus the shortening of the calf muscle and damage to the Achilles tendon that can make it impossible for women to walk without such shoes, give the male fetishists considerable satisfaction. A large part of J.J. Leganeur's site is dedicated to these problems. Messages from other fetishists are included on the site, and one correspondent writes, "I'd like to read some true stories about women that had theirs [sic] Achilles tendon permanently shortened. Could you tell me where I can find some to read?" (Leganeur, n.d.b). The problems section of the website has paragraphs on the women who are most likely to suffer from these problems and they are: "street-walking prostitutes and BDSM female submissives, who practice heavy bondage activities" (Leganeur, n.d.b). The BDSM (bondage and discipline, sadomasochism) submissives can be "made", presumably by their male partners, to:

> wear high heels all or most of the time. Some end up wearing high heels 24/7 . . . High heel shoes can also be locked on these women for days at a time. There are high heel shoes and boots that are made with padlocks and high heel shoe locking devices that are sold for bondage purposes . . . Standing in ballet boots press [sic] the calf muscles and Achilles tendons into their shortest size, usually making them sore. One of the reasons that ballet boots are made is to inflict punishment on those who wear them. Without sufficient padding, standing in ballet boots can even damage the toes, cause toes to bleed, lead to gangrene and require the toes to be amputated or chopped off.
>
> (Leganeur, n.d.b)

Leganeur gives a useful insight here into the interests of male sadists who torture women with these shoes and evinces a lipsmacking satisfaction with the pain involved. It suggests that behind the closed doors of some suburban homes in which men control women "slaves" very serious cruelty is taking place. In a 2004 case in Victoria a man was prosecuted for numerous crimes associated with keeping a woman as a slave in his garage, hosing her every couple of days with cold water in the yard. He was accused of forcing her, in front of his friends, to eat his faeces and stand naked on her head until she toppled onto carefully placed tacks, among other painful and degrading practices (Silkstone, 2004).

Cosmetic surgeons are developing a new and doubtless profitable specialism in cutting up or injecting women's feet so that they look better, particularly when they have become misshapen from wearing heels, or to enable the feet to fit into the fashionable heels of the moment. The surgeries they offer include, "shortening of the toes, narrowing of the feet, injecting the fat pad with collagen or other substances" (Surgicenteronline, 2003). A medical service called "CoolTouch", for instance, offers laser treatment to enable women to wear the crippling shoes with less pain. The treatment, which "plumps up the balls of the feet by stimulating collagen to form there", is described by a physician thus: "It's a laser that does not affect the epidermal layer, the top layer of skin. It causes destruction underneath. It stimulates collagen, the skin underneath [sic]; therefore, you're able to wear the shoes. The biggest problem is a burning under the ball of the foot" (*USA Today*, 2000). The treatment costs US$400 and lasts 3–6 months.

A website called Cosmetic Surgery Resource which provides patients with information on which surgeons specialize in particular practices tells women, "Cosmetic foot surgery is no joke. When sandal season comes, it's hard to enjoy it if gnarly toes make you hide. Sometimes foot surgery can relieve pain in addition to making your tootsies more attractive" (Cosmetic Surgery Resource, 2004). The surgery will most probably be performed to remove the deformities that high heels create, such as bunions. The website explains that after surgery women will have to, "spend a few days elevating your feet", because, "complications include post-operative infection, swelling or bleeding". The cost is US$5,000. Bunions are sometimes hereditary and do not necessarily cause pain except when forced into unsuitable shoes. They are also very likely to be the result of a lifetime of wearing high heels and women will seek treatment so that they can continue to wear such shoes.

Women can suffer terrible pain and disability from the surgery itself. A *New York Times* article describes the plight of a 60-year-old professor of speech pathology who undertook surgery to enable her to wear, at her daughter's wedding, the high heels she had abandoned because of the "searing pain" they caused. She had a bunion removed with the effect that: "The pain spread to my other toes and never went away . . . Suddenly, I couldn't walk in anything. My foot, metaphorically, died" (Harris, 2003).

She expects that she will never again be "able to walk barefoot or wear anything but specially designed shoes". The article explains that the professional podiatry association, American Orthopaedic Foot and Ankle Society (AOFAS) put out an official statement in December 2003 condemning unnecessary foot surgery. The AOFAS warns women that surgery should not be performed on feet for any reason apart from the alleviation of pain because the feet are so complex in their structure that a patient could completely lose the ability to walk. The article explains that more than half of the 175 members of the American Orthopaedic Foot and Ankle Society who responded to a recent survey said they had treated patients with problems that resulted from cosmetic foot surgery. Cosmetic foot surgery is being carried out in the UK too and a British foot surgeon warns that women should not seek treatment for bunions if they do not hurt: "Removing a bunion is a serious piece of surgery that involves slicing through the bone. There's a lot of pain. So I say, if it's not painful to start with, don't create more pain" (Lane and Duffy, 2004).

The podiatrists who are profiting from this cruel practice are unrepentant, however. Dr Suzanne Levine says that wearing high-heeled shoes is vitally important to women because they please men: "Take your average woman and give her heels instead of flats, and she'll suddenly get whistles on the street . . . I do everything I can to get them back into their shoes" (Harris, 2003). Such surgeons are not just performing surgery on conditions such as bunions and hammer toes, but on perfectly ordinary feet that their owners consider to be the wrong shape for high-heeled shoes and sandals. One problem they offer to correct is "Morton's toe", which is a long second toe that protrudes beyond the big toe. Apparently this, though entirely natural, is seen as unsightly in open-toed sandals or gets buckled when forced into unforgiving shoes, so surgeons cut them to make them shorter. Some women seek to get their little toes cut off, also, because they do not fit into the fashion shoes they wish to wear. There are clear parallels here with Chinese footbinding as women's feet are cut up to fit the expectations of men's foot and shoe fetishism. The savagery of this surgery, which can lead to serious difficulties in walking for life, is an example of the ways in which western beauty practices in the early twenty-first century have become more brutal and invasive.

WOMANBLAMING

Womanblaming is a common technique used to obscure the workings of male domination. It has been most used in relation to men's violence against women – that is, male criminologists, male lawyers, say that victims cause it by wearing the wrong clothes, or mothers cause it by being too clingy or too distant from their abusive sons, or wives cause it by being more educated than their abusive husbands (Jeffreys, 1982). All these explanations serve to divert attention from men's culpability and throw responsibility onto the subordinate sex class. The dominant class of men remains innocent and untouchable thereby. When women can be held responsible even when men's agency is clear, it is not surprising that womanblaming is particularly rife in relation to beauty practices where men apparently play no direct role.

The foot fetishist, J.J. Leganeur, resorts to womanblaming to explain footbinding. It was "not a matter of male domination at all" (Leganeur, n.d.a). In fact it was entirely and only to do with women:

> It was practiced by women. The mothers usually bound their daughters' feet . . . Chinese foot binding also has all the signs of a woman behind it. The process of foot binding is so horrifying and unwrapped bound feet are so grotesque that it would have frightened the hell out of any man. Foot binding was most likely invented or developed by a mother, who hoped that her daughter would marry an emperor or wealthy man.
>
> (Leganeur, n.d.a)

The radical feminist theorist Mary Daly explains that this womanblaming which disappears the responsibility of men is one of the criteria for recognizing what she calls "sado-rituals", which are enacted on women cross-culturally for men's delight. She says of footbinding: "Despite the blatant male-centeredness of this ritual, practitioners of the Rites of Right Scholarship allow themselves to write as if women were its originators, controllers, legitimators" (Daly, 1979, p. 140). She says that women are used in sado-rituals as "token torturers" with the result that "hate and distrust" are perpetuated among women. Daly calls the male scholarship which attributes responsibility to women "sado-scholarship", which is promoted to women in school textbooks, popular magazines and TV programmes and leads to "female self-loathing and distrust of other women" (1979, p. 141).

THE REVIVAL OF THE HIGH-HEELED SHOE

The high-heeled shoe lost some of its importance in western fashion in response to the feminist movement of the 1970s. Some of the gains women made at that time have been retained. "Sensible" shoes in which women can walk and run are available in shoe shops in fashionable styles. However in early 2002 the high street shoe shops in Melbourne were devoting the vast majority of their space to shoes with extremely high heels and very pointed toes – shoes to delight male foot fetishists and damage women severely. High heels had become, once again, high fashion, because the shoe fetishist designers brought them back. Devotees include fashion photographers such as Helmut Newton, the shoe designer Manolo Blahnik and the fashion designer Tom Ford who was quoted in Chapter 5 comparing women in high heels with baboons, who like to walk on tiptoe when they are feeling sexy.

Several male designers have contributed to the revitalizing of the extreme high heel as a trend in women's fashion, but the most famous is Manolo Blahnik. His shoes were publicized in television shows such as *Absolutely Fabulous* and *Sex and the City*. The extent of his fetishistic interest is clear in the fact that he is prepared to create shoes that cannot be worn: "the worlds's most adored shoemaker has created a pair of shoes so lethal that they will not actually go into production" (Tyrell, 2001. p. 5). The unwearable pair has a, "three-and-a-half-inch titanium heel tapering to a width of a mere one-tenth of an inch" (p. 5). For a serious foot fetishist the shoe is much more important than the woman. For Blahnik the shoe becomes a woman. He describes his shoes as if they are different types of women: "Now this one . . . is rather a chic woman. Very influenced by Marie Claire and Elle . . . This is a shoe for a Mediterranean girl . . . She's wearing a little Versace dress in lime. Tits pushed out . . . She's from Jaipur . . . She's come to Paris . . . A cocotte for our times" (McDowell, 2000, p. 125).

Blahnik says he needs to put care into designing the heel, not out of concern for the wearer but because if he does not make it correctly people will fall off and the shoe will not sell. The shoes are so fashionable that they have become compulsory for the women whose careers depend on them representing men's sexual ideals, such as Madonna. The pain and damage do not, apparently, matter to *Sex and the City*'s Sarah Jessica Parker, who is mugged in one episode for her Manolos. She says: "You have to learn how to wear his shoes; it doesn't happen overnight. But now I can race out and hail a cab. I can run up Sixth Avenue at full speed. I've destroyed my feet completely, but I don't care. What do you really need your feet for anyway?" (Tyrell, 2001, p. 5). Joan Rivers has said that Blahnik's shoes make her feel like a prostitute. She described his shoes as "slut pumps", adding, "You just put on your Manolos and you are automatically saying 'Hi, sailor,' to every man that walks by" (Tyrell, 2001, p. 5). Blahnik is a devotee of toe-cleavage, "And the secret of toe-cleavage – a very important part of the sexuality of the shoe. You must only show the first two cracks" (McDowell, 2000, p. 156).

Despite the fact that J.J. Leganuer is able to defend it, footbinding, if it continued today, is likely to be recognized by most as a harmful cultural practice. It fulfils all the criteria: it creates stereotyped roles for men and women, it emerges from the subordination of women and is for the benefit of men, it is justified by tradition, and it clearly harms the health of women and girl children. Though there are many similarities between footbinding and the wearing of high-heeled shoes it is unlikely that the latter practice would be commonly understood as a harmful cultural practice, even by those who do recognize that the west has a culture in which cultural practices can exist. This distinction is likely to rest on the issue of consent. It is clear that, as with female genital mutilation, a practice carried out on children cannot be consented to. Six- and seven-year-old girls have nowhere to go. They are dependent on those who require that they be mutilated. In theory adult women in the west can choose comfortable shoes, as Eleanor Roosevelt did. However, the continued importance of high-heeled shoes in fashion for women reflects the power of what Mary Daly calls the "sadosociety" (Daly, 1979), to require women to self-mutilate. High-heeled shoes, like the other practices of cutting up women's bodies that we will consider in the next chapter – breast implants, cosmetic surgery, piercing and cutting – can be understood as a form of self-mutilation by a group, women, with low social status (Jeffreys, 2000).

8

CUTTING UP WOMEN

Beauty practices as self-mutilation by proxy

In recent decades the beauty practices required of women and girls have become more and more invasive of the body. They require cutting, the shedding of blood and the placing of foreign objects under the flesh and skin. The degree of brutality involved is rather different from that of the 1960s and 1970s when the feminist critique of beauty practices was formed. At that time the creation of "beauty" was mostly confined to the surface of the body. Breast implants, for instance, have become a socially accepted aspect of beauty practices in American culture in the intervening period (Haiken, 1997). This practice is a severe form of mutilation of women's bodies. However, it is a practice that fits the rules of beauty as required under male dominance, and is thus not regarded with horror. As Andrea Dworkin points out, beauty practices frequently cause considerable pain and women are expected to suffer them according to the masochism that is thought to be "in their nature" (Dworkin, 1974).

Practices of self-mutilation which do not fit the rules of beauty, on the other hand, in which young women mutilate themselves in private, are seen as a reason for concern and socially undesirable (Favazza, 1996; Strong, 1998). What was once the private mutilation that women carried out in the privacy of their rooms as a result of abuse and low social status, became, in the 1990s, the basis of an industry of cutting and piercing, and a staple of men's pornographic diet on websites such as Body Modification Ezine (Jeffreys, 2000). Cutting and piercing, if carried out in studios by "artists", have now acquired the status of new everyday beauty practices. I shall argue here that there is a connection between private mutilation and those mutilations that are now part of the beauty industry and pornochic. All these practices are the stigmata of low social status. Women and other oppressed groups such as some gay men, are cutting up in private and in public, in socially acceptable ways such as cosmetic surgery and in ways that are not yet accepted, such as branding. They are carving into their bodies the hatreds of a woman- and gayhating society.

In the late twentieth century psychiatrists and psychotherapists noticed and sought to explain what appeared to be an epidemic of self-harm in western societies involving cutting, piercing, burning and in other ways damaging the body (Favazza, 1996). This epidemic, like the epidemic of eating disorders with which it is clearly linked (Shaw, 2002), affects young women in particular. It has been analysed by feminist practitioners and writers as an issue that seems very clearly to be linked to the condition of women, though male commentators have tended to ignore this aspect (Strong, 1998). Feminist analysis suggests that self-harm is connected with low social status and childhood or adulthood experiences of physical and sexual abuse. I have suggested elsewhere that practices in which women, and some men, request others to cut up their bodies, as in cosmetic surgery, transsexual surgery, amputee identity disorder and other forms of sado-masochism, should be understood as self-mutilation by proxy (Jeffreys, 2000). The proxy – such as the surgeon, the piercer in a piercing studio, the sadist – takes the role that in self-mutilation is more normally taken by the mutilator themselves, and in private. The proxy gains financial benefit, sexual excitement, or both, from carrying out the mutilation. Cutting up is mostly done to women but certain categories of men are also cut up and they will be considered here. As the practices of self-mutilation by proxy become more and more extreme it becomes increasingly necessary to subject them to political analysis and establish where limits may be drawn to prevent surgeons from aiding and abetting such self-harm.

SELF-MUTILATION

Self-mutilation is overwhelmingly a behaviour of girls and young women (Shaw, 2002). Its most common form is cutting with razors, or other sharp implements, of the forearm, though other areas of the body can be injured. It is related to childhood abuse. As Sarah Shaw puts it: "Studies abound linking childhood sexual and physical abuse and emotional neglect to the later development of self-injuring behavior" (Shaw, 2002, p. 193). It is a common behaviour. Marilee Strong estimates that 2 million young women in the USA regularly self-mutilate (Strong, 1998). The behaviour is usually carried out in private. Feminist analysis of women's self-injury suggests that it is engaged in to relieve the painful feelings associated with, "trauma, violations and silencing in a culture that fails to provide adequate opportunities for women's development, healing and expression" (Shaw, 2002, p. 201). The overwhelming majority of women in the ranks of self-injurers suggests that self-injury is associated with women's low status. Girls and women who have no outlet for the rage and pain they experience from male violence and abuse and from the other injuries of a male dominant culture, attack their own bodies. Often they are emotionally disassociated from their bodies, having learnt this technique to survive abuse. Self-mutilation breaches the barriers they have created and allows them to "feel". An increasing frequency of self-mutilation by young women fits into a context of increasing mental and physical health problems in teenage girls. The authors of an Australian study (Carr-Gregg *et al.*, 2003) say that risk-taking by girls in the form of marijuana use, binge drinking, smoking, unsafe sex and eating disorders is becoming more prevalent and at younger ages. Nineteen per cent of 12–13-year-old girls, for instance, are binge drinking weekly and the risk behaviour is symptomatic of psychological problems.

It is interesting, Sarah Shaw notes, that women's self-injury provokes social concern in a way that the injury of women by others or by themselves to accommodate the norms of fashion and beauty does not. Self-injury damages women's bodies in ways that men do not necessarily require for their sexual satisfaction and may even find offputting. Shaw sees women self-injurers as, "taking control of and objectifying their own bodies in ways that transgress cultural norms" (Shaw, 2002, p. 206). It is not, she says, "culturally tolerable for women to objectify and destroy their own bodies in ways that do not serve western aesthetics" (p. 206). Though some feminist analyses of self-injury almost seem to laud this behaviour as a form of positive resistance to patriarchy, Shaw does not: "In the end", she says, "self-injury undermines women's freedom, limits their possibilities and may blaze a trail toward suicide attempts" (2002, p. 209).

In the 1990s self-injury perpetrated by proxies became fashionable through the piercing, cutting and tattooing industry. The private self-mutilation born of despair and self-directed rage at abuse and oppression was exploited by piercing entrepreneurs. Piercing studios were set up in cities throughout the western world offering various forms of self-injury to make a profit for the perpetrators. The forms of injury provided by these studios and independent operators ranged from bellybutton piercings to the extremes of spearing straight through the torso as carried out by the Californian ex-advertising executive Fakir Musafar (Musafar, 1996). The practices stemmed from two main sources, punk fashion and gay male sadomasochism (Jeffreys, 2000). Commercial self-mutilation mainstreams the gay sadomasochism that once was seen as outré and transgressive by its exponents, and extends the practice to other social groups. It can be seen as the "mainstreaming-of-deviancy", one author argues (Leo, 1995). John Leo states unequivocally (p. 16) that: "The piercings of nipples and genitals arose in the homosexual sadomasochistic culture of the West Coast", and from the piercing shop The Gauntlet in particular. The Gauntlet by 1995 was a chain of three shops "about as controversial as Elizabeth Arden salons". "Rumbling through the biker culture and punk", Leo says, "piercing gradually shed its outlaw image and was mass marketed to the impressionable by music videos, rock stars and models" (1995, p. 16). I have argued elsewhere that the importance of sadomasochism in queer culture needs to be understood politically as arising from the loss of dominant masculine status that men suffer through homosexuality (Jeffreys, 2003).

Gay male fashion designers placed pierced models on their catwalks, and helped to inscribe a practice that had symbolized gayness, onto the bodies of conventional young women and some young men. The practices were enveloped in new age philosophy, said to be "tribal" in their reflection of the practices of African and other non-western peoples, and carried out by "modern primitives" (Camphausen, 1997). Rufus Camphausen in *Return of the Tribal* succinctly sums up the philosophy, "the great variety of practices aimed at adorning, beautifying, or even modifying the human body are the most ancient and most direct expression of human creativity, known and practiced all over the globe and at all times" (1997, p. 1). The practices can inflict quite extreme harm as in the "ball dances". Camphausen describes these as follows: "In recent years, more and more people have attended the 'ball dances' organized in various cities across the United States. Here, in the tradition of the Indian Taipusham festivals the more daring participants have balls hooked into their flesh and then dance until, as they say, the 'flesh rips'" (1997, p. 89). The devotees say the pain is "liberating" and "transforming".

However, the majority of those acquiring piercings and tattooings were simply being fashionable rather than deliberately pursuing pain and the mortification of the flesh. Camphausen argues that these practices of self-mutilation by proxy have gained social acceptance: "Once the domain of people at the fringe of society, tattooing (and piercing in its wake) is slowly becoming as accepted as lipstick and face-lifts" (1997, p. 2). A speaker at the annual meeting of the Society for Adolescent Medicine in San Diego in 2001 said, "What began with punks, gays, and Goths has now become fad and fashion for mainstream body piercing that we see in cheerleaders, jocks, nerds, and techies – in and out of school" (Brunk, 2001, p. 29).

An Australian study supports the notion that these practices are fashionable. It found that a high percentage of 14-year-old girls had piercings (Colman, 2001). Thirty per cent had ear piercings and 8 per cent had other parts of their bodies pierced. One in five women aged about 20 had had body piercing, excluding ears. Body piercing was less common among younger men, although it is notable that about one in eight younger men reported having undergone the procedure, and among men aged in their late 40s and early 50s, the prevalence of body piercing actually exceeded that of women. This may reflect, the study suggests, its popularity among older homosexual men. More young women than men, 7 per cent versus 3 per cent, said they had engaged in body piercing during the 12 months prior to the survey (Makkai and McAllister, 2001). Piercing represented very different values for the heterosexual young men, who sought to show how hard and masculine they were through mutilation in occupations such as the navy, or sought to join a subgroup in a prison setting. The study found that body decoration was "significantly associated with . . . injecting drug use" (Colman, 2001, p. 8), and injecting drug users "had their bodies pierced nine times oftener than the general population". This suggests that those engaging in one form of self-harm are likely to engage in another.

The practices of piercing and tattooing can cause severe physical harm and even medical emergencies. A professor of dermatology quoted in a piece called "Body Piercing and Branding Are the Latest Fads" says that "only 10%–15% [of piercings] get infected" (Donohue, 2000, p. 18). The majority of problems are caused by *Staphylococcus aureus* and *Streptococcus*. Another dermatologist who sees many pierced patients warns that infection with *Pseudomonas* can be dangerous: "Pseudomonas infection in the ear cartilage is an emergency" because it can "liquify ear cartilage" (Donohue, 2000, p. 18). Other problems included candidal infections of the navel and moist areas such as genitalia and the nose. Infections can arise from "trauma-induced tears". He warns that some patients should not have piercings because they form keloids or scar tissue and diabetic patients should not have piercings. Professor Goldman says that branding "hurts like hell", and "patients should be cautioned against branding themselves or their friends using paper clips or other metal objects", and "should be referred to someone who does it for a living" (Donohue, 2000, p. 18). Piercing has been known to cause a range of other infections including, "tuberculosis, tetanus, hepatitis, and toxic shock syndrome" (Hudson, 2001). Tongue piercing can create particular problems, such as "swallowing or inhaling the stud, deep cyst formation, scarring, damage to nerves and veins, and neuromas", as well as damage to teeth (Tongue Piercing, 2000, p. 22).

The normalization of body modification can create problems for those exponents of body modification who are motivated by the desire to demonstrate their "transgression" and "creative individuality". In its early days body modification was seen by its exponents as demonstrating radical politics. Piercing signified membership of the radical left. Shannon Bell explains the discomfort that mainstreaming caused for those wanting to show their outsider status. She chose to be tattooed to show her "separation from society" and "symbolic creativity" (Bell, 1999, p. 53). Having invested the pain and money to get tattooed Bell is worried that tattooing has become fashionable and that this erodes the rebelliousness of her gesture. She says of the new recruits having tattoos as part of a fad, "I am concerned that they are being duped into believing that tattoos have lost their stigma", and claims, "It takes a strong will and sense of self [identity] to withstand the blatant and piercing stares" (p. 53). She is reluctant to lose her understanding of herself as transgressive.

The mainstreaming of tongue piercing is revealed in a fundraising advertisement for Christian Aid in the *Guardian* newspaper in the UK in

1999. The photo in the advert shows a tongue protruding from lipsticked lips. The tongue is pierced and a small set of chain links hangs from the stud. The ad reads: "Wear your chain and let the world know you care about the Third World". Readers are asked to send in money to receive the chains, which do not have to attach to a piercing. They can wear them "on their clothing . . . with pride" (End Third World Debt, 1999). Christian Aid is an extremely respectable mainstream organization yet by 1999 it had adopted tongue piercing as a marketing motif. The organization saw no contradiction in expecting young women in the west to mutilate and chain up their tongues in order to unchain the poor countries of the world from debt. As many forms of body modification become normalized and available at the local chemist or studio, those seeking to be outcasts must engage in more extreme procedures and so body modification becomes more and more dangerous and destructive to the body. The outer reaches of body modification in the forms of castration and limb amputation will be considered later in this chapter.

SOCIALLY APPROVED SELF-INJURY

Cutting, piercing and tattooing have quickly become commonplace and socially acceptable among the new constituencies of young women and gay men, even though they are recent additions to the repertoire of beauty practices. It is not surprising then, as Sarah Shaw (2002) notes, that self-injury that is performed by proxies for the purposes of achieving the conventional beauty standards of this historical stage of male dominance is socially approved and has acquired a normative status presently in some areas of western culture. The most common form of severe self-mutilation by proxy is cosmetic surgery and this practice overwhelmingly affects women. I will examine and compare here the cases of two women who have been severely mutilated by cosmetic surgery in the fields of pornography and of art. One, Lolo Ferrari, is a French porn icon whose pimp involved her in more and more extreme mutilations. She died aged 30 after having 18 breast enlargement operations and numerous other forms of cosmetic surgery. There are thousands of websites devoted to her icon status. Orlan, on the other hand, is a French "performance artist" who has appeared in videos having extreme forms of cosmetic surgery performed on her body since 1990. She "performs" for the camera with stage scenery and the theatre crew in special costumes. Art critics use postmodern language to justify the mutilation of Orlan as transgressive and even as "feminism in action". I will seek to show the similarities between the forms of mutilation that these women have been subjected to, despite the apparent differences between the requirements of pornography and "art" for the mutilation of women.

Elizabeth Haiken, in *Venus Envy* (1997), shows how a revolution in social opinion and practice has normalized cosmetic surgery in American society. Between 1982 and 1992 the percentage of people in the USA who approved of cosmetic surgery increased by 50 per cent and the percentage who disapproved decreased by 66 per cent (Haiken, 1997, p. 4). The practice still overwhelmingly fulfils the criteria for a harmful cultural practice, with 80 per cent of the patients being women and the vast majority of surgeons being men. Cosmetic surgery, she says, began at the same time in the USA as the phenomenon of beauty pageants and the development of the beauty industry in the 1920s. Haiken points out that cosmetic surgery can be seen as an indication of the failure of feminist attempts to dismantle male domination: "Cosmetic surgery has remained a growth industry because, in greater numbers, American women gave up on shaping that entity called 'society' and instead turned to the scalpel as the most sensible, effective response to the physical manifestations of age" (1997, p. 172). Cosmetic surgery, as Haiken points out, was always about fitting women into the beauty norms of a sexist and racist society. Women who did not fit American norms had to cut up. Thus by the mid-century "Jewish and Italian teenage girls were getting nose jobs as high school graduation presents" (1997, p. 197).

Breast augmentation, however, is more recent than other types of cosmetic surgery and dates from the early 1960s. This places its origins in the so-called sexual revolution in which men's practice of buying women in prostitution was destigmatized through the ideology of sexual liberalism (Jeffreys, 1990, 1997b). The sex industry expanded swiftly in the USA through pornography and stripping. Breast augmentation was associated in the beginning with "topless dancers and Las Vegas showgirls" (Haiken, 1997, p. 246). The method of enlarging breasts for men's pornographic delight in this early period was silicone injections rather than implants. Strippers, Haiken tells us, were getting a pint of silicone injected into each breast through weekly injections. The origin of the practice lay in the prostitution industry created in postwar Japan to service US soldiers who found Japanese women too small for their taste: "Japanese cosmetologists pioneered the use of silicone . . . after such solutions as goats' milk and paraffin were found wanting" (1997, p. 246).

The effects on the health of victims of this harmful cultural practice were very severe. The silicone "tended to migrate". It could turn up in lymph nodes and other parts of the body and it could form lumps that would mask the detection of cancer. As Haiken comments: "At worst, then, silicone injections could result in amputation, and at the very least all recipients were expected to have 'pendulous breasts' by the time they were forty" (1997, p. 249). In 1975 it was reported that "surgeons suspected that more than twelve thousand women had received silicone injections in Las Vegas alone; more than a hundred women a year were seeking help for conditions ranging from discoloration to gangrene that developed anywhere from one to fourteen years later" (Haiken, 1997, p. 251). Silicone implants replaced injections but concerns about the health effects caused the American Food and Drug Administration to impose an almost total ban in April 1992. Women who received implants regularly lost sensation in their nipples after the surgery and suffered problems such as encapsulation when scar tissue rendered the breasts hard. Saline implants were favoured where silicone was outlawed. Nonetheless by 1995 when *Glamour* magazine asked men "'if it were painless, safe, and free, would you encourage your wife or girlfriend to get breast implants?' 55 percent said yes" (Haiken, 1997, p. 284). This figure does indicate where the pressure for women to have implants originates.

One impulse that underlies women's pursuit of breast implant surgery may be depression. Several studies have shown that there is an unusually high suicide rate among those who have implants. A 2003 Finnish study found that the rate was three times higher than among the general population (Kaufman, 2003). There is a controversy as to the reason for this high rate. Some researchers say it indicates that women who have implants are already depressed and have a tendency towards suicide. The high rate would then suggest that the surgery does not cure the depression. Indeed women might feel more depressed when they discover that large breasts do not make them feel better. Others say that the suicides may relate to the degree of pain and anxiety that women suffer because of the implants. Either way the suicide rate suggests that breast implants are not positively correlated with women's mental health.

The routinization of seriously invasive cosmetic surgery is evident in the discussion fora and message boards that the industry has set up in recent years to gain clients and encourage women to pay for their services. The message boards are sections of the websites of cosmetic surgery clinics and referral services. They are interesting because they demonstrate how forms of interaction that women have developed to deal with oppression – that is, gossip, sharing of experiences, encouragement and support – have been exploited to increase the profits of the industry. The discussions resemble a distorted form of consciousness-raising techniques. Women discuss their pain and distress but instead of this causing criticism of the process of exploitation in which they have been involved they support each other in going through with surgery and getting more. The boards are a consciousness-lowering medium.

One exchange, about tummy tucks, gives an impression of how serious the sequelae can be. Tenta writes that she had a tummy tuck 4 years ago, which "involved major complications". She had to go to hospital to have the "binder" cut off. She says, "At the time I had pubic area swelling and was told that it would go away. It has been 4 years and my pubic area still is swollen. I feel very uncomfortable and can't wear tights and usually purchase pants/skirts one size bigger" (Plastic Surgery Message Board. Tenta. Posted 4 June 2004). Danya replies that liposuction would probably solve the problem and explains that the mons pubis sometimes after a tummy tuck "gets pulled up because of the tension from having a nice flat tummy" (Plastic Surgery Message Board. Danya. Posted 6 June 2004).

Other problems that women discuss include swelling, bruising, pain, numbness, itching, smell, unwanted lumps, dents, and constipation. One woman, Calimom, complains on the Implantinfo Support Forum about pain: "My ps [plastic surgeon] has me massaging for 2–3 minutes every hour but today it really hurts. I'm very bruised and swollen below my breasts and it's starting to really burn there when I massage. Should I continue but just be gentler?" (Implantinfo Support Forum. Calimom. Posted 6 June 2004). On the same message board another woman, Emily, talks of the problems she has after both lipsuction and implants in her breasts after four days: "I was not expecting it to be this bad. Where my PS sucked out tissue on the side is just so painful. I just want to be able to wash my own hair, feed myself, and go to the bathroom alone . . . when should I really start feeling back to normal with pretty good usage of my arms? I don't know if I'll make it much longer!" (Implantinfo Support Forum. Emily. Posted 7 June 2004).

The surgeries that these women have had are the everyday practice of cosmetic surgeons in 2004. The message boards demonstrate the extent to which such surgery can now be the aspiration even of young teenage girls. A labiaplasty message board attached to lasertreatments.com has a message from a 14-year-old girl so desperate to have surgery on her labia and mons pubis that she has considered cutting up her own body:

> Hi I'm 14 and I've been wanting Labiaplasty too. (and lol I've gotten so mad I thought about taken the knife myself too!) It's bothered me for as long as I can remember and as much as guys say It's a turn-on I still hate it. . . . I was also looking into getting Liposuction of the Mons Pubis . . . and I know it seems weird to get liposuction there but I'm skinny but then fat there and it bothers me so much.
>
> (Lasertreatments.com. Kelly. Posted 16 January 2004)

Kelly is worried because her body is undergoing the ordinary changes of puberty. These can be frightening to young girls, particularly those with a tendency to eating disorders. Fortunately a woman responds to Kelly, telling her that it is normal for young girls of her age to be concerned about the way their body is developing and she should not consider altering it until she is fully grown.

THE PORNOGRAPHIC DEMAND FOR BREAST IMPLANTS: LOLO FERRARI

Ferrari is a woman who was constructed, and driven to her death, by men's pornographic demand for women with large breasts. Her life story serves as a grave example of the way men's fetish demands, in this case for large breasts, can be carved onto the bodies of women and the effect this can have on women's lives. Ferrari was in the *Guinness Book of Records* for possessing the biggest breasts in the world. They weighed one-eighth of her body weight. She died in March 2000, apparently of an overdose of prescription drugs. She had made several suicide attempts previously. She was born in 1963, had an unhappy childhood and was bulimic in her teens. Eating disorders frequently accompany other forms of self-mutilation in young women (Strong, 1998). Her first job was in a club as a waitress but by 1986 she was posing in porn magazines. She also posed topless for amateur photographers on the beach at Cannes. The cosmetic surgery operations began in 1990 after her marriage to Eric Vigne. Vigne sketched the results he would like to see for the surgeon and her chest was increased from 37 to 41 inches, her nose was reduced, her cheekbones accentuated, her lips filled with collagen and her eyes lifted. Her eyebrows were shaved and replaced with tattooed lines. There were more than 20 operations to come over the next 4 years with five to six surgeons operating on her. New implants took her chest size to 45 inches. Vigne befriended an aircraft engineer who made the mould that would be used for the silicone implants used to complete Ferrari's transformation into Lolo, which is the French slang term for "tit" (Greer, 2000; Henley, 2000).

Her pimp/husband, Vigne, was a transvestite interested in transsexuality. He had a fear of surgery so would not create the perfectly feminine face he wanted by cutting up his own. He used his wife as a canvass on which to create the extreme version of femininity that he found exciting. In this he bore some resemblance to the fashion designers who project exaggerated and degrading femininity onto women in their catwalk shows. Lolo's final implants contained 3.3 litres of silicone in each, taking her chest size to 51 inches. It is troubling that a cosmetic surgeon was prepared to do an operation that would create such damage. Vigne exhibited Lolo in night-clubs around Europe where thousands of men would go to see her breasts. He functioned as her pimp in various ways. He used her in porn films in the early 1990s and had a prostitution conviction for living off the immoral earnings of his wife. When he put her on display he would undo her dress to release her breasts, "'Three kilos,' he would say, pointing to one, 'drei kilos,' point to the other" (Peakin, 2000, p. 48). In one performance in 1999 Lolo fell from the stage unconscious. She was taking a great many drugs to anaesthetize herself and was unable to sleep easily because her breasts prevented lying on her front or back. Operations on her nose meant she had difficulty breathing. Just before her death she weighed only 48 kg. Lolo once said of the cosmetic surgery she had suffered: "All this stuff has been because I can't stand life. But it hasn't changed anything. There are moments when I disconnect totally from reality. Then I can do anything, absolutely anything. I swallow pills. I throw myself out of windows. Dying seems very easy then" (Henley, 2000).

Lolo chose her coffin some weeks before her death, but as it turned out she was found not to have committed suicide after all. Vigne, who was living off the earnings from the pornographic images compiled during her lifetime, was arrested by the French police on suspicion of her murder in March 2002. A new report by a team of three police scientists said that she had died of suffocation and not an overdose of prescription drugs as was previously thought (Henley, 2002).

William Peakin, however, in his article about Lolo's life and death, quotes Peter Stuart, managing editor of Rapido TV and an editor of *Eurotrash* which helped to pornographize Lolo, in order to engage in an exercise of womanblaming. Stuart says that the cause of her tragic life was her mother, rather than Vigne. He says that she was exploited by both men and women and "even exploited herself", but, "if you asked who caused her the most pain or damage in her life, Lolo would tell you it was her mother" (Peakin, 2000, p. 47). In fact in a search I performed the Rapido website is just one of over 10,000 which profit from pornographic photos of the dead woman. As we have seen in the case of other harmful cultural practices against women, they are blamed on women and the responsibility of men is made invisible.

Ferrari's experience may be the most extreme lengths to which breast implant sadism towards women can go, but there are other women following in her wake. The Australian magazine *NW*, which, like other women's gossip sheets, likes to cover the harmful practices carried out on celebrities, dedicated an article in 2001 to photos of women they considered to be seriously inconvenienced by what had been done to their chests (Renshaw, 2001). The UK model Jordan, had apparently had three "boob jobs" costing AU$28,350 leaving her frame "grossly out of proportion" with a size 32FF chest. The magazine helpfully includes a diagram showing how Jordan, on 20 cm heels, as she is pictured, has dangerously shifted her centre of gravity. Jordan's links with pornography are demonstrated by the fact that she "paraded around at Playboy king Hugh Hefner's 75th birthday party in London". She is an ex-Page 3 girl – the *Sun* newspaper's regular pornography page. A friend of the model explained, "Jordan admits she's always had low self-esteem and craves attention" (Renshaw, 2001, p. 20). In 1999 she took a drug overdose and her boyfriend left her over her "increasingly raunchy photo shoots" (Renshaw, 2002, p. 19). Jordan, with heavily collagened lips, is looking more and more similar to Lolo Ferrari. The US actor, Pamela Anderson, is going along the same path. She had breast implants taking her to a size 34D in 1989, and had them replaced by larger implants taking her to 34DD a few years later. She had the implants removed in 1999. In 2001 she had new implants put in and replaced these with larger ones almost immediately, according to *NW*. All this is despite the fact that she has had the problem of leaking implants (Renshaw, 2001, p. 21).

It is probably not surprising that the Spice Girls have been mutilated. The more closely a woman's occupation is geared to satisfying men's fetish imagination, as that of women entertainers is, the more likely it seems to be that they will have to have implants. Mel B had her first implants in 1999 and swiftly had another operation to increase the size (Renshaw, 2001). In 2001 she had the implants removed because they had hardened and she feared they would leak. She now, *NW* implies, has replacements that give her a much larger chest than previous versions did. Victoria Beckham apparently "hated her modest bust" as a schoolgirl and now "flaunts her vastly inflated chest". She had her first implants in 1999 and second in 2001 to size 34C. Her younger sister, we are told, had implants in 2002, paid for by "Posh", and at 24 had laser-resurfacing to combat wrinkes (Renshaw, 2001, p. 23).

The industry of sexually entertaining men requires that women have breasts large enough to satisfy men's breast fetishism. Anna Nicole Smith is an American former stripper who has become famous through her marriage to a rich man. Apparently the strip club which formerly employed her would only allow her to perform in less desirable hours because her breasts were not large enough. In 1990, at 22, she had two 450 cc silicone sacs implanted in each breast, increasing her bra size from 36A to 38DD. In 1991 the rich man, J. Howard Marshall, paid for another set of breast implants. Since then five further operations have increased her breasts to size 42DD. She has been "rushed to hospital three times for swelling and infection" (Renshaw, 2002, p. 18).

The body types featured in sexual entertainment spawn other forms of extreme mutilation of women besides breast implants. The hipster pants fashion, particularly as portrayed by Britney Spears, has led to a surge in lipo-surgery to create Britney-style flat stomachs. *NW* features a woman who undertook the 9-hour operation costing thousands of dollars because she was "so embarrassed by her belly" (Vokes-Dudgeon, 2002, p. 20). The patient, Hilary Coritore, explains, "I'd just like to feel proud of my figure, but right now I'm so ashamed of my belly – it just hangs there. Britney Spears has an amazing stomach, and I'd give anything to look like that. She wears all those low pants and I just wish I could have a stomach as flat as hers" (Vokes-Dudgeon, 2002, p. 20). In the operation she receives lipo-suction to her thighs and upper abdomen to help "show off" the tummy tuck which took place as follows: "A large 15cm-square slice of Hilary's belly is then cut off and thrown away. The whole area from Hilary's pubic bone up to her navel has been removed" (p. 20). She received breast implants at the same time to utilize the same incision. Cosmetic surgeons like to give the impression that they perform these mutilations for the sake of the women rather than to exploit women's low self-esteem to line their pockets. The surgeon in Coritore's operation says that "all my girls" in the compulsory "before" photograph of their almost naked bodies look "shy, timid and insecure", but, "the change I see in my patients in just a few days is so amazing" (Vokes-Dudgeon, 2002, p. 21).

Cosmetic surgeons seem to like to surgically construct their wives, as advertisements for their business, and, presumably, because they then have their favoured fetish objects easily available in their homes. One such is Ox Bismarchi who cut up his wife, Brazilian model Angela Bismarchi, ten times in 2 years (Renshaw, 2001, p. 28). He encouraged her to undertake more surgery and carried it out himself. He says: "When I look at her, I see my own creation." He is 25 years older than his 28-year-old wife. He gave her "Pamela Anderson-like breasts, a tiny waist and a totally flat stomach" as well as placing "non-absorbent gels" in his wife's "calves, lips and cheeks" (p. 28). He even gave her a dimple in her chin.

The cosmetic surgery carried out on women in the malestream entertainment industry is directed towards making them conform to men's sexual fantasies in order to earn their subsistence. In extreme forms women are made into freaks who cannot physically support the weight of their own breasts and whose faces are contorted masks, but the purpose is related to the dictates of the sexual corvée. The women are mutilated to provide feasts for men's eyes. In the case of the "performance artist" Orlan, the purpose, though still pornographic, is a little different. It is the process of cutting up her body, rather than its effects, that gives her fans satisfaction.

ORLAN – MUTILATION AS "ART"

Orlan's self-mutilation is usually represented as "art". However Orlan's "work" fits very well with other forms of mutilation of women in pornography and in pornographic culture. Her admirers, mostly French and male, can barely control their enthusiasm for her work, "By her daring, her radicalism, her incandescent and uncompromising passion, she sets thought on the contemporary body on deliberately tragic terrain" (Onfray, 1996, p. 39). Sarah Wilson says, "Orlan is O". She is, "The O in open. The O of other, as in the collective unconscious or obverse of ego. The religious O; the opening of lips; orifices; eyes; the double helix; the cell; the cold star; the O in chaos. *The Story of O*" (Wilson, 1996, p. 8). The most pretentious postmodern language is used by the apologists for Orlan's "art" so as to distinguish it from other forms of self-mutilation practice. Sarah Wilson employs postmodern theory to argue that: "The postmodern body is above all a text; yet Orlan cuts through her own skin, submits to the knife to create that text" (1996, p. 8). The feminist cultural studies theorist Susan Bordo is incisive in her criticism of the idea of body as text being applied to the damage done to women (Bordo, 1993).

Orlan has stagemanaged and performed as "art" numerous surgeries since 1990. In the operating theatre she wears designer clothing by Paco Rabanne and Issey Miyake and dresses the set and the performers in artistic costume. The surgeries are extreme even for cosmetic surgery. In Orlan's "art" many of the themes of this book come together – pornography, postmodern justification, fashion, cutting up. In the operations her ear is separated from her face, her skin from her flesh and her underchin hangs down almost entirely disconnected from her face. She undergoes extreme forms of mutilation of her face in which silicone implants are put in place not only in her cheeks but in her forehead so as to give her "horns". The aftermath of the operation is that Orlan's face is badly and painfully damaged. Wilson calls it, "Orlan's appallingly battered face covered with a rainbow of bruises" (Wilson, 1996, p. 16). The operations are videoed like any other pornographic performance but in this case the video is supposed to be "art". The operations were relayed live to the Pompidou Centre where "a round table of intellectuals were filmed reacting (uncomfortably) to the event" (1996, p. 11).

In the course of these surgeries Orlan ensures that scraps of her flesh are preserved so that they may become "reliquaries" that she can sell. As Kathy Davis expresses it, "these 'reliquaries' include pieces of her flesh preserved in liquid, sections of her scalp with hair still attached, fat cells which have been suctioned out of her face, or crumpled bits of surgical gauze drenched in her blood. She sells them for as much as 10,000 francs, intending to continue until she has 'no more flesh to sell'" (Davis, 1997, p. 171). This practice is similar to that of the porn model Houston, who we met in an earlier chapter, selling off the scraps of her labia left after her labiaplasty was filmed as pornography. "Art" and pornography are hard to separate here as female flesh is quite literally sold to male sadists.

The postmodern theorists who laud Orlan's work argue that she is a feminist and she says so herself. She supports cosmetic surgery, she says, because it enables women to make choices about their appearance. But she takes a stand against the "standards of beauty, against the dictates of a dominant ideology that impresses itself more and more on feminine (as well as masculine) flesh" (Orlan, 1996, p. 91). She understands that cosmetic surgery is, "one of the areas in which man's power over the body of woman can inscribe itself most strongly", but considers that it can be used to women's advantage, especially if the surgeon is a "feminist". A woman surgeon was engaged to operate on Orlan when male surgeons were not prepared to make Orlan "ugly" or wanted to "keep me 'cute'" (p. 91).

Orlan says she is "the first artist to use surgery as a medium and to alter the purpose of cosmetic surgery" (p. 91).

Orlan explains her performances by using that variety of postmodern feminist theory which argues that human beings can profitably become "cyborgs" – that is, incorporating some element of technology into the human body. She argues, for instance, that "the body is obsolete. It is no longer adequate for the current situation . . . We are on the threshold of a world for which we are neither mentally nor physically ready" (1996, p. 91). This is a world of technology that will affect the way humans live in their bodies and the form of human bodies. Thus she says, "My work is a struggle against the innate, the inexorable, the programmed, Nature, DNA (which is our direct rival as far as artists of representation are concerned), and God!" (p. 91). Kathy Davis explains that Orlan embodies a postmodern perspective which goes further than simply seeing the body as a social construction, "In her view, modern technologies have made any notion of a natural body obsolete . . . In the future, bodies will become increasingly insignificant – nothing more than a 'costume', a 'vehicle', something to be changed in our search 'to become who we are'" (Davis, 1997, p. 173).

There is another way of looking at Orlan's relationship to her body. Feminist critics have argued forcefully that the separation of mind from body, aka the mind/body split, is fundamental to the philosophy and practice of western male supremacy. In male philosophy the body is seen as weighing down the spirit. Men seek to separate from their bodies or control them, as they seek to control nature. Women are relegated to their bodies and to nature and are also subject to control. Masculine systems of science struggle with nature rather than working in harmony (Shiva, 1989). The body is represented in both Christian religion and existentialist philosophy as something that should be repudiated in favour of a higher state of being.

Orlan's work represents this misunderstanding. She creates a mind/body split and holds it up as transgressive. As a male admirer says, "This is the context of Orlan's work: the acceleration of man's mastery of nature" (Onfray, 1996, p. 35). In this case the nature in question is the body of a woman. She remarks, "My work is blasphemous. It is an endeavour to move the bars of the cage, a radical and uncomfortable endeavour!" (Onfray, 1996, p. 35). But in fact she can be seen as simply enacting the rules of male dominance, that woman's body must be controlled and punished. She fits perfectly into the sado-society, as Mary Daly (1979) describes it, and it is this that has occasioned her fame. If women artists want fame then the most surefire way to achieve this is to fulfil the requirements of the sadistic and pornographic scripts of male domination. Orlan used prostitution and pornography, for instance, to get noticed in her previous work. She provided kisses in exchange for money in one performance in 1977 and later held an exhibition entitled "Art and

Prostitution" (Wilson, 1996, p. 10). She wanted to exhibit a bed-sheet with semen stains on it and tried to get art dealers to engage sexually with her, but was unsuccessful. She is frequently partially nude in her performances, the easiest way for women to get noticed. In male dominant society women's work is not judged by the same rules that apply to men. To get men's attention women have to sexually objectify themselves. For male intellectuals who love to see women naked and cut up this seems to be effective. Orlan becomes an artist of genius instead of just another self-mutilating woman.

Orlan's performance requires disassociation, the practice of splitting the emotions off from the body that is a necessity for women and girls to survive the violation of child sexual abuse and prostitution (Herman, 1992). She advises her audience to disassociate from their feelings of distress when watching the surgeons mutilate her: "When watching these images, I suggest that you do what you probably do when you watch the news on television. It is a question of not letting yourself be affected by the images, and of continuing to reflect upon what is behind them" (Orlan, 1996, p. 84). She is anaesthetized to dull the pain of the surgery though, as she says, the procedures still cause her to suffer: "A few words about pain. I try to make this work as unmasochistic as possible, but there is a price to pay: the anaesthetic shots are not pleasant . . . After the operations, it is sometimes uncomfortable, sometimes painful. I therefore take analgesics" (1996, p. 92).

Orlan's experience is different from that of other cosmetic surgery victims who vie to undergo more and more extreme surgeries for pornographic attention, such as Houston or Pamela Anderson, only in that it is represented by her admirers as art. But some forms of pornography designed for elite male audiences have always been called art (Kappeler, 1986). It is likely that the consumers of Orlan's performances who see themselves as art afficionados share some characteristics with the male "devotees", ordinary pornophiles, who gain sexual excitement from pornographic websites which feature amputated women. In both cases women are cut up, and this is utilized by the male devotees as masturbatory material. Orlan may need to fool herself that she is engaged on a holier project but the effect on herself of the psychological damage created by disassociation, and on her admirers, may be little different. Orlan has become a heroine of the body modification movement of the 1990s and her practices of self-mutilation show considerable similarities with those engaged in by its members.

BODY MODIFICATION

In the 1990s, with the help of the Internet, the practice of self-mutilation by proxy developed into the "movement" of body modification. The current popularity of the practice of "body modification" is illustrated by the fact that my Internet search turned up 45,500 websites in response to this term in a search engine. In this "movement" that seems, like the rest of the piercing and cutting fashion, to owe its origins to punk, gay sadomasochism and now gothic culture, the mutilations are becoming very severe. Body modification extends to branding, penectomy and castration. Branding is increasing rapidly in popularity. Keith Alexander is a brander who started out as a piercer. He explains his craft: "Quickly removing the iron should result in a light scar. Leaving the iron in place . . . usually makes a heavier scar. Never push hard. Practicing on soft cardboard and room temperature chicken breast is a must. Vegetarian branders practice on Tofu. Really" (Alexander, 2003).

The major Internet resource for body modifiers is the Body Modification Ezine (BME, n.d.a). It shows the range of practices that are included under the umbrella of body modification. They become steadily more severe in their destruction of body tissue as time goes by. The site advertises piercers, cutters and branders with photos of their mutilations. The photos of mutilations serve as pornography for those who seek sexual excitement from seeing the blood and wounds. The site also works as a contact and networking site to put body modifiers in touch with each other and build the "body modification" community. The photos of modifications are arranged under a list of headings: piercing, which includes unusual ear piercings and "lobe stretching" plus "ear scalpelling", tongue piercing, nose piercing, eyebrow/bridge piercing, lip piercing, which includes "scalpelled and other large gauge lip procedures", navel piercing, nipple piercing, male genital piercing experiences, female genital piercing experiences, unusual piercing, which includes "uvula piercing" and "pocketing". The category of photos entitled Ritual/Culture includes a variety of suspensions in which people are hung from hooks through their flesh from backs or knees as in the "suicide suspension", and Lip Sewing. The category of scarification includes the "Burningskin Portfolio". The category entitled "Hard" includes such staples of gay sadomasochism as "castration play", "male chastity" and "cock torture play" among other forms of torture "play" on women.

There are other categories on offer which seem to target gay men, such as "Erotic heavy modded males", "Erotic pierced males", "Erotic tattooed males" and "Nailing", which is likely to be the gay sadomasochist practice of nailing the penis to planks of wood (see my discussion of this practice in Jeffreys, 1990). There is an implants category in which objects are placed beneath the skin, and a category of silicone injections (76 images), that will carry all the severe health risks that pertained to this practice when carried out on women's breasts in the 1960/1970s. There is "Tooth Art", Corsetry, Saline Injections into male and female genitals, Urethral Stretching and Penis Stretching, Urethral Reroutes, Subincision and Splitting of head and genitals including penises, Tongue Splitting and Uvula Splitting. There are photos of Female Nullo, and Eunuchs and Male Nullo which suggest castration and removal of genitals.

The body modification ezine site contains sets of photographs of heterosexual couples who met through body modification (BME, n.d.b). In one case the couple is kissing while suspended from hooks in their backs. In another set a body modification couple celebrate their marriage with an older grey-haired man, perhaps a parent, looking a little bemused at the modifications visible on the celebrants. Body modifiers only "transgress" social norms by attacking their own bodies. They marry just like other folks it seems. It is interesting to speculate on what will happen when they have offspring. Will the children be modified at an early age? Whole families of body modifiers could become members of the recently established "Church of Body Modification" in the USA that allows underage persons to become members with parental permission.

Body modifiers created the "Church of Body Modification" to give a spiritual dimension to their practices of self-mutilation (Church of Body Modification, 2003). Members "practice an assortment of ancient body modification rites which we believe are essential to our spiritual salvation". The Church is "currently awaiting nonprofit status from the Internal Revenue Service" (Church of Body Modification, 2003).

> The Church of Body Modification is the spiritual hub in which modified individuals around the world will find strength and procure the respect from society as equal intelligent, feeling human beings. Modified individuals will no longer be dismissed as a minority in our world. We have a voice and strong spiritual connection with our modifications. It is now that we will take back our traditions, whether old or new, and own our bodies so that we may practice our body rites. This is our birthright.

The Church campaigns for legislation that will protect the practice of body modification and prevent discrimination, such as an employer dismissing an employee because of a piercing or other form of visual modification. Interestingly there is a connection between the Church and cosmetic surgery. A co-founder of the Church, Steve Haworth, was "originally a designer and manufacturer of medical equipment (for plastic surgery)" (Steve Haworth, 2004).

Gay sadomasochism provides one important route through which "body modification" was mainstreamed. Sadomasochist symbolism of black leather and studs came to symbolize gayness in the 1970s and 1980s (Woods, 1995). Practices of mutilation in performance art, though represented as "transgressive", can be seen as demonstrating the abuse and oppression suffered by some gay men and their despair at the ravages of the AIDS epidemic. The work of the performance artist Ron Athey is typical. Athey is an "openly HIV-positive", "queer performer" who "presents his own infected body and performs upon it. He displays his pierced and tattooed skin, . . . is whipped . . . and then . . . his body is pierced onstage in front of you, right in your face, blood dripping onto the plastic-covered floor' (McGrath, 1995, p. 23). He also has his lips sewn together.

One particularly brutal variety of self-mutilation by proxy currently being carried out by men on each other is castration. This seems to be an offshoot of gay sadomasochism. One practitioner has been "convicted of castrating men for their sexual pleasure" in the USA (McKenna, 2003). Shuo-Shan Wang apparently started his career as a castrator in Australia where he performed four castrations on men before going on to a career of performing 50 over a few years. In the Australian case, because Wang was new to practising surgery, the procedure was practised on a dog before the castration of the dog's owner and his three friends. Though the men could be said to have consented to this amateur surgery, the dog was not in a position to. In the American case the victim was found wandering and bleeding in the road after the surgery and this led to Wang being charged with "practising medicine without a licence and dispensing prescription medicine without a licence" (McKenna, 2003). Wang found victims by advertising his services on "the website of an international network of men whose fetish is in having their testicles removed" (McKenna, 2003). The ability of the Internet to spawn forms of self-mutilation is once again in evidence. Wang did not charge for the 40-minute procedure and "shared some dessert with his patient before sending him on his way" (McKenna, 2003). It seems likely that Wang's payment lay in his pleasure in carrying out the procedure without anaesthetic for the satisfaction of both.

The most extreme form of "body modification" presently in vogue, besides amputation of genitals, is the amputation of limbs. The desire to have limbs amputated is overwhelmingly a male preoccupation. Recently "wannabes", those seeking limb amputation, have created a political movement to demand toleration, and limb amputation surgery on the public health service. This strategy carefully replicates that of the transgender movement. To this end the desire has been renamed Amputee Identity Disorder by its main proponents, psychotherapist Gregg Furth who is a "wannabe" and Scottish surgeon Robert Smith, who has carried out two voluntary leg amputations (Furth and Smith, 2002). The doctors and psychiatrists involved are most often those who have previously operated on or diagnosed patients identified as having "gender identity disorders". In 2000 the first book and the first documentary appeared in which amputation surgery is represented as a reasonable demand of an oppressed minority (BBC, 2000).

SELF-MUTILATION AND SOCIAL STATUS

The practices of mutilation that are being carried out on the bodies of women, girls and vulnerable categories of men in the early twenty-first century are savage and increasing in their brutality. Underlying the demand for these practices is the despair of those with low social status, particularly women and gay men. The harms of misogyny, sexual and physical abuse and gayhating, create the ability of those who self-mutilate to disassociate emotionally from their bodies, and to blame their bodies for their distress. The mutilations of Ferrari, Orlan and Ron Athey are crueller than nineteenth-century freak shows and should not be justified as art or performance. Rather, it is necessary to work out how to stop this epidemic of self-harm. These mutilation performances are the result of social harms and those who carry them out, as well as those men who watch them with sexual excitement, are both parasitic on these harms and help to perpetuate them.

Internet technology has provided a method by which the forms of mutilation can escalate through an online community of those who struggle to survive abuse and despair. Body modifiers now have a means to turn their private self-mutilation into an activity which will gain them positive recognition. More and more extreme practices are required to get the same attention. As I have explained elsewhere, male gay sadomasochism has connections with the harms of being sexually and physically abused, as well as bullied and harassed through childhood (Jeffreys, 2003). Though there is no reliable research on the connection between child abuse and adult sadomasochism there is some anecdotal evidence. Adult self-hating gay men sometimes do not consider their bodies worth anything but punishment and this can extend to death. The leading defendant in a famous trial of sadomasochists, the Operation Spanner case in the UK, remarked to an interviewer, Chris Woods, that he would not have minded if the branders and piercers had killed him. He was doing SM because of a "painful relationship with my father", and: "At one point I even got into the idea of being tortured to death" (Woods, 1995, p. 53). He suggested that "someone who's mentally fucked up" needs not torturing but "help". Woods comments that the defendants were "middle-aged, pre-liberation homosexual males, some of whom despised themselves so much that their pursuit of SM was an attempt at self-obliteration" (1995, p. 53).

The men who contacted the German cannibal, Armin Meiwes, seem to fit this category too (Wild, 2003). They were also prepared to be obliterated and one, Bernd-Juergen Brandes, was killed and eaten. Meiwes found his victim through cannibal discussion sites on the Internet and stated that there were thousands of cannibals in contact with each other through this medium. The Internet is crucial to the growth and spread of all forms of body modification. A forensic psychologist, Keith Ashcroft, saw the Meiwes case to be an example of extreme sadomasochism and connects the removal and consumption of the victim's penis, by both parties, to Body Dysmorphic Disorder, which, he says, also leads people to want to remove their legs – that is, amputee identity disorder (Wild, 2003). He says that disassocation, "where the person doesn't feel connected to the body and doesn't feel connected to the world", is a part of BDD. Disassociation is learnt most effectively through sexual and physical abuse in childhood when children seek to escape the abuse (Herman, 1992). Interestingly, Ashcroft also likens the sort of fetishistic behaviour that Meiwes engaged in with shoe fetishism: "It's a horrible anxiety – like any fetishes are, whether for shoes or anything else – that brings stress and worry. There is no joy in it" (Wild, 2003). Traditional psychologists do not offer social and political explanations for the behaviour and are likely, as has traditionally been the case in psychology and psychiatry (Jeffreys, 1982), to blame women for men's violence and the self-harm of victims. Only feminist psychologists (Herman, 1992; Shaw, 2002) offer such insights. Thus Ashcroft says that Meiwes' mother was "domineering" and his victim, Brandes, blamed himself for the death of his mother in a car crash (Wild, 2003). Such explanations conceal the forces of male dominant cultures that create these harms, and the violent behaviour of men which is most likely to underlie them.

As we have seen earlier in this volume definitions of what constitutes the behaviour of Body Dysmorphic Disorder look alarmingly like exaggerated versions of what is culturally required of women in everyday beauty practices – that is, excessive and compulsive checking in mirrors and adjustment of appearance (Phillips, 1998). The forms of mutilation that are socially approved because they make women more sexually attractive to men, cosmetic surgery and some forms of piercing and tattooing, are usually separated out from the wave of self-mutilations of more extreme or unusual varieties involved in body modification. It is not clear to me that they should be, however. The seriously invasive surgery involved in breast implantation, for instance, would be considered savage if it was carried out at a body modification convention. When it is done by surgeons in the name of relieving the supposedly ordinary distress of women about their appearance it can be seen as unremarkable. The connection between amputee identity disorder and cosmetic surgery is usefully made by Dan Edelman who asks: "When in both cases the language used implies a sense of Otherness with respect to one's body, wherein lies the difference in the decision to remove a 'foreign' limb versus tucking the tummy or lifting the face of a body that is not a 'home'?" (Edelman, 2000). In the face of an epidemic in the west of increasingly severe forms of self-mutilation it may be time to ask how the attacks on the body may be stopped. The fashion, beauty, pornography and medical industries which justify and promote these forms of self-harm are parasitic on the damage which male dominant western societies enact on women and girls and vulnerable constituencies of boys and men.

CONCLUSION

A culture of resistance

The practices I have examined in this book show that western culture is not "progressive" in comparison with non-western cultures in the cultural requirements for women's appearance. The enforcement mechanisms are likely, however, to be less severe, as women are not usually beaten in the street or in their families for failure to comply. But in the severity of their impact on women's health and lives the western practices fulfil the United Nations criteria for recognizing harmful traditional/cultural practices very well. Though recognition of these practices as harmful traditional/cultural practices does not offer an immediate solution it can help to clear away those veils of mystification that represent what western women are required to do to their bodies as just fashion, or medicine or choice. A growing understanding that these western practices are both culturally constructed and harmful will found the development of a culture of resistance.

Western beauty practices fulfil the first and most important criterion for a harmful traditional/cultural practice – that they should be harmful to the health of women and girls. There is little doubt, for instance, that cosmetic surgery practices that are becoming more and more brutal, lead to health problems and death. The death of Olivia Goldsmith, the US author of the novel on which the movie *First Wives Club* was based, shows that women are not protected by wealth or social privilege from destruction in the fulfilment of their sexual corvée (Kingston, 2004). She suffered a heart attack from a bad reaction to the anaesthetic during a routine cosmetic surgery procedure to tighten skin on her neck. The US sociologist, Deborah H. Sullivan (2002), explains in her book on American medicine's development of the cosmetic surgery industry that it is hard to establish figures for death and injury. However she describes the research carried out by the *Sun-Sentinel* newspaper in Florida into malpractice insurance claims, lawsuits, autopsy records, and newspaper accounts to establish the numbers of serious incidents of death and injury from cosmetic surgery in that state alone (Sullivan, 2002). They discovered that in the 26 months before the end of their research period, first quarter of 1999, there were 18 deaths. It may not be unreasonable to compare this rate of death and injury with those that result from practices such as female genital mutilation.

Unlike FGM, cosmetic surgery is not universal, but it is becoming more and more common and diverse in its forms. In the twenty-first century cosmetic surgery has become so normalized that a mainstream television show, *Extreme Makeover*, has a large primetime audience. In the American version people compete to have large numbers of severe surgical procedures carried out on their bodies to make their appearance more culturally acceptable (Moran and Walker, 2004). The Australian version is now being planned. There are forms of serious damage from other beauty practices too such as piercing and cutting, and the wearing of high-heeled shoes. Hammer toes, bunions, calf and heel injuries are indisputably harmful. There are likely to be less easily identifiable costs to mental health too from having to carry out everyday beauty practices and wear sexually objectifying costume in the street and at work.

Western beauty practices do not only arise from the subordination of women but should perhaps be seen as the most publicly visible evidence of that subordination. The crippling of feet, for instance, indicates the brutal strength of male dominance. That western beauty practices are for the benefit of men should be clear from the evidence of the innumerable websites on which men scream their demands that women get mutilated and celebrate the sexual stimulation this gives them. Some of the practices are newly savage or even new in kind but they resemble those practices that have traditionally been required of women in many cultures and which demonstrate women's lowly status. They unmistakably create the sexual difference that is such an important function of harmful cultural practices. They are justified by tradition, as in the popular wisdom that women have always wanted to be beautiful and that it is natural for men to be attracted to "beautiful" women. They are blamed on women and the role of men in enforcing and demanding these practices is concealed.

There is, however, a major difference in the way that harmful beauty practices are inscribed in culture and enforced on women in the west. This is the fact that they have been constructed into major industries that make large fortunes for transnational corporations and are a significant force in the global economy. The profitability of these practices to the cosmetics, sex, fashion, advertising and medical industries creates a major obstacle to women's ability to resist and eliminate them. There is so much money in these industries based on commercializing harmful cultural practices that they constitute a massive political force that requires the continuance of women's pain. The cosmetic surgery industry in the USA, for instance, is estimated to be worth US$8 billion yearly (Church *et al.*, 2003). While in non-western cultures harmful practices are enforced by families and communities they are not usually the foundation of huge and immensely profitable industries. They are perhaps therefore easier to identify and easier to target. Education can be used to change attitudes in the campaign to eliminate them. In the west these industries have political and economic clout and education will not be sufficient. In the place of religion and family the full force of powerful capitalist industries occupies cultural space.

A newly confident, mainstreamed and increasingly profitable international sex industry is a relatively new player in the business of beauty. But it has had very serious effects already in the pornographization of culture and the demand for more savage, invasive and brutal beauty practices. The international sex industry is becoming a more and more important market "sector" and is estimated by a 1998 report from the International Labour Organization to be worth 2–14 per cent of the economies of some Asian countries (Lim, 1998). The pornography and prostitution industries intersect with the entertainment and advertising industries to create images of women in the clothing and poses of prostitution on billboards, music videos, and mainstream television programmes such as *Sex and the City*. This cultural saturation with women as sexual playthings creates a powerful force to compel women to fulfil their sexual corvée. The gloves are off. More and more what is understood to be "beauty" is recognizably the look of prostitution.

In the west women are supposed to be empowered, possessed of opportunities and choices unimaginable only a generation ago, yet these same women are hobbled by clothing and shoes, maimed by surgery in ways that the feminist generation of the 1970s could not have imagined. Indeed much of the surgery is being conducted precisely on women of that 1970s generation as they discover that the sexual corvée knows no age boundaries. There is no longer a retirement age from this arduous, unpaid labour.

The new savagery of beauty practices may result from men having great difficulty adjusting to the change in relations between the sexes that women's new opportunities bring. Men's problems in adapting to women's greater equality are clear from the invigoration of the sex industry. Research on sex tourism shows that the men see their sexual access to obviously unequal unempowered women as a compensation for the dominance they feel they have lost over women in the west (O'Connell Davidson, 1995). Mail order bride company websites offer western men obedient and humble women from countries like Russia and the Philippines where dire poverty can command deference. In the west the threats that men face to their total cultural, political, economic dominance can be compensated for by the invigorated and newly brutalizing sexual corvée that women are having to demonstrate in streets and workplaces. Women may have the right to walk in public, and the right to work outside the home, but they must show their deference through their discomfort and pain. The cost is high.

For a culture of resistance to be created women need not only to recognize the harm to their health and status that beauty practices create, but to be prepared to abandon them. There are good reasons why even some feminists seek to justify beauty practices or downplay their significance. They may have, like most women, routinely watched what they ate, removed hair from their bodies and faces, worn "feminine" clothing as if it were natural, applied lipstick, for 30 or more years. The simple familiarity of beauty "rituals" might make them hard to identify as causes for concern, despite the physical and mental distress that they occasion, and the more and more serious forms that these practices are taking as botox takes over from anti-ageing cream, liposuction from panty girdles, and Brazilian waxing is added to the shaving of armpits and legs.

The feminist philosopher Sandra Bartky (1990) shows a sensitive awareness of why it can be difficult for women in general to criticize western beauty practices. She explains that women become locked into dependence on what she calls "the fashion–beauty complex" because it instills in them a sense of their own deficiencies, like "the church in previous times" and then "presents itself as the only instrument able, through expiation, to take away the very guilt and shame it has itself produced" (Bartky, 1990, p. 41). It offers "body care rituals" which are like sacraments. The effect is that women so locked into the fashion–beauty complex see feminism as both threatening "profound sources of gratification and self-esteem" and attacking "those rituals, procedures, and institutions upon which many women depend to lessen their sense of bodily deficiency" (p. 41).

The feminist critique of beauty practices, Bartky explains, "threatens women with a certain de-skilling, something people normally resist" (1990, p. 77). Women spend a great deal of time and money learning and practising to be beautiful. Especially if they feel they have mistressed this well, it may be difficult to accept that it was all for naught, and the skills have no value. Also women may be reluctant to "part with the rewards of compliance" which may have included male attention (p. 77). Feminism may threaten such women with "desexualization, if not outright annihilation", if their understanding of their value to others and themselves has been founded on beauty practices (p. 77). It is possible for women, Bartky says, to argue that makeup and all the practices of femininity are their individual choice because there are no obvious institutions requiring obedience to the dictates of beauty from women. Thus, "the production of femininity" can seem "either entirely voluntary or natural" (1990, p. 75). This, she says, leads to the "lie in which all concur", that: "Making up is merely artful play; one's first pair of high-heeled shoes is an innocent part of growing up and not the modern equivalent of foot-binding" (p. 75). But Bartky is at pains to make clear that the lack of formal sanctions does not mean that women "face no sanctions at all". Women face a "very severe sanction" under male dominance; that is, "the refusal of male patronage" (1990, p. 76). This may mean for the heterosexual woman, "the loss of a badly needed intimacy" and for both heterosexual women and lesbians, "the refusal of a decent livelihood" (p. 76). It may mean that she will find herself an outcast and unable to fit into the important social networks through which she has defined herself.

Bartky's work emerged from the powerful women's liberation movement of the 1970s when women all over the western world met in consciousness raising groups to examine the politics of personal life, and in particular the way that western beauty culture made them hate their bodies and engage in damaging beauty rituals. In 1973 I gave up beauty practices as part of that movement, supported by the strength of the thousands of heterosexual and lesbian women around me who were also rejecting them. I stopped dyeing my hair "mid-golden sable" and cut it short. I stopped wearing makeup. I stopped wearing high heels and, eventually, gave up skirts. I stopped shaving my armpits and legs. I have not gone back to these practices even though the political climate has changed and the strength of the women's liberation movement is no longer there to support the rejection of these cultural requirements.

The political culture of the 1980s and 1990s was the heyday of rogue capitalism. In support of this, governments deregulated business, reduced the role of states and told citizens they were consumers bearing the power of choice to control their lives. The popular political philosophies of the times reflected these ideas precisely. One was the liberal feminism of women like Naomi Wolf who told women they could "choose" to be powerful (1993). Another was the version more fashionable in the academy, a postmodern feminism that told women they had agency and could be empowered, once again by choice (Davis, 1995). Susan Bordo explains that both these parallel philosophies echoed the consumer culture of the time as exemplified in the Nike "Just Do It" advertisements (Bordo, 1997). Women were strongly discouraged from looking at the material forces that constrained their lives. During this time women were likely to say that they wore makeup for "themselves" or "for other women". It was considered churlish to remark that they might engage in beauty practices because they were required in a male supremacist culture to service men's interests rather than their own.

But times change. As Susan Bordo expressed it in 1997: "Freedom. Choice. Autonomy. Self. Agency. These are powerful words in our culture, fighting words. But they are also words that are increasingly empty in many people's experience" (p. 57). In the twenty-first century a strong anti-globalization movement is challenging the idea that citizens are given any real power through consumer "choice", and is mounting an opposition to the power of transnational corporations to profit from oppression and pain in many forms that can readily include the beauty industry. The new era that is beginning may offer new possibilities for women to reject beauty practices, and find the strength to counter the negative consequences that they may face. Susan Bordo says of women's ability to reject or embrace beauty practices that: "To act consciously and responsibly means understanding the culture we live in, even if it requires that we are not always 'in charge'" (1997, p. 51). *Beauty and Misogyny* has sought to aid women's understanding of western beauty culture and enable such responsible action. Bordo encourages women to act by saying that, "Seemingly minor gestures of resistance to cultural norms can lay deep imprints on the lives of those around us" (1997, p. 64). She points out that the opposite is also true. When women encourage their daughters to go to slimming clinics, for instance, that gesture of "capitulation" will have negative effects. It will be easier for women to come out from under the rule of western beauty practices when a new and supportive feminist movement emerges to support such resistance. But even without this development women can refuse their sexual corvée. The more that women resist and the further they push this resistance the easier it will be for other women to join in. These gestures of resistance will help to create the world beyond beauty practices.

Opposition to beauty practices, however, should not simply be the responsibility of individuals. The UN Convention on the Elimination of All Forms of Discrimination Against Women (CEDAW; UN, 1979) requires states to take action to counter the cultural attitudes that underlie harmful cultural practices. The countering of such attitudes will require state regulation or elimination of the powerful industries that play such a significant role in creating them.

It is the responsibility of governments to regulate the practices of the medical profession since it is clear that self-regulation does not prevent the practices that surgeons are prepared to carry out from escalating in harm. As Deborah Sullivan argues, those members of the medical profession who are promoting and profiting from cosmetic surgery are motivated by greed, and taking medicine back to the nineteenth century when quacks were able to practise through fraud and deception with serious risks to health for monetary gain (Sullivan, 2002). The medical profession is involved through cosmetic surgeries, whether for beauty purposes or for what is commonly called "sex-reassignment" surgery, in political/cultural regulation. The expression "sex-reassignment" actually expresses this political purpose quite well. Those who are unhappy within one status category are reassigned, by medical practitioners as agents of the state, to a new one. I have argued elsewhere that this surgery needs to be understood as a violation of human rights for this reason (Jeffreys 1997a). It is political surgery in the same way that lobotomies carried out on homosexuals in the gayhating 1950s in the west have been identified as surgery for a politically oppressive purpose. Though cosmetic surgeries that create artificial hymens, for instance, may be understood as political/cultural regulation, carried out to fulfil the cultural requirements of women's degraded status, the political/cultural role of breast implant surgery or labia mutilation carried out on western women may not seem so clear but the impetus is the same.

It may be because the medical profession can be such an effective handmaiden of male dominance that its activities are likely to escape critical scrutiny and regulation. However, the medical profession can be required to restrict its activities to the creation and maintenance of health, rather than being permitted to expand its role as an arm of the fashion–beauty complex. Regulation would lead, of course, to discussion of whether some cosmetic surgeries are necessary to assuage the mental agony associated with having an imagined physical flaw. Such discussions have taken place in the Netherlands where breast implant surgery is permitted at public expense when it is deemed necessary for mental health (Davis, 1995). The problem with recognizing mental distress as a reason for surgery is that the medical profession is just one element of an apparatus that creates that distress in the first place. The very promotion of surgical solutions leads to an expectation that culturally proscribed physical attributes should be excised or altered. Medicine both follows the dictates of culture, as in the creation of artificial hymens or big breasts, and creates those dictates. When the degree of damage that the surgeons are prepared to inflict reaches the stage of breast implants, labiaplasty, limb amputation, or "sex-reassignment" surgery there is good reason to introduce legislation to stay the surgeon's hand.

There is another area in which state intervention could counter the attitudes that underlie harmful beauty practices. I have sought to demonstrate throughout this book that the international prostitution industry, particularly in the form of pornography, has been a powerful motor force in the production of savage surgical beauty practices in the last two decades. But it has produced harmful fashion and everyday beauty practices too. The normalization of the pornography industry has led to a fashion requirement that young women provide men with unpaid sexual titillation in public space through adopting the dress codes of prostitution.

There are good grounds for prohibiting the production of pornography that go beyond its role in the creation of beauty practices. The harms of pornography include the experience of the women, girls and young men used in its production; that is, the insertion of men's penises, fingers, arms in their mouths, vaginas and anuses over many hours while they dis-associate emotionally or take drugs to survive. This practice of pornography constitutes a form of sexual violence in itself (Jeffreys, 2003). The harms also include the damage done to the status of all women and to the possibility of relations of equality between women and men. So far as beauty is concerned, the pornography industry and the wider international sex industry construct contemporary cultural requirements for how women's faces, breasts, bodies, genitals, clothes and shoes, should look. This has far-reaching implications for women's mental and physical health and for the possibility of women's equality. States that are concerned with women's equality can choose to regulate and seek to end the commercial sexual exploitation of women in pornography and prostitution. Sweden has done this for prostitution by introducing legislation penalizing the "buying of sexual services" in 1999 (Ekberg, 2004). This legislation can be expanded to cover pornography.

The ending of the sex industry that could be achieved by penalizing men's demand would go a long way towards the creation of a culture in which women can thrive and have dignity. Another element in the creation of the present culture of self-harm for women in the west is the advertising industry that relies on sexism to sell a great many things, including beauty products and practices, to women. Feminist theorists such as Susan Bordo (1993) have pointed out the power of this industry in creating harm for women. Cultural change will require a serious attempt by states to regulate advertising so that it is not the most potent source of the attitudes that CEDAW speaks of, those that underlie harmful cultural practices.

What would a world without harmful beauty practices look like? In such a world the creation of sexual difference/deference through appearance would become obsolete. Women would not be required to perform their sexual corvée. The practices of physical care that they exercised on their bodies would not be directed to servicing men's sexual interests. They would not need to engage in any of the practices of femininity that cause women so much physical pain, expense and expenditure of mental and temporal energies. Depilation and makeup would become unnecessary. Women would be able to wear comfortable shoes suited to their activities – standing, walking, running for the bus. If women chose to wear skirts then this would be explicitly for the comfort they offered, and their suitability for certain activities rather than because they were compulsory. As the wearing of skirts became less common, fewer girls and women would have to spend time worried about how to place their legs when sitting, about whether anyone could see their knickers, about whether they would be revealed on a windy day or when bending over.

In fact in the future beyond harmful beauty practices women might not have to concern themselves so often in a day with what their clothes were doing, such as whether they were showing too much breast cleavage or too little toe cleavage. A look in the mirror in the morning could be cursory before they strode or skipped out of the house without caring who looked at them or what they saw. All these things are presently the privileges of men, but they could be gained by women. It should not be a privilege only of men to be barefaced, to walk with both feet on the ground, swinging arms or with hands in capacious pockets that serve instead of handbags, uninterrupted, while ruminating on the day, by the regulatory comments, whistles and stares of men. Indeed some women already live as if they have this freedom and so help to create it for others. The word "dignity" is much used in the Universal Declaration of Human Rights (UN) and in the international human rights community. It is worth considering what this word might mean if it were applied to women's appearance, to clothes, shoes, hair and faces. The physical and mental freedoms that the ending of harmful beauty practices offer to women are worth campaigning for.

The elimination of harmful beauty practices requires an overturning of the culture of sexual difference/deference. Sexual difference/deference is the very basis of western culture and envisioning a world beyond it is challenging. Male domination may not survive the public dismantling of the signs of this difference/deference because it is necessary to male dominance that the subordinate sex class of women can be identified. Identifiable sexual difference is also a pleasure to men, as the psychologist Flugel pointed out in 1930. The removal of this compulsory requirement that women sexually service men in public spaces is likely to meet with great resentment and resistance. Men will lose something valuable, and women have a great deal to gain. Sexual difference is not biological, but a cultural requirement to show and maintain women's subordination. If there is to be a serious advance in the status of women in the west then this bastion of male dominance will have to be breached.

REFERENCES

ABGender (n.d.). America's Most Popular Transgender Resource and Shopping Directory. Retrieved 17 September 2002 from http://www.ABGender.com/

Abu-Odeh, Lama (1995). Post-Colonial Feminism and the Veil: Considering the Differences. In Olsen, Frances E. (ed.) *Feminist Legal Theory*. Volume I. Aldershot: Dartmouth, pp. 523–534.

Adams, Gerald (1985). Attractiveness through the Ages: Implications of Facial Attractiveness Over the Life Cycle. In Graham, Jean Ann and Kligman, Albert M. (eds) *The Psychology of Cosmetic Treatments*. New York: Praeger, pp. 133–151.

Adult Video News (2000, July). Houston on EroticBid: Pussy Debut Busted by Cops. Loose Lips. Rocco and the Stripper. Retrieved 12 February 2004 from http://www.adultvideonews.com/archives/200007/loose0700.html

Adult Video News (2002a, August). The 25 Events That Shaped the First 25 Years of Video Porn. http://www/adultvideonews.com/cover/cover0802_01.html

Adult Video News (2002b, August). Innerviews. Getting Her Jolly's and Looking For More. Retrieved 12 February 2004 from http://www/adultvideonews.com/inner/iv0802_01html

Afshar, Haleh (1997). Women, Marriage and the State in Iran. In Visnathan, Nalini, Duggan, Lynn, Nisonoff, Laurie and Wiegersma, Nan (eds) *The Women, Gender and Development Reader*. London: Zed Books, pp. 317–320.

Alexander, Keith (n.d.). Keith Alexander's Modern American Bodyart. Retrieved 12 October 2003 from www.modernamerican.com/aboutb.htm

Alter, Gary (n.d.). Remodelling of Labia Major and Pubis. Retrieved 24 September 2002 from www.altermd.com/female/Publis.htm

Ananova (2001, 19 September). High Heels Still Biggest Cause of Women's Foot Pain. Retrieved 6 October 2001 from http://www.ananova.com/news/story/sm_402596.html?menu=

Anders, Charles (2002). *The Lazy Crossdresser*. Emeryville, CA: Greenery Press.

Avedon, Richard (1998). *The Naked and the Dead. Twenty Years of Versace*. London: Jonathan Cape.

Bahr, David (1998, 22 December). Eye Candy. The *Advocate*, p. 59.

Barry, Kathleen (1995). *The Prostitution of Sexuality*. New York: New York Uuniversity Press.

Bartky, Sandra Lee (1990). *Femininity and Domination. Studies in the Phenomenology of Oppression*. New York: Routledge.

Bell, Shannon (1999). Tattooed: A Participant Observer's Exploration of Meaning. *Journal of American Culture*, Summer, 22, 2: 53–58.

Ben-Tovim, David I., Walker, Kay, Gilchrist, Peter, Freeman, Robyn, Kalucy, Ro and Esterman, Adrian (2001, 21 April). Outcome in Patients with Eating Disorders: A 5-year Study. The *Lancet*, 357, 9264: 1254–1257.

Benjamin, Harry and Masters, R.E.L. (1964). *Prostitution and Morality*. London: Souvenir Press.

Bentley, Toni (1984). The Heart and Sole of a Ballerina's Art: Her Toe Shoes. *Smithsonian*, June, 15: 88–89.

Bergler, Edmund (1987). *Fashion and the Unconscious*. Madison, CT: International Universities Press. (Original work published 1953)

Blanchard, Ray (1989). The Concept of Autogynephilia and the Typology of Malegender Dysphoria. *The Journal of Nervous and Mental Disease*, 177, 10: 616–623.

Blanchard, Ray (1991). Clinical Observations and Systematic Studies of Autogynephilia. *Journal of Sex and Marital Therapy*, 17, 4, Winter: 236–251.

Blanchard, Ray (1993). The She-Male Phenomenon and the Concept of Partial Autogynephilia. *Journal of Sex and Marital Therapy*, 19, 1, Spring: 69–76.

Blank, Hanne and Kaldera, Raven (eds) (2002). *Best Transgender Erotica*. Cambridge, MA: Circlet Press.

Blow, Isabella and LaChapelle, David (1998, September). The New Surrealists (stylist Isabella Blow and photographer David LaChapelle) *Interview*. Retrieved 5 March 2002 from http://www.findarticles.com/cf_0/m1285/n9_v28/21076317/p1/article.jhtml

Body Modification Ezine (n.d.a). BME Site Map. Retrieved 4 June 2003 from http://www.bmezine.com/sitemap.htm

Body Modification Ezine (n.d.b). Couples Who Met through BME. Retrieved 4 June 2003 from http://www.bmezine.com/ritual/love5.htm

Bomis: The Lipstick Fetish Ring (n.d.) Retrieved 24 February 2004 from http://www.bomis.com/rings/lipstick/

Bordo, Susan (1993). *Unbearable Weight. Feminism, Western Culture and the Body*. Berkeley, CA: California University Press.

Bordo, Susan (1997). *Twilight Zones: The Hidden Life of Cultural Images from Plato to OJ*. Berkeley, CA: University of California Press.

Bornstein, Kate (1994). *Gender Outlaws: On Men, Women and the Rest of Us*. London: Routledge.

Brady, Shirley and Figler, Andrea (2003, 11 August). Porn Sent Packing. *CableWorld*. Media Central Inc., p. 31.

British Broadcasting Corporation (BBC) (1997, 20 July) Cutting Up Rough. *The Works*. Arts Documentaries for BBC2. Retrieved 14 June 2002 from www.bbc.co.uk/works/s3/mcqueen/subinfo/shtml

British Broadcasting Corporation (BBC) (2000, 17 February). Complete Obsession. *Horizon*. Retrieved 18 February 2004 from www.bbc.co.uk/science/horizon/1999/obsession_script.shtml

British Broadcasting Corporation (BBC) (2001, 6 March). Feet Suffer for Fashion.

BBC News. Retrieved 5 June 2002 from http://news.bbc.co.uk/1/hi/health/1205560.stm

Brownmiller, Susan (1984). *Femininity*. London: Paladin.

Brunk, Doug (2001, 1 September). Body Piercing Considered Mainstream by Adolescents. *Family Practice News*, 31, 17: 29.

Burns, Janice Breen (2003, 26 July). Thought for the Day. Quote of the Week. *The Age*. Melbourne, Australia: John Fairfax Publications.

Butler, Judith (1990). *Gender Trouble: Feminism and the Subversion of Identity*. New York & London: Routledge.

Butler, Judith (1993). *Bodies that Matter: On the Discursive Limits of "Sex"*. New York and London: Routledge.

Califia, Pat (1994). *Public Sex. The Culture of Radical Sex*. Pittsburgh, PA: Cleis Press.

Callaghan, Karen A. (ed.) (1994). *Ideals of Feminine Beauty. Philosophical, Social, and Cultural Dimensions*. Westport, CT: Greenwood Press.

Camphausen, Rufus C. (1997). *Return of the Tribal: A Celebration of Body Adornment, Piercing, Tattooing, Scarification, Body Painting*. Rochester, VT: Park Street Press.

Cardona, Mercedes M. (2000, 27 November). Young Girls Targeted by Makeup Companies; Marketers Must Walk Fine Line Not To Upset Parents. *Advertising Age*, 71: 15.

The Carnal Knowledge Network (n.d.). Personal Grooming. Removing Unpleasant Or Unsightly Hair! Retrieved 4 December 2002 from www.carnal.net/public/module/html

Carr-Gregg, Michael R.C., Enderby, Kate C. and Grove, Sonia R. (2002, June). Risk Behaviour of Young Women in Australia. *Medical Journal of Australia*, 178, 12: 600–604.

Carter, Keryn (2000). Consuming the Ballerina: Feet, Fetishism and the Pointe Shoe. *Australian Feminist Studies*, 15, 31: 81–90.

Carvel, John (2002, 13 July). Women Still Earn Half As Much As Men, DTI Admits. The *Guardian*.

Castleman, Michael (2000, 6 September). Porn-Star Secrets. Salon.com. Retrieved 19 October 2002 from http://archive.salon.com/sex/feature/2000/09/06/hair_removal/print.html

Church of Body Modification (n.d.). Retrieved 4 April 2003 from www.churchofbodmod.com

Church, Rosemary, Weaver, Lisa Rose and Cohen, Elizabeth (2003). Plastic Surgery Becoming More Common. *Insight*. CNN International. Cable News Network. Retrieved 1 March 2004 from http://web.lexis-nexis.com.mate.lib.unimelb.edu.au/universe/document?_m=afd02569d2d87f8b74404858889f4f4e&_docnum=1&wchp=dGLbVtz-zSkVb&_md5=137bf02dfeeb444546f3470e48ae2d0f

Cindoglu, Dilek (1997). Virginity Tests and Artificial Virginity in Modern Turkish Medicine. *Women's Studies International Forum*, March, 20, 2: 253–262.

Colman, Adrian (2001, September). Body Piercing. *Youth Studies Australia*, 20, 3: 8.

Confessore, Nicholas (2002, 7 February). Porn and Politics in a Digital Age. *Frontline. American Porn*. Public Broadcasting Service. Retrieved 4 October

2003 from http://www.pbs.org/wgbh/pages/frontline/shows/porn/special/politics.html

Cook, Blanche Wiesen (1992). *Eleanor Roosevelt.* New York: Viking.

Coomaraswamy, Radhika (1997) Report of the Special Rapporteur on Violence Against Women, Its Causes and Consequences, Ms Radhika Coomaraswamy. E/CN.4/1997/47. Retrieved 28 February 2004 from http://www.unhchr.ch/Huridocda/Huridoca.nsf/TestFrame/043c76f98a706362802566b1005e9219?Opendocument

Coomaraswamy, Radhika (2002). Cultural Practices in the Family that Are Violent Towards Women. Report of the Special Rapporteur on Violence Against Women. E/CN.4/2002/83. Retrieved 28 February 2004 from http://www.unhchr.ch/Huridocda/Huridoca.nsf/TestFrame/42e7191fae543562c1256ba7004e963c?Opendocument

Corinthians (1957). *The Bible, Authorized Version.* London: The British and Foreign Bible Society.

Cosmetic Surgery Resource (n.d.). Cosmetic Foot Surgery. Retrieved 21 January 2004 from http://www.cosmeticsurgeryresource.com/Cosmetic-Foot-Surgery.html

Daly, Mary (1979). *Gyn/Ecology: The Metaethics of Radical Feminism.* London: The Women's Press.

Davies, Jessica (2001, 20 April). A Vogue for Porn. *The Times.*

Davis, Kathy (1995). *Reshaping the Female Body: The Dilemma of Cosmetic Surgery.* New York: Routledge.

Davis, Kathy (1997). "My Body is My Art". Cosmetic Surgery as Feminist Utopia? In Davis, Kathy (ed.) *Embodied Practices: Feminist Perspectives on the Body.* London: Sage.

Dellinger, Kirsten and Williams, Christine L. (1997). Makeup at Work: Negotiating Appearance Rules in the Workforce. *Gender and Society*, April–May, 11, 2: 151–178.

Delphy, Christine (1993). Rethinking Sex and Gender. *Women's Studies International Forum*, 16, 1: 1–9.

Devor, Holly (1999). *FTM. Female-to-Male Transsexuals in Society.* Bloomington and Indianapolis: Indiana University Press.

Doezema, Jo (1998). Interviews NWSP Coordinator, Cheryl Overs. In Kempadoo, Kamala and Doezema, Jo (eds) *Global Sex Workers. Rights, Resistance, and Redefinition.* New York and London: Routledge, pp. 204–209.

Donohue, Maureen (2000, 15 February). Body Piercing and Branding Are the Latest Fads. *Family Practice News*, 30, 4: 18.

Dorkenoo, Efua (1994). *Cutting the Rose. Female Genital Mutilation: The Practice and Its Prevention.* London: Minority Rights Publications.

Dr Becky (1998). Janice Raymond and Autogynephilia. Retrieved 10 October 2002 from http://www.drbecky.com/Raymond.html.

Dworkin, Andrea (1974). *Woman Hating.* New York: E.P. Dutton.

Eagleton, Terry (1996). *The Illusions of Postmodernism.* Oxford: Blackwell.

The Economist (2003, 24 May). Special Report: Pots of Promise – The Beauty Business. *The Economist*, 367, 8325: 71.

Edelman, Dan (2000). The Thin Red Line: Social Power and the Open Body.

Cambridge Scientific Abstracts. Retrieved 5 June 2002 from www.csa.com/hottopics/redline/oview/htm

Egan, Timothy (2001, 23 October). Wall Street Meets Pornography. *New York Times*.

Eicher, Joanne B. (2001). Dress, Gender and the Public Display of Skin. In Entwhistle, Joanne and Wilson, Elizabeth (eds) *Body Dressing*. Oxford and New York: Berg, pp. 233–252.

Ekberg, Gunilla (2004). The Swedish Law that Prohibits the Purchase of Sexual Services. Best Practices for Prevention of Prostitution and Trafficking in Human Beings. *Violence Against Women*, 10, 10: 1187–1218.

Ellis, Henry Havelock (1913). *Studies in the Psychology of Sex. Volume 2. Sexual Inversion*. Philadelphia, PA: F.A. Davis.

Ellis, Henry Havelock (1926). *Studies in the Psychology of Sex. Erotic Symbolism, the Mechanism of Detumescence and the Psychic State in Pregnancy*. Philadelphia, PA: F.A. Davis.

End Third World Debt (1999, 15 June). End Third World Debt. A Radical Statement. The *Guardian*.

Enloe, Cynthia (1989). *Bananas, Beaches and Bases: Making Feminist Sense of International Politics*. London: Pandora.

Ephesians (1957). *The Bible, Authorized Version*. London: The British and Foreign Bible Society.

Erickson, Kim (2002). *Drop-Dead Gorgeous. Protecting Yourself from the Hidden Dangers of Cosmetics*. Chicago, IL: Contemporary Books.

Eriksson, Marianne (2004). Draft Report on the Consequences of the Sex Industry in the European Union (2003/2107 (INI)). Brussels: European Parliament, Committee on Women's Rights and Equal Opportunities.

Etcoff, Nancy (2000). *The Survival of the Prettiest. The Science of Beauty*. New York: Anchor Books.

Evans, Caroline (2001). Desire and Dread: Alexander McQueen and the Contemporary Femme Fatale. In Entwhistle, Joanne and Wilson, Elizabeth (eds) *Body Dressing*. Oxford and New York: Berg, pp. 201–214.

Evans, David T. (1993). *Sexual Citizenship: The Material Construction of Sexualities*. London: Routledge.

Express (2002). A Model Shows Off an Outfit by New Designer Award Winner Toni Maticevski at the Melbourne Fashion Festival Yesterday. Picture: Simon Schluter. *The Age*. Melbourne, Australia: John Fairfax Publications, p. 16.

Fallon, Patricia, Katzman, Melanie A. and Wooley, Susan C. (eds) (1994). *Feminist Perspectives on Eating Disorders*. New York: Guilford Press.

Farley, Melissa, Baral, Isin, Kiremire, Merab and Sezgin, Ufuk (1998). Prostitution in Five Countries: Violence and Post-Traumatic Stress Disorder. *Feminism and Psychology*, 8, 4: 405–426.

Farrow, Kevin (2002). *Skin Deep. A Guide to Safe, Chemical-Free Skincare and Cleaning Products*. Melbourne, Australia: Lothian Books.

Fashion Icon (2002). Everything You Always Wanted to Know about Bikini Waxing . . . But Didn't Know Who to Ask. Retrieved 11 September 2002 from http://www.fashion-icon.com/brazil.html

Favazza, Armando (1996). *Bodies Under Siege. Self-mutilation and Body*

Modification in Culture and Psychiatry. Baltimore and London: The Johns Hopkins University Press.

Finkelstein, Joanne (1991). *The Fashioned Self*. Cambridge: Polity Press.

Finkelstein, Joanne (1996, 30 August). Heel! *The Australian Financial Review Magazine*. Sydney, Australia: John Fairfax Publications.

Fitzmaurice, Eddie (2001, 14 October). Catwalk "Pornography". *The Sun-Herald*. Sydney, Australia: John Fairfax Publications.

Flugel, J.C. (1950). *The Psychology of Clothes*. London: The Hogarth Press. (Original publication 1930)

Freedland, Jonathan (2002, 16 July). Nation in Bondage. When Porn is Used to Sell Pot Noodle, It Is Time for Society to Change Its Attitude Towards Sex. The *Guardian*.

Frost, Liz (1999). "Doing Looks": Women, Appearance and Mental Health. In Arthurs, Jane and Grimshaw, Jean (eds) *Women's Bodies: Discipline and Transgression*. London and New York: Cassell, pp. 117–136.

Frost, Liz (2001). *Young Women and the Body. A Feminist Sociology*. Basingstoke, Hampshire: Palgrave.

Frye, Marilyn (1983). *The Politics of Reality*. Trumansburg, NY: The Crossing Press.

Furth, Gregg M. and Smith, Robert (2002). Amputee Identity Disorder: Information, Questions, Answers and Recommendations about Self-Demand Amputation. Bloomington, IN: 1st Books.

Fyfe, Melissa (2001, 8 January). Magazine in Row Over Genital Surgery Article. *The Age*. Melbourne, Australia: John Fairfax Publications.

Gaines, Steven and Churcher, Sharon (1994). *Obsession: The Lives and Times of Calvin Klein*. New York: Birch Lane Press.

GenderPAC (n.d.). Retrieved 18 March 2001 from http://www.gpac/index.html

Giobbe, Evelina (1991). "Prostitution: Buying the Right to Rape". In Burgess, Ann Wolpert (ed.) *Rape and Sexual Assault III. A Research Handbook*. New York: Garland Publishing.

Girl Talk (2002). Online Discussion Board. Retrieved 10 July 2002 from http://boards.substance.com/messages/get/sbcell17/57.html

Goddess Tika's Lipsticked Luvs (n.d.). Retrieved 5 June 2002 from http://members.aol.com/lpstkluv/tika.html

Gottschalk, Karl-Peter (1995). Leigh Bowery. Goodbye to the Boy from Sunshine. Retrieved 23 February 2004 from http://easyweb.easynet.co.uk/~karlpeter/zeugma/inters/bowery.htm

Graham, Dee L.R., with Edna I. Rawlings and Roberta K. Rigsby (1994). *Loving to Survive: Sexual Terror, Men's Violence and Women's Live*. New York: New York University Press.

Graham, Jean Ann and Kligman, Albert M. (eds) (1985). *The Psychology of Cosmetic Treatments*. New York: Praeger.

Greer, Germaine (2000, November). Sex 2000? *HQ*, pp. 98–101.

Grosz, Elizabeth (1994). *Volatile Bodies. Toward a Corporeal Feminism*. St Leonards, NSW: Allen and Unwin.

Guillaumin, Colette (1996). The Practice of Power and Belief in Nature. In Leonard, Diana and Adkins, Lisa (eds) *Sex in Question: French Materialist Feminism*. London: Taylor and Francis, pp. 72–108.

Haiken, Elizabeth (1997). *Venus Envy. A History of Cosmetic Surgery*. Baltimore, MD: The Johns Hopkins University Press.

Halberstam, Judith (1998). *Female Masculinity*. Durham, NC and London: Duke University Press.

Halbfinger, David M. (2002, 1 September). After the Veil, a Makeover Rush. *New York Times*, section 9, p. 1.

Harris, Gardiner (2003). Cosmetic Foot Surgery a "Scary Trend". *New York Times*. Retrieved 3 February 2004 from http://www.broward.com/mld/charlotte/living/health/7455892.htm

Hausman, Bernice (2001). Recent Transgender Theory. *Feminist Studies*, 27, 2, Summer: 465–490.

Henley, Jon (2000, 16 March). Larger than life. The *Guardian*.

Henley, Jon (2002, 2 March). Husband Arrested for Lolo Ferrari's Murder. The *Guardian*.

Henley, Nancy (1977). *Body Politics: Sex, Power and Nonverbal Communication*. Englewood Cliffs, NJ: Prentice-Hall.

Herman, Judith (1992). *Trauma and Recovery: The Aftermath of Violence – From Domestic Abuse to Political Terror*. New York: Basic Books.

Hidden Woman (n.d.). Retrieved 17 September 2002 from http://www.hiddenwoman.com

Hill, Amelia (2002, 21 April). I'll Be Ready in 21 Minutes, Dear. The *Observer*.

Hint Fashion Magazine (n.d.). Chic Happens. Retrieved 1 March 2001 from http://www.hintmag.com/chichappens/chichappens1-3-01.htm

Hirschberg, Lynn (2001, 8 July). Questions for Jean-Paul Gaultier. An Artist? Moi? The *New York Times Magazine*, p. 13.

Hochswender, Woody (1991, October). Appearance at Work. Is a Fashionable Image Empowering – or Does It Undermine Authority? *Vogue*, pp. 230–238.

Holland, J., Ramazanoglu, C., Sharpe, S. and Thomson, R. (1998). *The Male in the Head: Young People, Heterosexuality and Power*. London: Tufnell Press.

Hollander, Anne (1994). *Sex and Suits*. New York: Alfred A. Knopf.

Holliday, Ruth (2001). Fashioning the Queer Self. In Entwhistle, Joanne and Wilson, Elizabeth (eds) *Body Dressing*. Oxford and New York: Berg, pp. 215–231.

Home Office (2000). *The BSE Inquiry: The Report*. London: Home Office. Online at http://www.bseinquiry.gov.uk/index.htm

Hoodfar, Homa (1997). Return to the Veil: Personal Strategy and Public Participation in Egypt. In Visnathan, Nalini, Duggan, Lynn, Nisonoff, Laurie and Wiegersma, Nan (eds) *The Women, Gender and Development Reader*. London: Zed Books, pp. 320–325.

Hot Supermodels (n.d.). Hot Supermodels. Elle MacPherson. Retrieved 8 August 2002 from http://www.hot-supermodels.com/elle.htm

Hudepohl, Dana (2000, February). I Had Cosmetic Surgery on My Genitals. *Marie Claire*.

Hudson, Patrick (n.d.). Plastic Surgery After Pregnancy. Retrieved 19 September 2001 from www.phudson.com/postpartum.html

Hudson, Tori (2001, May). Body Piercing. *Townsend Letter for Doctors and Patients*, p. 156.

Implantinfo Support Forum (2004, 6 and 7 June). Retrieved 7 June 2004 from http://forums.implantinfo.com/cgi-local/support

iVillage (n.d.). Why get a Brazilian Bikini Wax. Retrieved 19 September 2001 from www.substance.com/b...hremoval/article/0,11462,217750,00.htm

Jackson, Stevi and Scott, Sue (2002). *Gender. A Sociological Reader*. London: Routledge.

Jameson, Fredric (1998). *The Cultural Turn: Selected Writings on the Postmodern, 1983–1998*. London and New York: Verso.

Jeffreys, Sheila (1982). The Sexual Abuse of Children in the Home. In Friedman, Scarlet and Sarah, Elizabeth (eds) *On the Problem of Men*. London: The Women's Press, pp. 56–66.

Jeffreys, Sheila (1985/1997). *The Spinster and Her Enemies. Feminism and Sexuality 1880–1930*. London: Pandora; Melbourne: Spinifex.

Jeffreys, Sheila (1990). *Anticlimax: A Feminist Perspective on the Sexual Revolution*. London: The Women's Press; New York: New York University Press.

Jeffreys, Sheila (1996). Heterosexuality and the Desire for Gender. In Richardson, Diane (ed.) *Theorising Heterosexuality*. Buckingham: Open University Press, pp. 75–90.

Jeffreys, Sheila (1997a). Transgender Activism. *Journal of Lesbian Studies*, 1 3/4: 55–74.

Jeffreys, Sheila (1997b). *The Idea of Prostitution*. Melbourne: Spinifex Press.

Jeffreys, Sheila (2000). Body Art and Social Status: Piercing, Cutting and Tattooing from a Feminist Perspective. *Feminism and Psychology*, November: 409–430.

Jeffreys, Sheila (2003). *Unpacking Queer Politics. A Lesbian Feminist Perspective*. Cambridge: Polity Press.

Jenny (n.d.). How to Wear High Heels. Retrieved 20 October 2000 from http://freespace.virginnet.co.uk/jenny.ntegroup/wearing5/htm

Johnson, Douglas F. (1985). Appearance and the Elderly. In Graham, Jean Ann and Kligman, Albert M. (eds) *The Psychology of Cosmetic Treatments*. New York: Praeger, pp. 152–160.

Kaplan, E. Ann (1993). Madonna Politics: Perversion, Repression, or Subversion. In Schwichtenberg, Cathy (ed.) *The Madonna Connection. Representational Politics, Subcultural Identities, and Cultural Theory*. St Leonards, NSW: Allen and Unwin, pp. 149–165.

Kappeler, Susanne (1986). *The Pornography of Representation*. Cambridge: Polity Press.

Kaufman, Marc (2003, 2 October). Breast Implants Linked to Suicide. The *Washington Post*.

King, Elizabeth (2001, 28 November). The New Frontier. *The Age*. Melbourne, Australia: John Fairfax Publications.

Kingston, Anne (2004, 24 January). First Wife Author's Final Exit. Olivia Goldsmith's Death Offers Useful Lessons to Us All. *Saturday Post*. Canada, p. 1.

Kirp, David L., Yudof, Mark G. and Franks, Marlene Strong (1986). *Gender Justice*. Chicago, IL: University of Chicago Press.

Ko, Dorothy (1997a). The Body as Attire: The Shifting Meanings of Footbinding in Seventeenth-century China. *Journal of Women's History*, Winter, 8, 4: 8–28.

Ko, Dorothy (1997b). Bondage in Time: Footbinding and Fashion Theory. *Fashion Theory*, 1, 1: 2–28.

Ko, Dorothy (2001). *Every Step a Lotus. Shoes for Bound Feet.* Berkeley, CA: University of California Press.
LabiaplastySurgeon.com (n.d.). Frequently Asked Questions and Things You Should Know. Retrieved 10 November 2002 from http://www.labiaplastysurgeon.com/faq.html
LaBruce, Bruce (2000, 29 November). Porn Free. The *Guardian.*
LaBruce, Bruce (2001, 15 March). New York's Steep Slopes. *Eye Weekly.* Retrieved 19 September 2001 from http://www.eye.net/eye/issue/issue_03.15.01/columns/feelings.html
Lane, Megan and Duffy, Jonathan (2004, 13 January). The Stigma of Plastic Surgery. *BBC News Online Magazine.* Retrieved 3 February 2004 from http://news.bbc.co.uk/2/hi/uk_news/magazine/3389229.stm
Lasertreatments.com (2004). Re: Labiaplasty. Retrieved 18 March 2004 from http://lasertreatments.com/www.board/messages/3717.html
Lawrence, Anne (n.d.a). Sexuality and Transsexuality: A New Introduction to Autogynephilia. Transsexual Women's Resources. Retrieved 17 September 2002 from www.annelawrence.com
Leganeur, J.J. (n.d.a). East (Chinese) Footbinding vs. West (French) High Heels. Retrieved 22 September 2002 from http://www.2heels.com/b.html
Leganeur, J.J. (n.d.b). High Heel Foot Problems. Retrieved 24 February 2004 from http://www.2heels.com/contents.html
Leganeur, J.J. (2000). *All About Wearing High Heels.* New York: Xlibris Corporation.
Lehrman, Karen (1997). *The Lipstick Proviso.* New York: Anchor Books.
Leibovich, Lori (1998, 14 January). From Liposuction to Labiaplasty. Salon.com. Retrieved 24 February 2004 from http://archive.salon.com/mwt/feature/1998/01/14feature.html
Lemon, Brendan (1997, 10 June). Gucci's Gay Guru. *The Advocate.* n735: 28–33 Online. http://web2.infotrac.galegroup.com/itw/infomark/162/849/47224869w2/purl=rc1_EAIM_0_A20164877&dyn=3!xrn_1_0_A20164877?sw_aep=unimelb
Leo, John (1995, 31 July). The "Modern Primitives". *U.S. News and World Report,* 119, 5: 16.
Lerner, Gerda (1987). *The Creation of Patriarchy.* New York: Oxford University Press.
Levine, Martin P. (1998). *Gay Macho. The Life and Death of the Homosexual Clone.* New York: New York University Press.
Levy, Howard S. (1966). *Chinese Footbinding. The History of a Curious Erotic Custom.* New York: William Rawls.
Liberty Women's Health (n.d.). Expert Labial, Labia Reduction Surgery. Retrieved 21 October 2002 from wysiwyg://33http://www.libertywomenshealth.com/9.htm
Lichtarowicz, Ania (2003, 24 October). Modern Life Increased Rickets Risk. *BBC News.* Retrieved 24 February 2004 from http://news.bbc.co.uk/1/hi/health/3210615.stm
Lim, Lin Lean (ed.) (1998). *The Sex Sector. The Economic and Social Bases of Prostitution in Southeast Asia.* Geneva: International Labour Office.
Lipstick and Leather Books (n.d.). Retrieved 12 October 2002 from http://lipstickandleather.info/
Lister, Ruth (1997). *Citizenship: Feminist Perspectives.* Basingstoke: Macmillan.

Lloyd, Fran (1994). *Deconstructing Madonna*. London: Batsford.
Lloyd, Joan Elizabeth (n.d.). Lovers' Feedback Forum. Shaving. Retrieved 12 October 2002 from www.joanelloyd.com
Loy, Jen (2000, 29 May). Pushing the Perfect Pussy. *Fabula*. Retrieved 12 October 2002 from http://www.alternet.org/story.html?StoryID=9217
Low, Lenny Ann (2003, 17 December). Designs From Artist Who Broke Every Taboo. *Sydney Morning Herald*. Retrieved 17 December 2003 from http://www.smh.com.au/articles/2003/12/17/1071336997757.html?from=storyrhs
McCann, Edwina (2003, 8–9 March). Cabaret Kylie Brings Galliano Guests to Heel. The *Weekend Australian*. Sydney, Australia.
McClosky, Deirdre N. (1999). *Crossing. A Memoir*. Chicago, IL: Chicago University Press.
McCorquodale, Duncan (ed.) (1996). *Orlan: ceci est mon corps, ceci est mon logiciel*. London: Black Dog Publishing.
McCouch, Hannah (2002, April). What Your Bikini Waxer Really Thinks. *Cosmopolitan*, pp. 92–94.
McDowell, Colin (2000). *Manolo Blahnik*. London: Cassell and Co.
McGrath, John Edward (1995). Trusting in Rubber. Performing Boundaries During the AIDS Epidemic. *The Drama Review*, 39, 2 (T146), Summer: 21–38.
Mackay, Jill Campbell (2001, 16 September). Sick Chic. *Cyprus Mail*. Retrieved 22 September 2002 from www.cyprus-mail.com/September/16/column2.htm
McKenna, Michael (2003, 6 April). Fetish "Doctor" Castrated 50 Men. The *Sunday Mail*. Brisbane, Queensland.
MacKinnon, Catharine (1989). *Towards a Feminist Theory of the State*. Cambridge, MA: Harvard University Press.
Mackrell, Judith (2000, 4 January). The Magical Feet of Ballerina Sarah Wildor. The *Guardian*.
McRobbie, Angela (1997). *More!* New Sexuality in Girls' and Women's Magazines. In Angela McRobbie (ed.) *Back to Reality? Social Experience and Cultural Studies*. Manchester: Manchester University Press.
Maguire, Kevin (2002, 28 May). Blair Risks New Row by Inviting Porn Tycoon to Tea. The *Guardian*.
Makkai, Toni and McAllister, Ian (2001). Prevalence of Tattooing and Body Piercing in the Australian Community. *Communicable Diseases Intelligence*, 25, 2: 67–72.
Marwick, Arthur (1988). *Beauty in History. Society, Politics and Personal Appearance c. 1500 to the Present*. London: Thames and Hudson.
Masson, Jeffrey Moussaieff (1984). *The Assault on Truth: Freud's Suppression of the Seduction Theory*. New York: Farrar, Strauss and Giroux.
Media Awareness Network (n.d.). Calvin Klein – A Case Study. Retrieved 8 August 2002 from http://www.media-awareness.ca/eng/med/class/teamedia/ckstudy.htm
Miller, Rachel (1996). *The Bliss of Becoming One*. Highland City, FL: Rainbow Books.
Miss Vera (n.d.). Miss Vera's Finishing School For Boys Who Want To Be Girls. Retrieved 17 September 2002 from http://www.missvera.com/
Moran, Jonathan and Walker, Kylie (2004, 17 January). Going to Extremes. *Townsville Bulletin/Townsville Sun*. Australia.
Mower, Sarah (2002, June). Alex in Wonderland. *Vogue*, pp. 44–45.

Mugler, Thierry (1998). *Fashion, Fetish, Fantasy*. London: Thames and Hudson.

Musafar, Fakir (1996). Body Play: State of Grace or Sickness? In Favazza, Armando *Bodies Under Siege. Self-mutilation and Body Modification in Culture and Psychiatry*. Baltimore and London: The Johns Hopkins University Press, pp. 325–334.

National Transgender Advocacy Coalition (2000). Retrieved 17 September 2002 from http:www.ntac.org/

Nicholson, David (2002, 31 July). Could Sex Save 3G Mobiles? Porn Could Popularise Next Generation Mobile Phone. The *Guardian*.

Nussbaum, Martha (2000). *Sex and Social Justice*. New York: Oxford University Press.

O'Brien, Glenn (ed.) (1992). *Madonna. Sex*. London: Martin Secker and Warburg Ltd.

O'Connell Davidson, Julia (1995). British Sex Tourists in Thailand. In Maynard, Mary and Purvis, June (eds) *(Hetero)sexual Politics*. London: Taylor and Francis, pp. 42–65.

O'Hagan, Sean (2004, 17 October) Good Clean Fun? The *Observer*.

Onfray, Michel (1996). Surgical Aesthetics. In McCorquodale, Duncan (ed.) *Orlan: ceci est mon corps, ceci est mon logiciel*. London: Black Dog Publishing, pp. 31–39.

Orlan (1996). This is My Body . . . This is My Software. In McCorquodale, Duncan (ed.) *Orlan: ceci est mon corps, ceci est mon logiciel*. London: Black Dog Publishing, pp. 82–93.

Ousterhout, Douglas (1995). Feminization of the Transsexual. Retrieved 17 September 2002 from http://www.drbecky.com/dko.html

Paglia, Camille (1992). *Sex, Art, and American Culture*. New York: Vintage Books.

Parriott, Ruth (1994). *Health Experiences of Twin Cities Women Used in Prostitution: Survey Findings and Recommendations*. Unpublished. Available from Breaking Free, 1821 University Avenue, Suite 312, South, St Paul, Minnesota 55104, USA.

Peakin, William (2000, 18–19 November). Dangerous Curves. *The Australian Magazine*, pp. 42–52.

Peiss, Kathy (1998). *Hope in a Jar. The Making of America's Beauty Culture*. New York: Metropolitan Books, Henry Holt and Company.

Peiss, Kathy (2001). On Beauty . . . and the History of Business. In Philip Scranton (ed.) *Beauty and Business. Commerce, Gender, and Culture in Modern America*. New York: Routledge, pp. 7–23.

Pertschuk, Michael J. (1985). Appearance in Psychiatric Disorder. In Graham, Jean Ann and Kligman, Albert M. (eds) *The Psychology of Cosmetic Treatments*. New York: Praeger, pp. 217–226.

Phillips, Katharine A. (1998). *The Broken Mirror. Understanding and Treating Body Dysmorphic Disorder*. Oxford: Oxford University Press.

Phillips, Lynn (2000). *Flirting with Danger: Young Women's Reflections on Sexuality and Domination*. New York and London: New York University Press.

Ping, Wang (2000). *Aching for Beauty. Footbinding in China*. Minneapolis: University of Minnesota Press.

Plastic Surgery Message Board (2004, 4 June and 6 June). Retrieved 7 June 2004 from http://beautysurg.com/forums/printthread.php

Plummer, David (1999). *One of the Boys. Masculinity, Homophobia, and Modern Manhood*. Binghamton, NY: Harrington Park Press.
Porter, Charlie (2003, 9 December). How Stella lost her groove. The *Guardian. G2*, p. 6.
Preston, John (1993). *My Life as a Pornographer and Other Indecent Acts*. New York: Masquerade Books.
Psurg Surgical Art Gallery (n.d.). Retrieved 17 September 2002 from www.psurg.com/women/htm
Puwar, Nirmar (2004). Thinking About Making a Difference. *British Journal of Politics and International Relations*. 6: 65–80.
Raymond, Janice G. (1994). *The Transsexual Empire*. New York: Teachers College Press. (Original publication 1979)
Ready for Brazilian Waxing? (2004, 25 February). Advertisement in The *Melbourne Times*, p. 15.
Renshaw, Helen (2001, 29 October). Plastic Fantastic. *NW*, pp. 20–28.
Renshaw, Helen (2002, 21 January). Plastic Surgery Disasters. *NW*, pp. 16–19.
Reyes, Renee (n.d.). T-Girls Survival Guide. Retrieved 17 September 2002 from www.reneereyes.com
Reynaud, Emmanuel (1983). *Holy Virility*. London: Pluto Press.
Rich, Adrienne (1993). Compulsory Heterosexuality and Lesbian Existence. In Abelove, H., Barale, M.A. and Halperin, D.M. (eds) *The Lesbian and Gay Studies Reader*. London: Routledge, pp. 227–254.
Robotham, Julie (2001, 27 June). Hair Dye Linked to Cancer. *The Age*. Melbourne, Australia: John Fairfax Publications.
Rocky Mountain Laser Clinic (n.d.). Permanent Hair Removal for Trans-Genders. Retrieved 17 September 2002 from http://www.rockymountainlaser.com/
Rofes, Eric (1998). The Ick Factor: Flesh, Fluids, and Cross-Gender Revulsion. In Miles, Sara and Rofes, Eric (eds) *Opposite Sex. Gay Men on Lesbians, Lesbians on Gay Men*. New York: New York University Press, pp. 44–65.
Rogers, Lesley (1999). *Sexing the Brain*. London: Weidenfeld and Nicolson.
Roiphe, Katie (1993). *The Morning After: Sex, Fear and Feminism on Campus*. Boston, MA: Little, Brown and Co.
Roof, Judith (1998). 1970s Lesbian Feminism Meets 1990s Butch-Femme. In Munt, Sally R. (ed.) *Butch/Femme. Inside Lesbian Gender*. London: Cassell.
Rose, Pania (2003, 2 November). New York Times. The *Sunday Age Magazine. Sunday Life*. Melbourne, Australia: John Fairfax Publications.
Rossi, William A. (1989). *The Sex Life of the Foot and Shoe*. Ware, Hertfordshire: Wordsworth Editions. (Original publication 1977)
Rottnek, Matthew (ed.) (1999). *Sissies and Tomboys. Gender, Nonconformity and Homosexual Childhood*. New York: New York University Press.
Rudd, Peggy J. (1999). *My Husband Wears My Clothes. Crossdressing from the Perspective of a Wife*. Katy, TX: PM Publishers.
Russell, Diana (ed.) (1993). *Making Violence Sexy: Feminist Views on Pornography*. Buckingham: Open University Press.
Saban, Stephen (2002, 29 June). Mr Outrageous. *The Age. Good Weekend*. Melbourne, Australia: John Fairfax Publications, pp. 30–33.
Saeed, Fouzia (2001). *Taboo! The Hidden Culture of a Red Light Area*. Karachi: Oxford University Press.

Saharso, Sawitri (2003, February). Culture, Tolerance and Gender: A Contribution from the Netherlands. *The European Journal of Women's Studies*, 10, 1: 7–27.

Schulze, Laurie, White, Anne Barton and Brown, Jane D. (1993). "A Sacred Monster in Her Prime": Audience Construction of Madonna as Low-Other. In Schwichtenberg, Cathy (ed.) *The Madonna Connection. Representational Politics, Subcultural Identities, and Cultural Theory*. St Leonards, NSW: Allen and Unwin, pp. 15–37.

Schwichtenberg, Cathy (ed.) (1993a). *The Madonna Connection. Representational Politics, Subcultural Identities, and Cultural Theory*. St Leonards, NSW: Allen and Unwin.

Schwichtenberg, Cathy (1993b). Madonna's Postmodern Feminism: Bringing the margins to the center. In Schwichtenberg, Cathy (ed.) *The Madonna Connection. Representational Politics, Subcultural Identities, and Cultural Theory*. St Leonards, NSW: Allen and Unwin, pp. 129–145.

Shave My Pussy (n.d.). More Fine No Cost XXX Sites. Retrieved 11 September 2002 from www.allbjsinc.com/shavemypussy/

Shaw, Sarah Naomi (2002, May). "Shifting Conversations on Girls' and Women's Self-Injury: An Analysis of the Clinical Literature in Historical Context". *Feminism and Psychology*, 12, 2: 191–219.

Shiva, Vandana (1989). *Staying Alive. Women, Ecology and Development*. London: Zed Books.

Silkstone, Dan (2004, 20 February). Lawyer Ridicules Brainwashing, Slavery Claims. *The Age*. Melbourne, Australia: John Fairfax Publications, p. 5.

Skin Doctors Dermaceuticals (2002, 13 October). Kiss Your Thin Lips Goodbye Today! Advertisement. *The Sunday Age. Television Magazine*. Melbourne, Australia: John Fairfax Publications, p. 7.

Smith, Joan (2000, 22 March). Falling for Madonna. The *Guardian*.

Smith, Helena (2004, 12 May). Has Prince Charles Found His Spiritual Home on a Greek Rock?: Visits Spark Claims of Royal's Commitment to Orthodoxy. The *Guardian*.

Steele, Valerie (1996). *Fetish. Fashion, Sex and Power*. Oxford: Oxford University Press.

Steve Haworth (2004). Steve Haworth. Body Modification. Retrieved 27 February 2004 from http://steve.htcbodypiercing.com/about.html

Strong, Geoff (2001, 26 December). Ban on Cosmetic Chemical Mooted. *The Age*. Melbourne, Australia: John Fairfax Publications.

Strong, Marilee (1998). *A Bright Red Scream: Self-Mutilation and the Language of Pain*. New York: Viking.

Strovny, David (n.d.). Mutual Grooming: Shaving For Sex. Retrieved 22 September 2002 from http://www.askmen.com/love/love_tip_60/63_love_tip.html

Sullivan, Deborah A. (2002). *Cosmetic Surgery. The Cutting Edge of Commercial Medicine in America*. New Brunswick, NJ: Rutgers University Press.

Summers, Leigh (2001). *Bound to Please: A History of the Victorian Corset*. Oxford and New York: Berg.

Surgicenteronline (2003, 30 December). Cosmetic Foot Surgery to Beautify Feet has Serious Risks. Retrieved 12 February 2003 from http://www.surgicenteronline.com/hotnews/3ch30102541.html

Swain, Jon (1998, 28 February–1 March). Seriously Chic. The *Weekend Australian*, pp. 4–6.

Tggalaxy (n.d.). Transgendered Galaxy. Retrieved 17 September 2002 from http://tggalaxy.com/contacts.html

Tgnow.com (n.d.). Personal Advice and Answers. Retrieved 17 September 2002 from www.tgnow.com

Thompson, Denise (2001). *Radical Feminism Today*. London: Sage.

Tinsley, Emily G., Sullivan-Guest, S. and McGuire, John (1984). Feminine Sex Role and Depression in Middle-Aged Women. *Sex Roles*, 11, 1/2: 25–32.

Tom, Emma (2002, 29–30 June). Stick With Your Job If It Fits. The *Weekend Australian*.

Tongue Piercing (2000, 8 April). *Chemist and Druggist*, p. 22.

Townsel, Lisa Jones (1996, September). Working Women: Dressing for Success. *Ebony*, pp. 60–65.

Transformation (n.d.). Transvestite Transformation. Retrieved 17 September 2002 from http://www.transformation.co.uk

Transgender Forum (n.d.). All I Gotta Do Is, Act Naturally. Retrieved 17 September 2002 from http://www.geocities.com/westhollywood/village/1003/BeautyTips.htm

Transgender Magazines (n.d.) Retrieved 17 September 2002 from http://www.transgender.magazines.co.uk

Transsexual Magic (n.d.). Retrieved 17 September 2002 from http://www.geocities.com/ aureliamagic/

Tyrell, Rebecca (2001, 14 November). Better than Sex. *The Age. Today*. Melbourne, Australia: John Fairfax Publications, p. 5.

United Nations (1979). Convention on the Elimination of All Forms of Discrimination Against Women. Geneva: United Nations. Retrieved 3 March 2004 from http://www.unhchr.ch/html/menu3/b/e1cedaw.htm

United Nations (1995). Fact Sheet No. 23 on *Harmful Traditional Practices Affecting the Health of Women and Children*. Geneva: United Nations.

USA Today (2000, 14 November). Other Ways To Stay Forever Young. *USA Today, Health*. Retrieved 12 June 2002 from www.usatoday.com/life/health.alternative/lhalt014.htm

Vance, Carole A. (ed.) (1984). *Pleasure and Danger: Exploring Female Sexuality*. London: Routlege and Kegan Paul.

Vitzhum, Virginia (1999, 7–13 May). A Change of Dress. *Washington City Paper*.

Vokes-Dudgeon, Sophie (2002, 21 January). I want Britney's belly. *NW*, pp. 20–21.

Walker, Susannah (2001). Black is Profitable. The Commodification of the Afro, 1960–1975. In Philip Scranton (ed.) *Beauty and Business. Commerce, Gender, and Culture in Modern America*. New York: Routledge, pp. 254–277.

Walkowitz, Judith (1992). *City of Dreadful Night: Narratives of Sexual Danger in Late-Victorian London*. London: Virago.

Walter, Natasha (1999). *The New Feminism*. London: Virago.

Webb, Terri (1996). Autobiographical Fragments from a Transsexual Activist. In Ekins, Richard and King, Dave (eds) *Blending Genders*. London and New York: Routledge, pp. 190–195.

Weeks, Jeffrey (1977). *Coming Out. Homosexual Politics in Britain from the Nineteenth Century to the Present*. London: Pluto Press.

Weinberg, Martin S., Williams, Colin J. and Calhan, Cassandra (1994). Homosexual Foot Fetishism. *Archives of Sexual Behaviour*, 23, 6: 611–626.

Wild, Abigail (2003, 6 December). Why On Earth would Someone Want to be Eaten by This Man? *The Glasgow Herald*. Scottish Media Newspapers Limited.

Wilson, Cintra (1999, 30 June). The Emperor's New Guitars. Salon.com. Retrieved 12 September 2001 from www.salon.com/people/col/cintra/1999/06/30/clapton/

Wilson, Elizabeth (1985). *Adorned in Dreams: Fashion and Modernity*. Berkeley, CA: University of California Press.

Wilson, Sarah (1996). L'histoire d'O, Sacred and Profane. In McCorquodale, Duncan (ed.) *Orlan: ceci est mon corps, ceci est mon logiciel*. London: Black Dog Publishing, pp. 8–17.

Wittig, Monique (1996). The Category of Sex. In Leonard, Diana and Adkins, Lisa (eds) *Sex in Question: French Materialist Feminism*. London: Taylor and Francis, pp. 24–29.

Wolf, Naomi (1990). *The Beauty Myth*. London: Chatto and Windus.

Wolf, Naomi (1993). *Fire with Fire: The New Female Power and How it Will Change the 21st Century*. New York: Random House.

Woods, Chris (1995). *State of the Queer Nation. A Critique of Gay and Lesbian Politics in 1990s Britain*. London: Cassell.

Wynter, Bronwyn, Thompson, Denise and Jeffreys, Sheila (2002, April). The UN Approach to Harmful Traditional Practices: Some Conceptual Problems. *International Feminist Journal of Politics*, 4, 1: 72–94.

Young, Lola (1999). Racializing Femininity. In Arthurs, Jane and Grimshaw, Jean *Women's Bodies: Discipline and Transgression*. London and New York: Cassell, pp. 67–89.

Zawadi, Aya (2000, October). Mutilation by Choice. *Soul Magazine*. Winnipeg, Manitoba, Canada. Retrieved 15 January 2001 from http://www.soulmagazine.com/Neo/Body/

INDEX

Abu-Odeh, Lama 37–9, 40
abuse *see* child abuse
Academy Awards 88
Adult Video News (AVN) 67–8, 69, 70, 78
advertising 70–5
Advocate, The (magazine) 94, 104
Afghan Ministry of Women's Affairs 41
Afghanistan 41–2
African women, female genital mutilation 35–6
African-American women: and makeup 113–14, 115, 117; and white beauty ideals 113–14
Afro hairstyle 114
Afshar, Haleh 38
Age, The (newspaper) 71
agency 14, 38, 175; beauty practices as an expression of 2, 5–6, 16–17, 27; Madonna as model of 76; and the veil 38, 39
agents, postmodern abandonment 14
AIDS (acquired immunodeficiency syndrome) 167
Air Force One 68
Alaia, Azzadine 92
Alexander, Keith 165
Alter, Gary 82, 85
American Academy of Orthopaedic Surgeons 142
American Orthopaedic Foot and Ankle Society (AOFAS) 145
amputation, limb 4, 167, 169, 177
Amputee Identity Disorder 167, 169
Anders, Charles 47–8, 55, 59, 64
Anderson, Pamela 73, 160, 164
anorexia 122–3
anti-ageing creams 126
appearance training 122–3
arch stretchers 134, 138
arm hair 120–1
asexuality, of not conforming to western beauty practices 122–3
Ashcroft, Keith 169
Asher, Bill 69
AT&T 70
Athey, Ron 167, 168
autogynephilia 50, 51–2, 56, 61
Avedon, Richard 99

Babylon 43
"ball dances" 152
ballet 128, 135–8
Barrett, Michele 14
Barrymore, Drew 103
Bartky, Sandra 7, 8, 15, 106, 107, 174–5
"beauty aid" 41
beauty contests 113
beauty courses 113
beauty standards, construction of 113–14
Beckham, Victoria 160
Bell, Shannon 153
Benjamin, Henry 110
Bentley, Toni 136, 137
Bergler, Edmund 96
big business 112, 113
binge drinking, teenage 151
Bismarchi, Angela 161
Bismarchi, Ox 161
black women 113–14, 115, 117
Blahnik, Manolo 147
Blair, Tony 68

Blanchard, Ray 50, 51–2
bleaching: arm hair 120; skin 113
Bloch, Iwan 23
Blow, Isabella 103
body: grip of culture on 5–27; as obsolete 163; sense of Otherness regarding 169; as separate from the self/women's alienation from 8; as text 2
body dysmorphic disorder (BDD) 108–9, 125, 169
body hair 44–5; cult of 82; *see also* depilation
body hatred 20
body modification 164–7, 168–9
Body Modification Ezine (BME) 121, 165–6
body/mind split 163
bondage 93
bondage and discipline, sadomasochism (BDSM) 143
Bordo, Susan 15–16, 162, 175, 176, 178
Bornstein, Kate 48, 66
Bouquet, Carole 65
Bovine Spongiform Encephalopathy (BSE) 126
Bowery, Leigh 103
Bowery, Nicola Bateman 103
Brandes, Bernd-Juergen 168, 169
branding 149, 153, 165
breast augmentation/implants 16, 31–2, 149, 154–61, 169, 177; depression and 156; health risks of 155–6, 157, 158–61; porn stars and 77–8, 154–5, 158–61; silicone injections 155–6
breast growth (gynaecomastia) 47
brides, mail order 173
Brownmiller, Susan 108–9
bunions 144, 145
burkha 34–5, 41; health costs of wearing 34
butch shift 52, 94, 95
Butler, Judith 2, 17–18, 116

Cadente, Stella 73
Califa, Pat (Patrick) 51, 66
Callaghan, Karen 27
Camphausen, Rufus 152
cancer 124, 125
cannibalism 168–9
capitalism 41–2; rogue 5, 175
carcinogens 124–5
Carnal Knowledge Network 119–20
Castleman, Michael 79
castration 29, 165, 166, 167
Chanel 92
Charles, Prince 43–4
chatshows 15–16
cheek implants 78
child abuse: physical 150, 168, 169; sexual 53, 150, 164, 168, 169
children: and makeup use 118–19; women represented as 100
China 42; *see also* footbinding
choice 2, 5–6, 9–14, 16–17, 27–8, 32, 34–8, 174–5; and gender 17; illusion of 3, 7; impoverished 36–7; and makeup wearing 114, 118–20; and transsexualism 52, 65; and the veil 38, 39, 40
Christian Aid 153–4
Christianity: and the covering of women 42–4; womanhating sentiments of 43–4
Church of Body Modification 166
Cindoglu, Dilek 86
class *see* sex class
Clinton, Bill 67–8
clothing: enveloping 34–5; revealing 71; and sexual difference 23–4; skirts 140, 178; workplace 116–17; *see also* fashion; headcovering; high-heeled shoes; veiling
coal tar 124
coercion 3, 5, 174–5; of makeup wearing 114, 118–20; and pornographization of the beauty industry 81–2; and the veil 38; and the workplace 9
collagen 126
college appraisals, of female appearance 113
consent, of the victim 4
consumer culture 175
Convention on the Elimination of All Forms of Discrimination Against Women (CEDAW) 29, 45, 176, 178
Coomaraswamy, Radhika 32–5
Coritore, Hilary 160–1
corsets 32, 91–3
cosmeceuticals 124

cosmetic surgery 1, 7; as art 161–4; cheek implants 78; deaths from 171–2; economics of 172, 176; foot practices 144–5; as harmful cultural practice 28, 30–1, 45; health risks of 30–1, 36, 83, 155–61, 171–2; liposuction 157, 160–1; as morality 16; normalization 155, 172; political role 176–7; and pornography 77–8, 154, 155, 158–61; regulation 177; and sadism 159; as self-mutilation by proxy 4, 149–50, 154–64, 169–70; and transfemininity 55, 158; tummy tucks 156–7, 160–1; *see also* breast augmentation/implants; labiaplasty
Cosmopolitan (magazine) 80, 82
Costin, Simon 102
covering women 42–4; *see also* veiling
creams, anti-ageing 126
cultural imperialism, western, and the exportation of harmful cultural practices 41–2
cultural studies perspectives: on footbinding 133–4; on Madonna 76
cultural turn 13–20
cultural values 31–2
culture: grip on the body 5–27; popular 14, 15–16, 18; pornographization of 67; of resistance 171, 174–6; of survival 121, 126, 135; *see also* harmful cultural practices
cutting 149, 150, 151, 154, 165
cybersex 59
cyborgs 163

Daily Express (newspaper) 68
Daily Mail (newspaper) 77
Daily Star (newspaper) 68
Daly, Mary 77, 111, 135, 146, 148, 163
dancing, pole 73
dancing girls 132
Davies, Jessica 70–1
Davis, Kathy 16, 162, 163
deferential nature of women 24, 45; *see also* inequality; male dominance; oppression of women; subordination of women
deficiency, promotion of feelings of 8
Dellinger, Kirsten 114–15, 116
Delphy, Christine 27
department stores 111
depilation 44–5, 107, 119–22; arm waxing 120–1; genital 78–86; ingrown hairs 120; laser hair removal 55; leg shaving 119–20
depression 156
Desmond, Richard 68
deviancy, mainstreaming of 151
Diana, Princess of Wales 44
dieting 30, 35–6
dignity 34, 89, 105, 179
Dirie, Waris 113
discrimination against women, CEDAW against 29, 45, 176, 178
dissociation 164, 168, 169
"doing looks" 16–17, 20
domestic labour 64
domestic violence 10–11
dominatrices 60–1, 91, 93, 98, 100–1
Dr Becky 52
drag 17–18, 55, 95
Dworkin, Andrea 6–7, 8, 10, 107, 108, 132, 133, 149

Eagleton, Terry 14
Ebony (magazine) 117
economic issues: of cosmetic surgery 172, 176; and the exportation of western beauty practices 41–2; of the makeup industry 110–11, 112; of the porn industry 67, 69–70, 173; profits of the beauty industry 33; of the transfeminine makeover industry 54, 55; women's employment in the beauty industry 42
Economist, The 33
Edelman, Dan 169
Egypt 39, 40
Eicher, Joanne 88
Ellis, Havelock 51, 129–30
employment: female jobs in the beauty industry 42; and the subordination of women 111
empowerment: Madonna as model of 76; through makeup wearing 107, 115
Engels, Friedrich 22
Enloe, Cynthia 121–2
entitlement, female 112
entrepreneurs, female 110–11, 112
environmental pollution 125

Environmental Protection Agency (US) 124, 125
equality, female, masculine resentment of 173
Erickson, Kim 124, 125
erotica, fashion 70–5
Etcoff, Nancy 13
European Union (EU): Cosmetics Directive 126; Women's Committee on the impact of the sex industry in Europe 70
Eurotrash (TV programme) 159
Evans, Caroline 97
Eve, fall of 44
Extreme Makeover (TV show) 172

Fanon, Frantz 7–8
fantasies, sexual: masturbatory 50; men's practice of femininity as 49–50, 51–3, 55–63, 66
fashion 87–106; democratic 89–90; dignified 89, 105; and gay misogyny 94–105; gendered nature 87–90; male 88–90, 106; playing with gender and 18; pornographization 70–5, 90–1, 96, 98–103; and prostitution 75, 77, 86, 98; psychoanalytic views 96; sadomasochism and 91–4; sex acts and 74–5; suits 89; theory 105–6; *see also* clothing; high-heeled shoes
fashion designers: female 94–5; gay male 3, 87, 91–2, 94–105, 152; and high-heeled shoes 147; pornographic influences on 90
"fashion erotica" 70–5
fashion models 94, 96–100, 152; black 113; sex acts and 74–5
fashion photographers 3; pornographic influences 90, 102–3; sadomasochistic influences 91, 92
fashion–beauty complex 174, 177; as central producer and regulator of femininity 8
Fath, Jacques 92
female genital mutilation (FGM) 28, 30, 33, 111, 112, 172; comparison with dieting 35–6; comparison with labiaplasty 83; reversal 86
female masculinity 66
females-to-constructed-males (FTMs) 49, 53
femininity: as behaviour of subordination 24–7, 46; and body dysmorphic disorder 108–9; exaggerated/extreme versions 54, 55, 56, 76, 158; fashion–beauty complex as central producer and regulator of 8; fetishistic 55; fossilized form of 57; as learnt behaviour 65; male versions of 95, 104, 105, 158; men's practice of as sexual fantasy 49–53, 55–63, 66; political construction 24–5; of pornography 54, 56; as sex toy 66; as social construction 46, 53; as societal Stockholm syndrome 26; *see also* transfemininity
femme fatale 98
Ferrari, Lolo 154, 158–60, 168
fetishism: attempted normalization of 129–30; cannibalistic 169; fashion and 90, 91–4, 98, 100; lipstick and 59–61; as male phenomenon 129–30; of pornography 77–8; *see also* foot fetishism
fetishistic femininity 55
fingernails 118, 124, 125
Finkelstein, Joanne 105, 106
Fleming, Teresa 117–18
flesh, selling over the Internet 78, 162
flooding procedure 122–3
Flugel, J.C. 23, 90, 179
Flynt, Larry 69, 70
Food and Drug Administration (US) 156
foot fetishism 128–48, 169; arch stretchers 134, 138; and ballet 137–8; and footbinding 134; as most frequent fetish 129
footbinding 111, 112, 128, 130–6, 147–8; as chastity belt 131; comparison with high heels 130, 131, 132, 138, 145, 148; movement against 132; origins 132; process 130; and prostitution 131, 132–3; restricted movement produced by 130–1; as ritual passed from mother to daughter 134–5, 146; sexual myths regarding 140; and womanblaming 146
forced feeding 30
Ford, Tom 95, 101–2, 104, 147
formaldehyde 124

Foucault, M. 15
free market 5, 28, 67
Freedland, Jonathan 71
freedom: beauty practices as threat to 6–7; sexual 67
French Revolution 89–90
Frost, Liz 16–17, 20
Frye, Marilyn 2
fun, beauty practices as 16, 17
Furth, Gregg 167

gait: desexed 140; restricted 131, 132, 135–6, 139, 140
Galliano, John 94, 103
Gan, Stephen 104
Gaultier, Jean-Paul 92, 95, 105
gay men: disgust towards the female body 104–5; exclusion from male dominated culture 95, 104, 152; fashion designers 3, 87, 91–2, 94–105, 152; fetishism of 130, 142; ideal gay male 95; misogyny and fashion 94–105; sadomasochism 52, 91–4, 151–2, 165–8; self-mutilation by proxy 4; *see also* homosexuality
gayhating 149
gelatine 126
gender: abolition of 65; construction as result of constraint 17–18; dominance/subordination dichotomy in gay culture 53; playing with/ performance of 18, 76–7, 116, 117, 140; as product of male dominance 48, 66; as sex toy 66; as social construction 17
gender dysphoria 29, 50; heterosexual dysphoria 50, 52; homosexual/ androphilic dysphoria 50, 52
gender essentialism, transsexualism's defence of 47, 48–9, 58, 65–6
gender reassignment surgery *see* sex reassignment surgery
GenderPAC 58
General Motors 70
genitals: ageing 85; hair removal 78–86; surgery 82, 85–6; *see also* hymen repair surgery; labiaplasty
Girl Talk (online discussion forum) 120–1
Glamour (magazine) 156
Goldman, Professor 153
Goldsmith, Olivia 171
Graham, Dee 25–7
Graham, Heather 73
Granger, Ethel 93
Granger, Will 93
Greek Orthodox Christianity 43–4
grooming behaviours 107–27; construction of beauty standards 113–14; courses for 113; excessive 108–9; *see also* depilation; makeup
Grosz, Elizabeth 2
Guardian (newspaper) 71, 72, 94, 137, 153–4
Gucci 101, 104
Guillaumin, Colette 20–1
gynaecomastia (breast growth) 47

Haiken, Elizabeth 36, 83, 155
hair: Afro hairstyle 114; bleaching 113; dyeing 107, 124; perming 42, 107; straightening 113–14; *see also* body hair
hair removal *see* depilation
Halberstam, Judith 66
Hamilton, James 88
Hammurabi 43
Hamnett, Katherine 74
harmful cultural practices 3, 27, 171, 176; exportation of western 41–2; western beauty practices as 28–45, 123–4
Hausman, Bernice 48
Hawn, Goldie 73
Haworth, Steve 166
"He-Man" hoax 96
headcovering/headscarfs 39, 42–4
health, effects of western beauty practices on 171; cosmetic surgery 30–1, 36, 83, 155–61, 171–2; dieting 36; high-heeled shoes 142–5, 172; makeup 122–7; *see also* mental health
health insurance 51, 52
Hefner, Hugh 159
helplessness, projection of male onto women 96
Henley, Nancy 25, 27
heterosexuality: compulsory 22; gaining an appearance of through wearing makeup 115
Hezbollahis (Party of God) 38, 40
Hidden Woman (transfeminine makeover store) 54

high-heeled shoes 45, 94, 102, 128–9; comparison with footbinding 130, 131, 132, 138, 145, 148; as complimenter of men 129; demonization of the alternatives 138–9; health risks of wearing 142–5, 172; as marker of female fragility 128; men's demand for 138–42; pain of wearing and male sexual excitement 128, 140–1, 143–4; and prostitution 133; revival 146–8; and sadism 139, 143–4; and sadomasochism 142, 143; sexual myths regarding 140; toe cleavage 138, 147; and womanblaming 145–6
HIV (human immunodeficiency virus) 167
Hof, Denis 69
Hollander, Anne 89
Holliday, Ruth 18
Hollywood film industry 70, 88
homosexuality 51; and femininity 52; as socially constructed behaviour 95; *see also* gay men; lesbians
honour killings 33, 36
Hoodfar, Homa 38–40
Hopkins, Ann 117
hormone disrupters 124, 125
hormone therapy 47, 48, 49, 55, 59
Houston (porn star) 78, 162, 164
human rights 179; violations 176
hymen repair surgery 36–7, 85–6, 176–7

"ick factor" 104–5
ideals: gay male 95; of white beauty 113–14
ideology 14–15; of beauty and fashion 15; dominant 16; and relations of ruling 15; retention of 14
Iman 113
immigrant communities, and hymen repair surgery 36–7, 86
implants: of body modification 165; *see also* breast augmentation/implants
in-laws 39
inequality: construction through makeup wearing 116; income 31; *see also* deferential nature of women; male dominance; oppression of women; subordination of women
interests: postmodern abandonment of 14; subordination of women's 63
Internet: body modification and 164–7, 168–9; chatrooms 59; cosmetic surgery and 156–7; pornography and 67, 69–70, 86; selling body flesh over 78, 162; transfemininity and 3, 46–7, 49, 53–7, 59–60, 66
intersexuality 21
Iran 38, 40
Islamic society 37–44, 86; veiling 37–40, 42–4

Jameson, Fredric 13–14
Johnson, Douglas 123
Jolie, Angelina 102
Jordan 159–60
Judaism 43

Kalabari tribe 88
Kaliardos, James 104
Kaplan, Ann 76
Karen, Donna 94–5
kiddy porn 72–3, 100
Klein, Calvin 72–3, 104
Ko, Dorothy 132–5

labial elongation 33–4
labiaplasty 28, 33–4, 177; comparison with female genital mutilation 83; health damaging effects 36, 83; and the porn industry 78, 82–5, 86; selling the trimmings of 78, 162; and teenage girls 157
labour: domestic 64; spent on beauty practices 31
Labour Party 68
LaBruce, Bruce 72
LaChapelle, David 102–4
Lacroix, Christian 92
"ladyboys" 56
Lagerfeld, Karl 82
Lancet (journal) 34, 36
laser hair removal 55
lashing 38, 40
latex 100
Lawrence, Anne 51–2
lead poisoning 124
leather 93
leg shaving 119–20
Leganeur, J.J. 132, 141, 143, 146, 147
Lehrman, Karen 1–2, 12–13

Lemon, Brendan 94
Leo, John 151
Lepore, Amanda 102, 103
Lerner, Gerda 43
lesbianhating 53
lesbians: culture of resistance 175; and the fashion industry 94, 98; and fetishism 130; gay male revulsion towards 104; and makeup use in the workplace 115; oppression of 53; shoe choice 138; transsexual 53; transsexual 'men' as 50, 57; when the wives of transvestites feel like 63
Levine, Suzanne 145
Levy, Howard S. 131
liberal feminism 9–10, 36–7; defence of western beauty practices 1–2, 5–6, 10, 11–13
Liberty Women's Health 85–6
limb amputation 4, 167, 169, 177
Lip Sewing 165
liposuction 160–1; mons pubis 157
lips, "Perfect Pout" 126
lipstick wearing 44–5, 107; history of 110; men's fetishism of 59–61; as symbol of subordination 61
Lister, Ruth 31

MacKinnon, Catharine A. 1, 8, 10, 24, 65
Mackrell, Judith 137
MacPherson, Elle 73, 74
Madonna 12, 98, 147; cult of 75–7, 86
magazines (women's): sexual content 18–19; women's creative interpretations of 18–19
mainstreaming: of deviancy 151; of piercing 153–4; of pornographic beauty practices 82–5, 86, 177–8; *see also* normalization
makeup 107–27; children's use of 118–19; and choice 114, 118–20; coercive nature of wearing 114, 118–20; comparison with the veil 37–40; and the construction of inequality 116; costs of not wearing 44, 115; as culture of survival 121, 126; divisive nature 116; economic issues surrounding 110–11, 112; as empowering 107, 115; health effects 123–7; history of 109–13; lipstick wearing 44–5, 59–61, 107, 110; and male dominance 114–22; as marker of women's inferior status 61; and mental health 122–3; as "paint" 110; playful wearing of 116; as shared and pleasurable women's culture 112, 115–16, 126; time sacrifices of wearing 118; and transfemininity 59–61; unthreatening look of 115; and the workplace 111–12, 114–15, 117–18; *see also* lipstick
makeup artists 3
male dominance: coercive nature 175; through cosmetic surgery 155; through fashion 105; through female high-heeled shoe wearing 128, 172; female implementers of 111; through female wearing of makeup 37–8, 114–22; and femininity 24–7; gay male exclusion from 95, 104, 152; gender as product of 48, 66; and harmful cultural practices 28, 29, 30, 37–8, 39; masculinity as product of 66; through the medical profession 86, 177; and the mind/body split 163; through notions of sexual difference 20–4; overturning of 179; and the public/private distinction 10–11; and self-mutilation 155, 163, 164, 169–70; and transfemininity 61, 65; through the veil 37–8, 39; and womanblaming 145–6; *see also* deferential nature of women; inequality; oppression of women; subordination of women
male opinions 119
male sexual desire 172, 178; aroused by fashion 88, 90–1, 93, 102; aroused by showing skin 88; construction of beauty for 32, 37–8, 44, 45; cosmetic surgery and 155, 156, 158, 160; female compliance with through makeup wearing 115, 126; gained from foot fetishism and high heels 128, 129, 131, 139–41; and harmful cultural practices 28; visual nature 91–2
male submission, controllable 91
males-to-constructed-females (MTFs) 49, 50–2, 54
Malta 42–3
Marie Claire (magazine) 83–4
Marks and Spencer 118

marriage 22; "gay" 49; rape 11
Marshall, J. Howard 160
Marx, Karl 22
Masaki 120
masculinity: as behaviour of domination 26, 27; female 66; idealized forms of 94; as product of male dominance 66
masochism: and ballet 137; of transfemininity 46–7, 49, 51–2, 54, 58–62; *see also* sadomasochism
Masson, Jeffrey 96
Masters, R.E.L. 110
masturbatory fantasies 50
Maticevski, Toni 71
McCloskey, Donald (Deirdre) 51, 52, 57–8
McQueen, Alexander 95, 97–9, 102, 103, 104
McRobbie, Angela 18–19
Media Awareness Network 72
medical profession 176–7; as handmaiden of male dominance 86, 177; and transfemininity 46–7, 50–1
Meiwes, Armin 168–9
Mel B (Spice Girl) 160
Mellen, Polly 100
Members of Parliament 31, 44–5
mental health 7, 31, 122–3, 172
Mercier, Laurent 103–4
middle-aged women, invisibility of 123
Miller, Rachel 50, 62
mind/body split 163
mirror checking 108
Miyake, Issey 162
mons pubis 157
morality, cosmetic surgery as 16
Moran, Josie 74
Morton's toe 145
Moss, Kate 73, 74
Mower, Sarah 99
Mugler, Thierry 92, 100–1
muhaggaba (veiled one) 39
multiculturalism 36
Musafar, Fakir 92, 151

nail polish 124, 125
Nailing 165
nakedness 98–9; divesting of social status through 88; gay male revulsion at female 104
narcissism 8
National Institute of Occupational Safety and Health (US) 124
National Transgender Advocacy Coalition (NTAC) 49
naturalized behaviours: female subordination as 8; femininity as 65, 174; grooming as 32, 41, 107, 108, 121–2, 174
Network of Sex Work Projects 77
neurotoxins 125
New York Post (newspaper) 73
New York Times (newspaper) 41, 144
Newton, Helmut 74, 92, 147
normalization: of cosmetic surgery 155, 172; of fetishism 129–30; of pornographic beauty practices 4, 67–9, 70, 86, 177–8; of prostitution 77, 110, 132–3; *see also* mainstreaming
Nussbaum, Martha 35–6
NW (magazine) 159, 160

objects *see* sex objects, women as
occupational therapists 122–3
Operation Spanner case 168
opinions, male 119
oppression of women 53; through beauty practices 1–2, 5, 7–8, 20, 113; through clothing 93; through exportation of western beauty practices 42; as failure to exercise personal power 13; through footbinding 133, 135; makeup and the survival of 116; through notions of sexual difference 20–4; postmodern interpretations 15; psychological 7; through sexual violence 19; and the veil 39, 40; *see also* deferential nature of women; inequality; male dominance; subordination of women
oral sex 110
Orlan, mutilation as art 154, 161–4, 168
Otherness, and one's body 169
Ousterhout, Douglas 55
Overs, Cheryl 77

Paglia, Camille 75–6
pain, desire of men to see women in 128, 130, 140–1, 143–4
Pakistan 132

Parker, Sarah Jessica 147
partners, and conformity to western beauty practices 119–20
patriarchal religion 42–4; *see also* Christianity; Islam
patriarchal reversal 77
patriarchy, resistance to 151
Paul, St 43
Paul, Ru 100
Peakin, William 159
Peiss, Kathy 38, 42, 109–11, 112–13
penectomy 165
"Penthouse effect" 82
performance art 154, 161–4, 166–7
Pertschuk, Michael 122–3
philanthropy, beauty industry as form of 41
Phillips, Katharine 108, 109
Phillips, Lynn 19
physical abuse, childhood 150, 168, 169
physical freedom, beauty practices as threat to 6–7
piercing 1; of body modification 165; and gay men 151–2; infections from 153; mainstreaming 153–4; as mark of transgression 153; as self-mutilation by proxy 4, 149, 151–4, 165, 169; and straight men 152–3; tongue 153–4; women and 152
Ping, Wang 135
Playboy (magazine) 82
podiatrists 144–5
pole dancing 73
pollution 125
popular culture 14, 15–16, 18
porn stars 68; contract girls 70
pornography 4, 67–86, 163–4; and advertising 70–5; Awards Show 68; beauty practices 77–86; body modification as 165; and cosmetic surgery 77–8, 154–5, 158–62, 164; distribution 70; economic issues 67, 69–70, 173; ending 178; exaggerated femininity of 54, 56; and fashion 70–5, 90–1, 96, 98–103; gay 72, 95; and genital hair removal 78–86; hard core 69; influence on mainstream beauty practices 4, 177–8; kiddy porn 72–3, 100; and Madonna 75–7; normalization 4, 67–9, 70, 86, 177–8; pole dancing 73; and the rise of sadomasochism 91; and the sexual revolution 67; transgendered 59–60, 66
Porter, Charlie 94
postmodern feminism 2, 6, 13–20, 175
postmodern perspectives: on cosmetic surgery 161–3; on fashion 87, 106; on footbinding 133–4; gender as performance 140; on Madonna 76–7
Pot Noodle advertising 71
power 15; beauty practices as display of feminine 16; and fashion 98, 101; and space 25; and touch 25
Prada, Miuccia 94–5
prejudice, against those who do not conform to western beauty practices 32, 44, 115, 122–3
Price-Waterhouse 117
private sphere 10–11
propylene glycol 124–5
prostitution 4, 73, 163–4; Babylonian 43; economic issues 173; ending 178; and fashion 75, 77, 86, 98; and the female domination of men 75–6, 77; and footbinding 131, 132–3; and high heels 133; influence on mainstream beauty practices 177–8; and makeup 110; normalization 77, 110, 132–3, 177–8; and the rise of sadomasochism 91, 92; and the shaping of cultural expectations of women 92; and transsexualism 53, 55–6
Pseudomonas 153
psychiatry: and makeup wearing 122–3; and transfemininity 46
psychoanalysis 96, 129
psychological oppression 7
public space: women's entry into and makeup use 111–12; women's entry into and the veil 112
public/private distinction, and male supremacy 10–11
punk fashion 92, 151, 152, 165
Puwar, Nirmal 31

queer theory 104; and gender 17–18, 66; and makeup 116; and transfemininity 48, 65

Rabanne, Paco 162
racism 115

radical feminism: critique of beauty 2, 5–13; in patriarchal reversal 77; on the public–private distinction 10–11
rape 19; marital 11
Rapido TV 159
Raymond, Janice G. 47, 65, 66
religion: patriarchal 42–4; *see also* Islamic society
religious indoctrination 40
reproduction, and beauty 13
resistance to beauty practices 171, 174–6; resentment towards 32, 44, 115, 122–3
Reyes, Renee 57
Reynaud, Emmanuel 24
Richardson, Terry 74–5
rickets 34
risk behaviours, of teenage girls 151
rituals, female beauty 134–5, 146, 174
Rivers, Joan 147
Rofes, Eric 104–5
role models, Madonna as 75–7
Roosevelt, Eleanor 139, 148
Rose, Pania 73
Rossi, William 128, 130, 133, 138, 139–41
rubber 94
Rudd, Peggy 48, 61

sadism: and cosmetic surgery 159; and high heels 139, 143–4; *see also* pain, desire of men to see women in
sado-rituals 111, 146
sado-scholarship 146
sado-society 148, 163
sadomasochism 4; of cosmetic surgery/piercing 150; and fashion 91–4; gay male 52, 91–4, 151–2, 165–8; and high heels 142, 143; of male dominance 24; transgendered 60, 66
Saeed, Fouzia 132
Saharso, Sawitri 36–7
Sati 33
scarification 165
Schon, Mila 73
Schwichtenberg, Cathy 76–7
science 28
self-harm 149–54; socially approved 154–7; as taking control 151
self-mutilation by proxy 4, 149–70; body modification 164–7, 168–9; consent of the victim 4; cosmetic surgery 4, 149–50, 154–64, 169–70; Lolo Ferrari 154, 158–60, 168; Orlan 154, 161–4, 168; self-harm 149–54; and social status 149, 150, 168–70; socially approved self-harm 154–7
self-mutilation websites 121, 164–7, 168–9
sex: as performance for men 19; women as category of 22–3, 76
sex class, women as subordinate 22, 24, 146, 179; enforcement through fashion 87; marked through western beauty practices 32
sex industry *see* pornography; prostitution
sex objects, women as 8, 30–1, 37–9, 41, 173; fashion and 88, 93, 94
sex reassignment surgery 29, 48, 51–2, 176–7; as harmful cultural practice 29; as inalienable right 51; Internet research on 59; as sign of privilege and prosperity 58
sex roles: androgynous/masculine of women 123; cultural construction 21; destruction 27; maintenance through beauty practices 44, 45; transsexualism as enforcement of 47, 48–9
sex toys, femininity as 66
sexism: transsexualism as form of 47; *see also* deferential nature of women; inequality; oppression of women; subordination of women
sexual abuse, childhood 53, 150, 164, 168, 169
sexual desire *see* male sexual desire
sexual difference 65; maintenance by beauty practices 7, 20–4, 30, 31, 125, 172; creation through fashion 87–91, 105, 106; indicated through footbinding 132; as obsolete notion 27, 178, 179; indicated through shoe fashions 128, 142
sexual fantasies: masturbatory 50; men's practice of femininity as 49–50, 51–3, 55–63, 66
sexual freedom 67
sexual harassment 39, 40
sexual objects, women as 13, 42, 44, 164; and footbinding 132; and high heels 140; objectification process 8; in the workplace 9

sexual revolution 67, 92, 110
sexual service, of women 23
sexual violence 19, 69
shaving: legs 119–20; red bumps from 120, 121; underarm irritation 121
Shaw, Debra 97
Shaw, Sarah 150, 154
Shields, Brooke 72
shoes *see* high-heeled shoes
Shulman, Alexandra 71
silicone 155–6
Sisley 74
skin: bleaching 113; feminine displays of 87, 88
skirts 140, 178
slenderness 33
Smith, Anna Nicole 160
Smith, Robert 167
social control, through symbolic manipulation 27
social status, subordinate 31, 32, 46, 61, 65; divesting through nakedness 88; and self-mutilation 149, 150, 168–70
societal Stockholm syndrome 25–6
Society for Adolescent Medicine 152
Soul Magazine 83
Soviet Union 42
space 25
Spears, Britney 86, 160
Spice Girls 160
"spinster/sexual deviate" perspective of feminism 90
standards of beauty, construction 113–14
Stanton, Elizabeth Cady 88
Staphylococcus aureus 153
starvation 30
Steele, Valerie 91, 93
Stevens, Tabitha 78
Stockholm syndrome 25–6
Streptococcus 153
stripping 155
Strong, Marilee 150
Strovny, David 81–2
Stuart, Peter 159
Stubbs, Robert S. 85
submission, male, controllable 91
subordination of femininity, sought by men 46, 49, 50, 51–2, 60–1, 66
subordination of gay men 95, 104
subordination of women: through cosmetic surgery 31; through employment 111; through fashion 87, 105–6; femininity as behaviour of subordination 24–7, 46; interests 63; makeup as marker of 61; as naturalized behaviour 8; through popular culture 14; through the private sphere 10–11; through notions of sexual difference 20–4; as social construction 179; through veiling 40; through western beauty practices 2, 5–10, 15, 26–7, 31, 32, 45, 172; *see also* deferential nature of women; inequality; male dominance; oppression of women; social status, subordinate
suicide 156, 158, 159
suicide suspension 165
suits 89
Sullivan, Deborah 176
Summers, Leigh 92
Sun (newspaper) 159
survival cultures: footbinding as 135; makeup wearing as 121, 126
sweet-sixteen parties 135

t-girls 57
Taglioni 136, 137
Taipusham Indians 152
talc 125
Taliban 41
tallow 126
tattooing 151–4, 169; as mark of transgression 153
teenagers: binge drinking 151; and labiaplasty 157; sweet-sixteen parties 135
Thompson, Denise 14, 15
time sacrifices, of makeup wearing 118
Times, The (newspaper) 70–1
Tinsley, Emily 123
tobacco industry 68
toe cleavage 138, 147
Tom, Emma 73
Tom of Finland 95
tomboys 65, 115
touch 25
toluene 125
Trans-Gender Education Association (TGEA) 58, 61
transfemininity 3, 46–66

transgression, marks of 153, 166–7
transsexual surgical castration 29
transsexualism 3, 45, 46–66; conservatism of 49, 61–2, 65–6; and cosmetic surgery 158; definitions 46–53; discrimination against 49; distinction from transvestism 47–8; females-to-constructed-males 49, 53; makeover industry 53–8; males-to-constructed-females 49, 50–2, 54; minority status 49; sexist nature/prevention of gender role disruption 47, 48–9, 58; as social construction 47, 49; women's soul in a man's body narrative 50–1; *see also* sex reassignment surgery
transvestism 3, 30, 45, 46–66; conservatism of 61–2, 65–6; and cosmetic surgery 158; definitions 46–53; distinction from transsexualism 47–8; and fashion 99, 100; heterosexual 57–8, 61–2; makeover industry 53–8; prevalence 62; sexual excitement of 50; vanity/primping 64; wives 57, 58, 61–4
tribalism 152
triclosan 124
Trojan (model) 103
tummy tucks 156–7, 160–1
Turkey 86
Tutsi women 33–4

underarm shaving 121
Ungaro 92
United Nations (UN): CEDAW 29, 45, 176, 178; on harmful cultural practices 3, 27, 28–35, 45, 123–4, 171, 176; Universal Declaration of Human Rights 179
urolagnia 130

vaginal rejuvenation surgery 82, 85
Valentine, Vicky 55–6
Valentino 92
values, cultural 31–2
veiling: comparison with makeup 37–40; readoption 38–9; and women's entry into the public space 112
Veronica Vera 54
Versace, Donatella 94–5
Versace, Gianni 92, 93, 99–100
victim, consent of 4
victim feminists 6
Vigne, Eric 158, 159
violence against women: domestic 10–11; pornographic 69; sexual 11, 19, 69
virgin/whore dichotomy 37–8, 41
virginity, hymen repair surgery 36–7, 85–6, 176–7
Visionaire (magazine) 104
Vogue (magazine) 41, 42, 70–1, 98, 112, 116
vulva, hairless 78–9

Walkowitz, Judith 111
Wallace, Michelle 114
Walter, Natasha 1–2, 12
Wang, Shuo-Shan 167
water sports 130
waxing: arms 120–1; Brazilian 79–81, 82, 83–4; general bikini line 120
western cultural imperialism, and the exportation of harmful cultural practices 41–2
Westwood, Vivienne 73
white ideal of beauty 113–14
Wildor, Sarah 137
Williams, Christine L. 114–15, 116
Wilson, Cintra 102
Wilson, Elizabeth 98, 105–6
Wilson, Sarah 161–2
Wintour, Anna 41
Wittig, Monique 20–3, 65, 76
wives: status 31; of transvestites 57, 58, 61–4; *see also* brides, mail order
Wolf, Naomi 8–10, 175
womanblaming 145–6, 159
women's liberation movement 8, 175
Woods, Chris 168
workplace: and clothing 116–17; coercive influence of beauty practices in 9; Islamic women in 39–40, 112; and makeup use 111–12, 114–15, 117–18

Xianzhong, Zhang 141

Zawadi, Aya 83
Zeitgeist 15